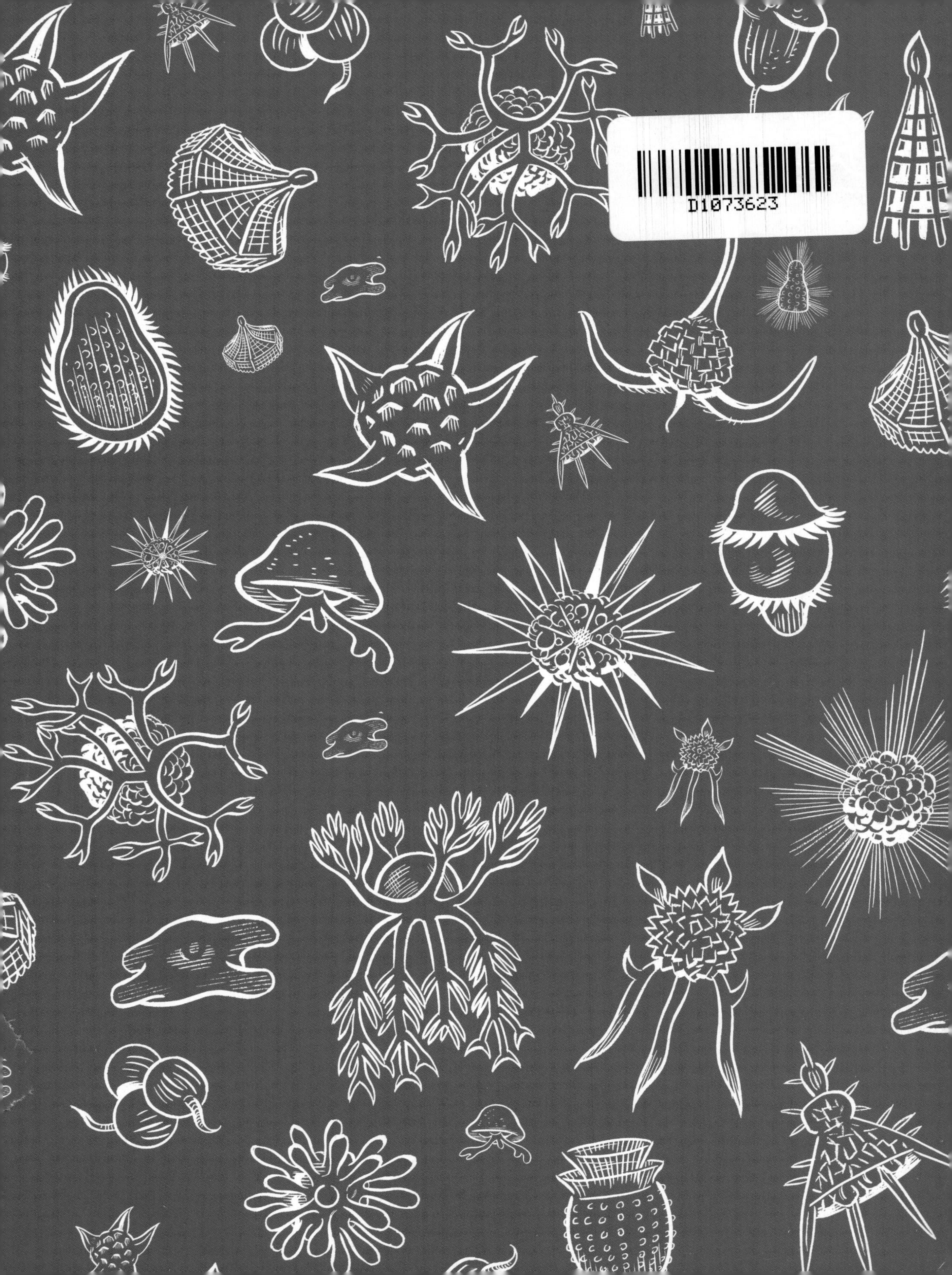

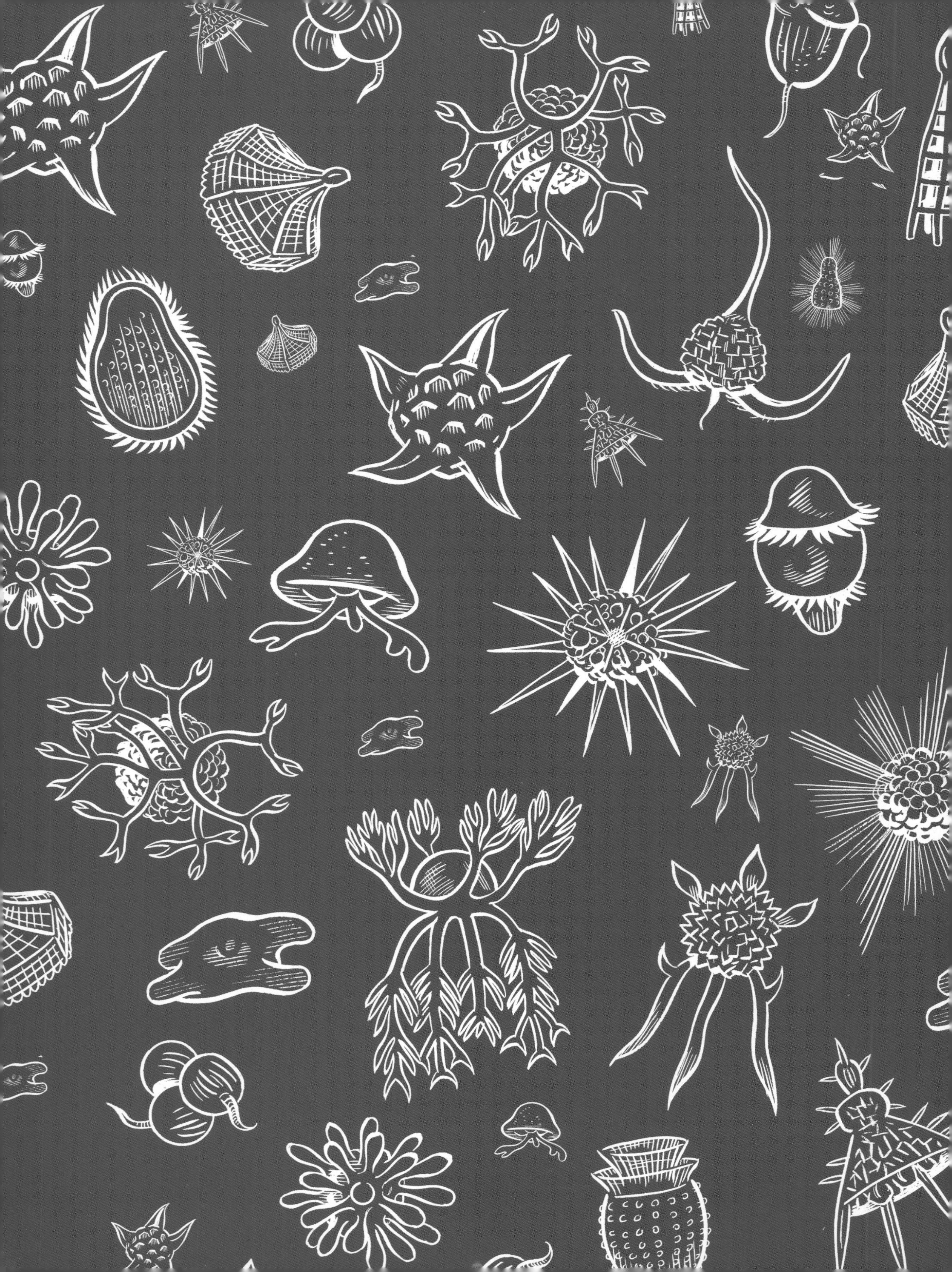

DAVID BORING

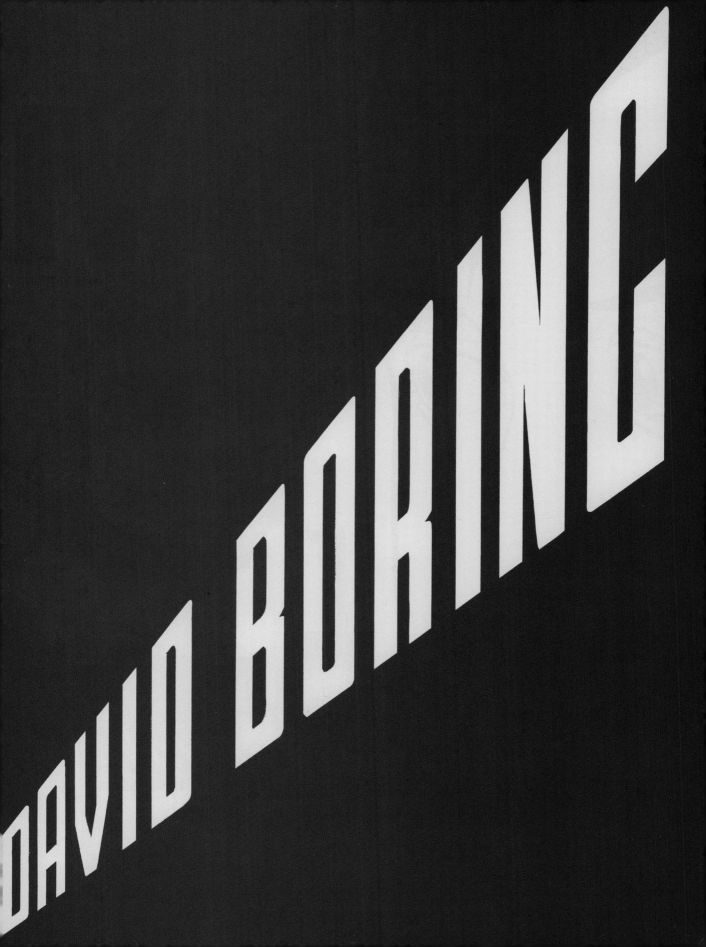

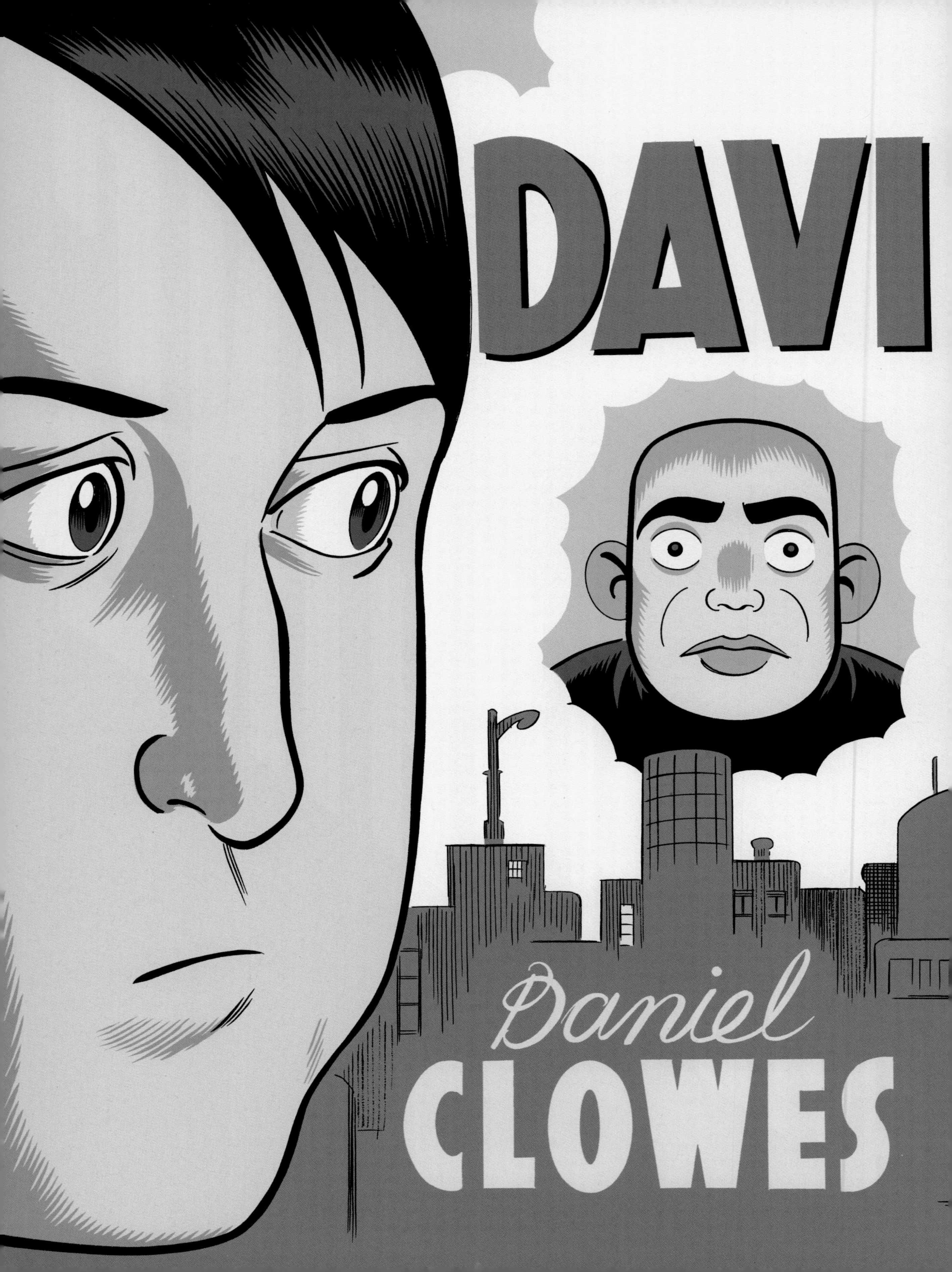
DAVI
Daniel
CLOWES

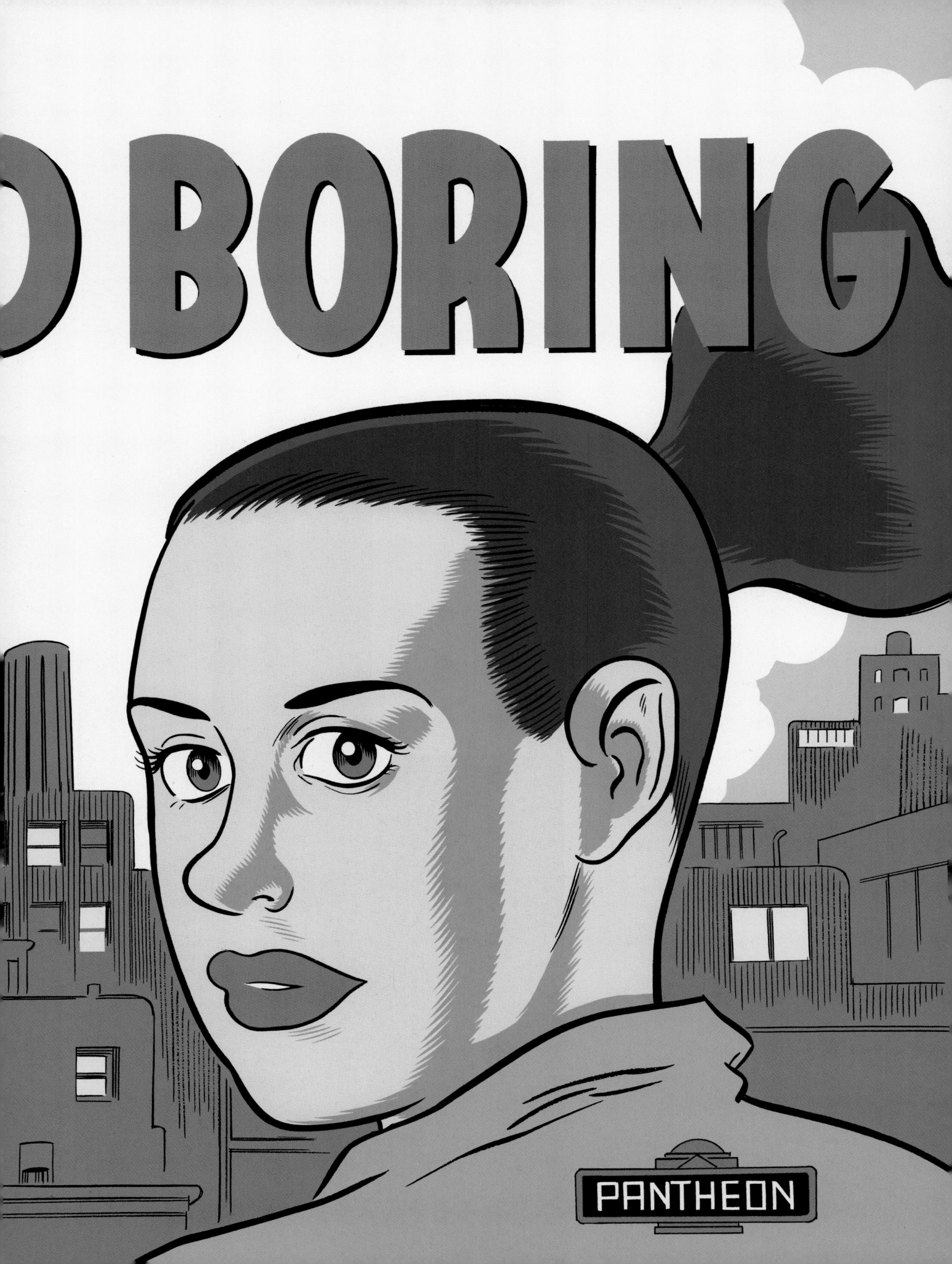

O BORING
PANTHEON

ALL RIGHTS RESERVED UNDER
INTERNATIONAL AND PAN-AMER-
ICAN COPYRIGHT CONVENTIONS.
PUBLISHED IN THE UNITED
STATES BY PANTHEON BOOKS,
A DIVISION OF RANDOM HOUSE,
INC., NEW YORK, AND SIM-
ULTANEOUSLY IN CANADA BY
RANDOM HOUSE OF CANADA
LIMITED, TORONTO. ORIG-
INALLY PUBLISHED IN HARDCOVER
BY PANTHEON BOOKS, A
DIVISION OF RANDOM HOUSE,
INC., NEW YORK, IN 2000.

PANTHEON BOOKS AND COLOPHON
ARE REGISTERED TRADEMARKS
OF RANDOM HOUSE, INC.

PORTIONS OF THIS WORK WERE
ORIGINALLY PUBLISHED IN EIGHT-
BALL. EIGHTBALL IS PUBLISHED
BY FANTAGRAPHICS BOOKS.

LIBRARY OF CONGRESS CATALOG-
ING-IN-PUBLICATION DATA
 CLOWES, DANIEL.
DAVID BORING / DANIEL CLOWES
  p. cm.
ISBN 0-375-71452-9
I. TITLE
PN6727. C565 D38 2000
741. 5'973--dc 21
00-039194

WWW. PANTHEONBOOKS. COM

BOOK DESIGN: DANIEL CLOWES.

BIG-DOT SEPARATIONS AND
TECHNICAL SUPERVISION: JOHN
KURAMOTO.

PRINTED IN SINGAPORE.

FIRST PAPERBACK EDITION.

9 8 7

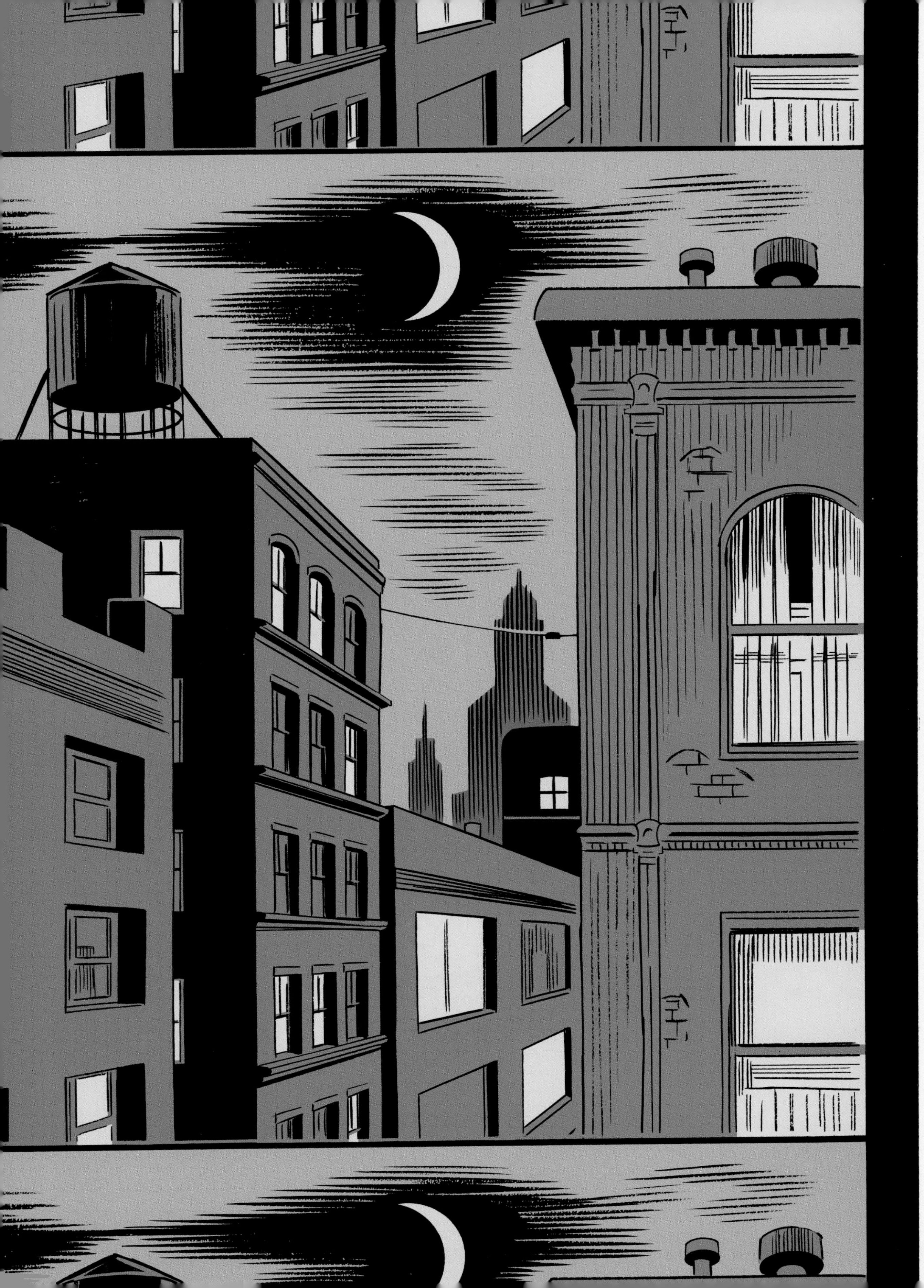

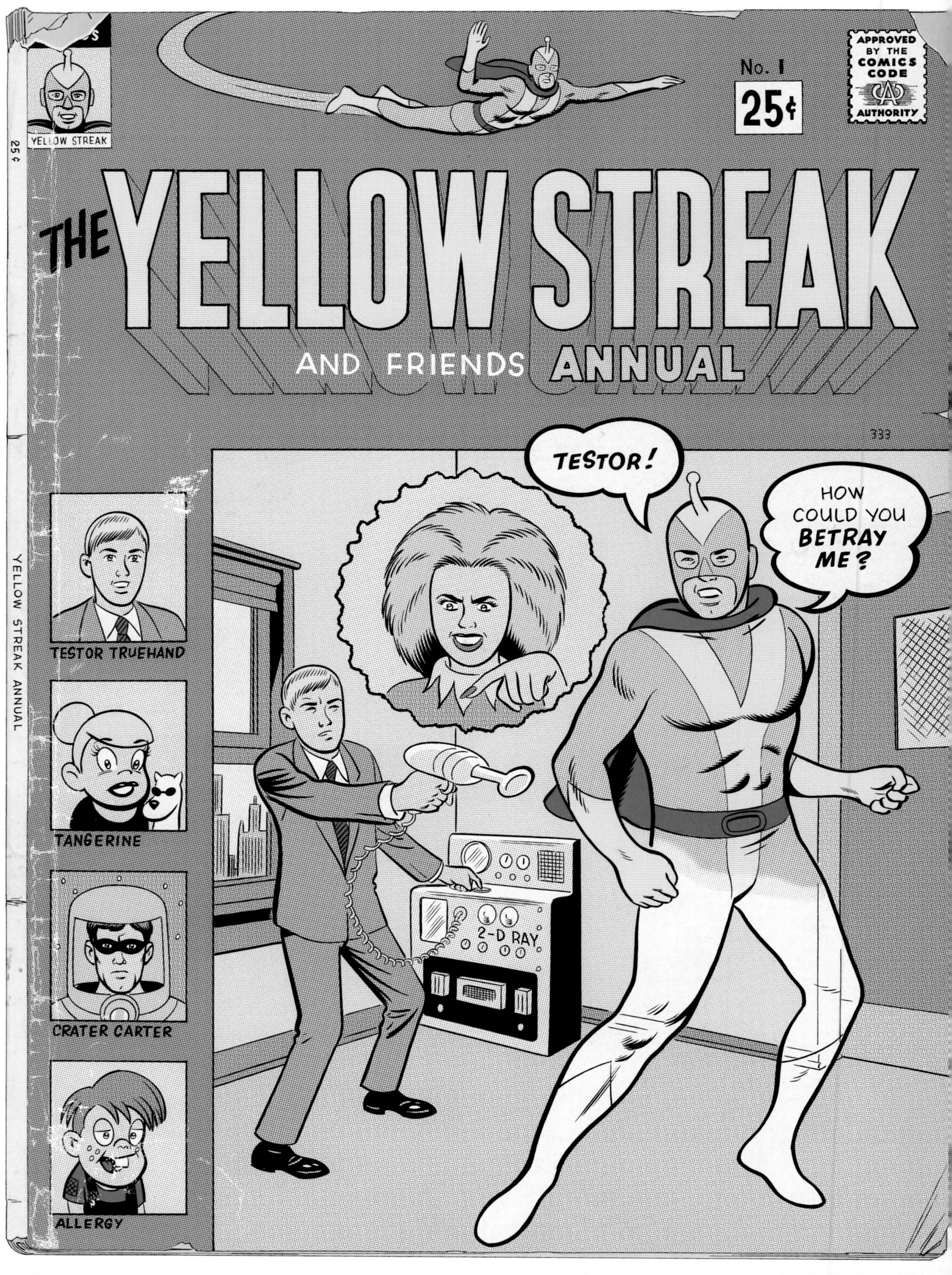

YELLOW STREAK
No. 1
25¢
APPROVED BY THE COMICS CODE AUTHORITY
THE YELLOW STREAK
AND FRIENDS ANNUAL
333
TESTOR!
HOW COULD YOU BETRAY ME?
2-D RAY
TESTOR TRUEHAND
TANGERINE
CRATER CARTER
ALLERGY
25¢
YELLOW STREAK ANNUAL

HERE, BY SOME MIRACLE OF CIRCUMSTANCE, I WAS, NAKED, ABOUT TO HAVE SEXUAL INTERCOURSE WITH WHAT THE CONSENSUS OF THE DAY WOULD HAVE HELD AS A PERFECTLY BEAUTIFUL WOMAN.

HER SKIN WAS SMOOTH AND ELASTIC, DAPPLED WITH GIRLISH YELLOW FUZZ. HER TRIM, ATHLETIC FIGURE WAS BLAH BLAH ETC. ETC....

SHE HAD RECENTLY BEEN ASKED TO MODEL FOR A SPORTSWEAR CATALOG AND WAS CONSIDERED 'VERY PROMISING' BY HER ACTING TEACHERS.

SHE WAS NOT DISPLEASED WITH MY THRUSTS (SHE BIT HER LIP AND MADE BREATHY NOISES) BUT I KNEW FROM THE START THAT I PROBABLY WOULDN'T GET ANOTHER CHANCE IF SHE WASN'T (AT LEAST) OVERWHELMED BY MY ENTHUSIASM.

I BELIEVE IN 'EXPERIENCING THE MOMENT' IN ITS PRESENT TENSE, WITHOUT DWELLING ON BYGONE ASSOCIATIONS OR A TRAGIC AFTERMATH...

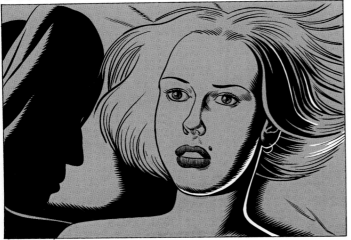

THE BREATHY NOISES TRAILED OFF AND I COULDN'T HELP BUT FEEL THAT AT ANY MOMENT SHE MIGHT EXTRACT HERSELF FROM THE SITUATION AND DASH OFF TO A JUST-REMEMBERED PARTY TO MINGLE IN HER NATURAL ELEMENT AMONG B-LIST ACTORS AND THE CHILDREN OF MILLIONAIRES.

A STORY IN THREE ACTS
BY
DANIEL CLOWES

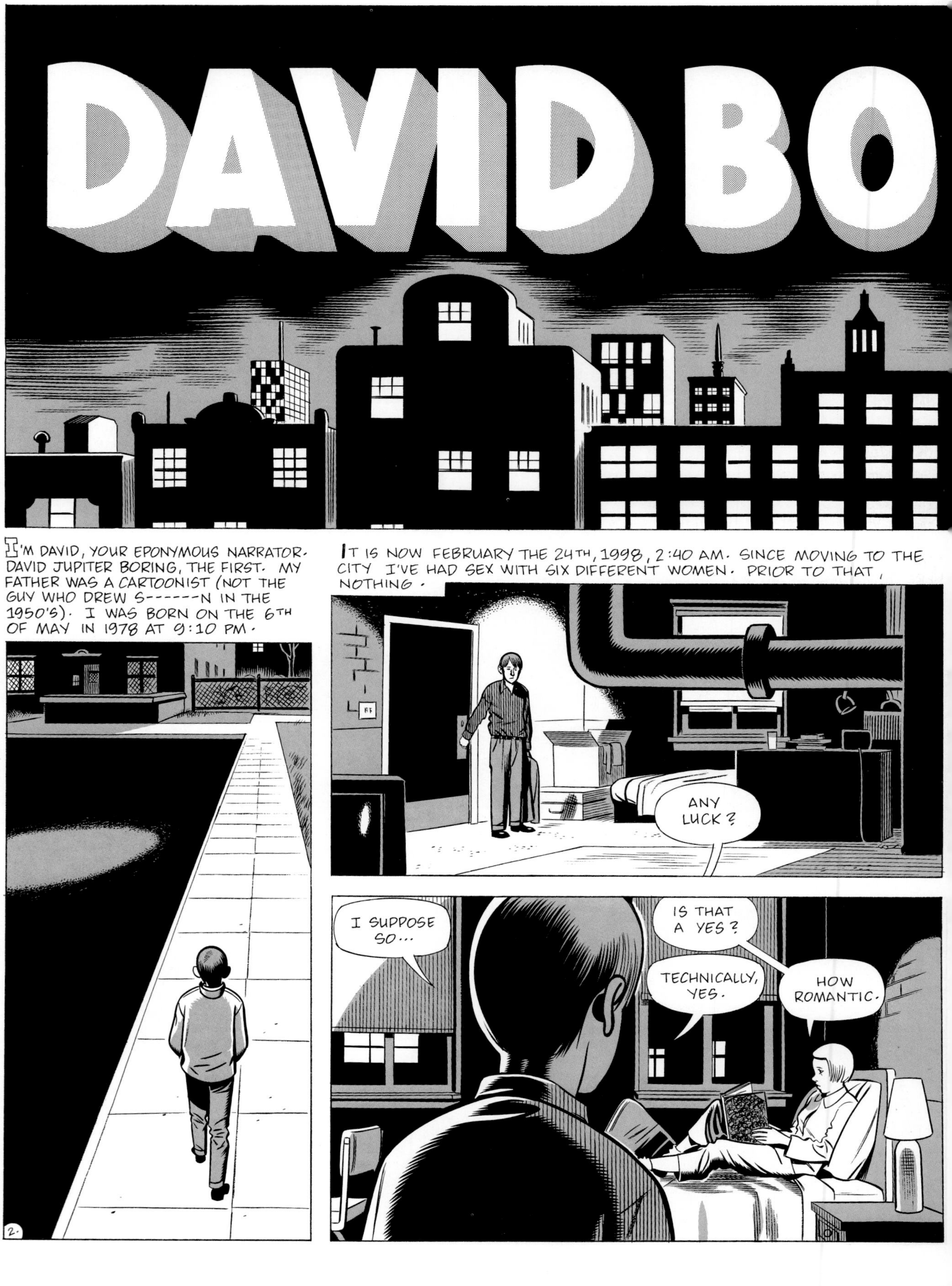

DAVID BO
I'M DAVID, YOUR EPONYMOUS NARRATOR. DAVID JUPITER BORING, THE FIRST. MY FATHER WAS A CARTOONIST (NOT THE GUY WHO DREW S------N IN THE 1950'S). I WAS BORN ON THE 6TH OF MAY IN 1978 AT 9:10 PM.
IT IS NOW FEBRUARY THE 24TH, 1998, 2:40 AM. SINCE MOVING TO THE CITY I'VE HAD SEX WITH SIX DIFFERENT WOMEN. PRIOR TO THAT, NOTHING.
ANY LUCK?
I SUPPOSE SO...
IS THAT A YES?
TECHNICALLY, YES.
HOW ROMANTIC.

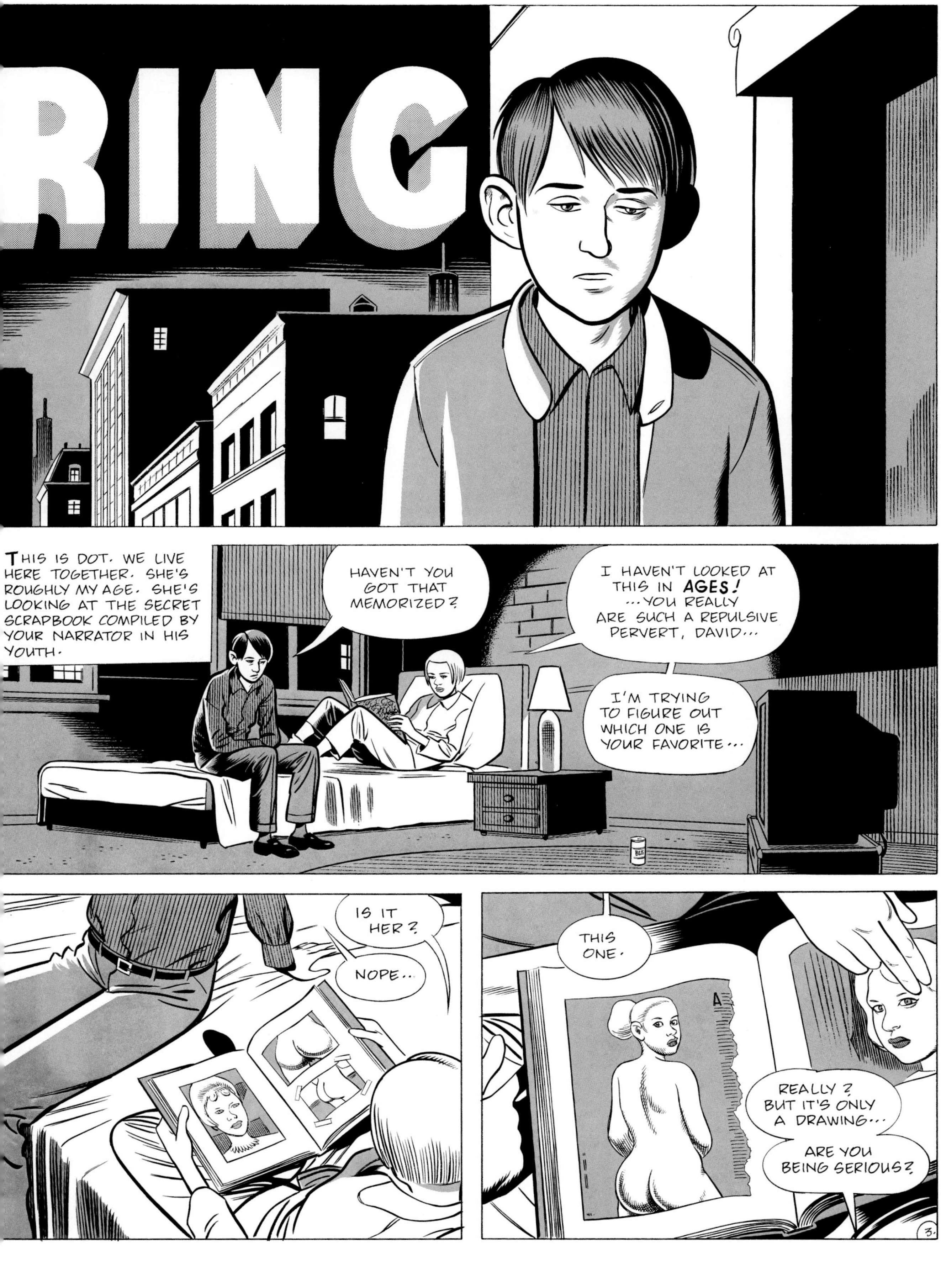
RING
THIS IS DOT. WE LIVE HERE TOGETHER. SHE'S ROUGHLY MY AGE. SHE'S LOOKING AT THE SECRET SCRAPBOOK COMPILED BY YOUR NARRATOR IN HIS YOUTH.
HAVEN'T YOU GOT THAT MEMORIZED?
I HAVEN'T LOOKED AT THIS IN AGES! ...YOU REALLY ARE SUCH A REPULSIVE PERVERT, DAVID...
I'M TRYING TO FIGURE OUT WHICH ONE IS YOUR FAVORITE...
IS IT HER?
NOPE...
THIS ONE.
REALLY? BUT IT'S ONLY A DRAWING...
ARE YOU BEING SERIOUS?
3.

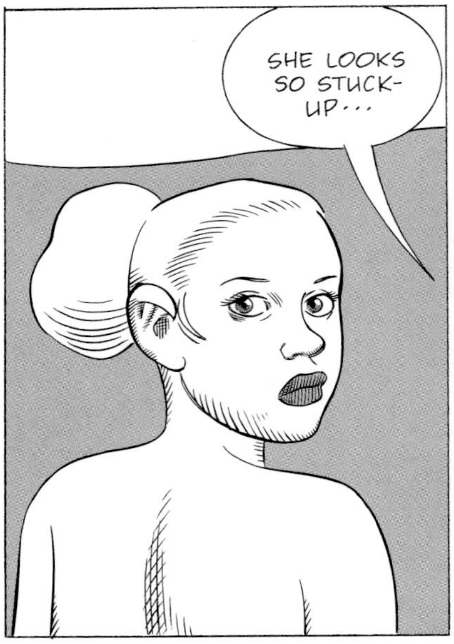
SHE LOOKS SO STUCK-UP...

NEXT TO OUR BUILDING IS A VACANT LOT FILLED WITH GARBAGE. IT BEGAN WITH A LAYER OF TYPICAL FLOTSAM (TIRES, SOFA, MATTRESS) BUT AS THE LEVEL CONTINUES TO RISE (THE FIRST FLOOR IS NEARLY SUBMERGED) DISCARDED OBJECTS SEEM MORE AND MORE TO HAVE BEEN LEFT FOR THEIR SYMBOLIC VALUE...

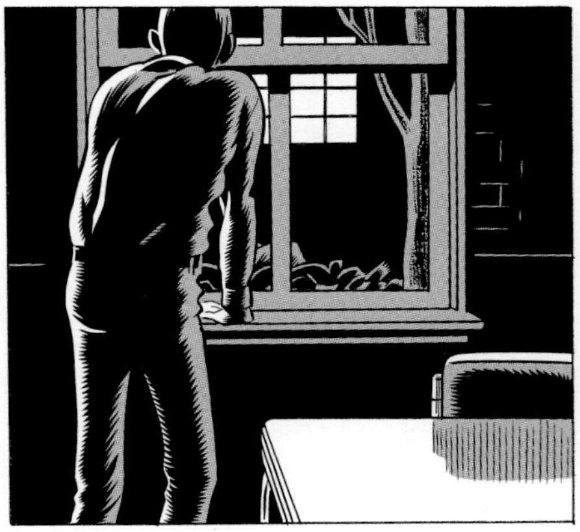

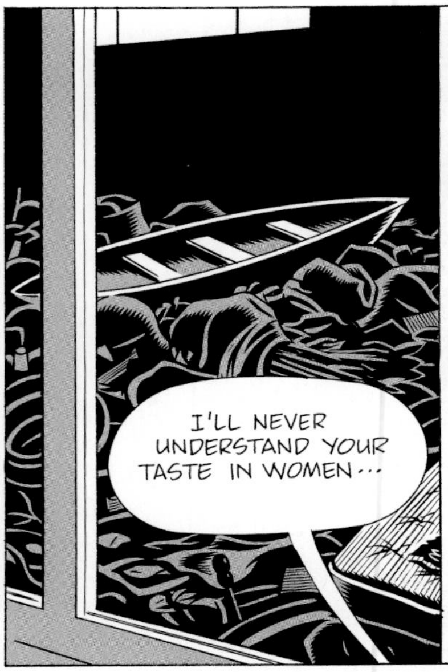
I'LL NEVER UNDERSTAND YOUR TASTE IN WOMEN...

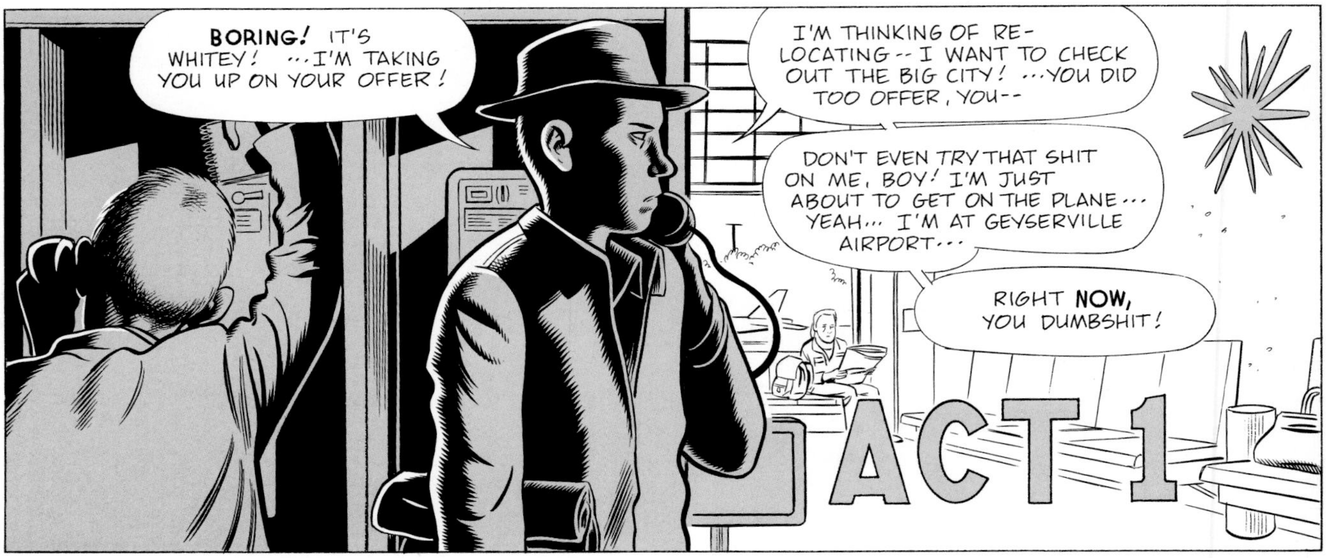
BORING! IT'S WHITEY! ...I'M TAKING YOU UP ON YOUR OFFER!
I'M THINKING OF RE-LOCATING -- I WANT TO CHECK OUT THE BIG CITY! ...YOU DID TOO OFFER, YOU--
DON'T EVEN TRY THAT SHIT ON ME, BOY! I'M JUST ABOUT TO GET ON THE PLANE... YEAH... I'M AT GEYSERVILLE AIRPORT...
RIGHT NOW, YOU DUMBSHIT!
ACT 1

I GREW UP IN THE COUNTRY, IN MERRYVALE TOWNSHIP, WITH MY MOTHER (MY FATHER ESCAPED WHEN I WAS VERY YOUNG. HIS WORKS WERE THEREAFTER FORBIDDEN, THOUGH I SAVED A FEW SECRET ISSUES). I WAS EDUCATED AT HOME UNTIL I WAS 14, AT WHICH TIME I WAS SENT TO THE LOCAL HIGH SCHOOL (GO HOOTOWLS) WHERE I BEFRIENDED WHITEY, A CYNICAL HAYSEED WITH PRETENSIONS OF URBANITY WHO HAD BEEN THE SCHOOL PUNCHING BAG BEFORE MY ARRIVAL.

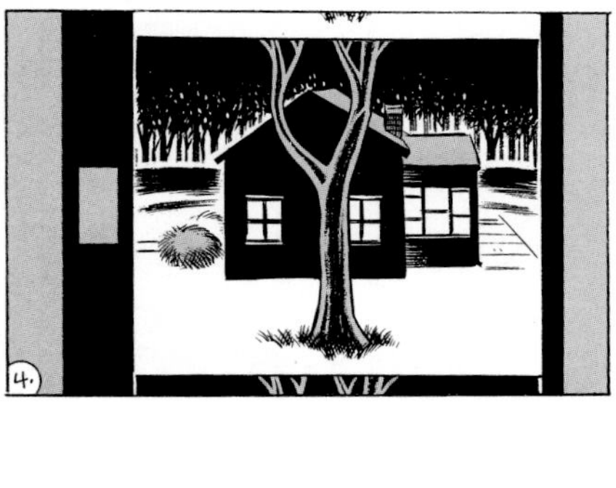

I SPENT MY SENIOR YEAR IN A SCHOOL FOR "GIFTED" CHILDREN IN LIVERBROOK, AT WHICH I DID POORLY BUT HAD THE GOOD FORTUNE TO MEET DOT, MY ONLY TRUE FRIEND IN THIS MISERABLE LIFE (SO FAR). WE MADE SUPER-8 MOVIES AND TALKED IN ENDLESS GYNECOLOGICAL DETAIL ABOUT THE GIRLS IN OUR CLASS (AND ONE PARTICULARLY BRALESS MATH TEACHER).

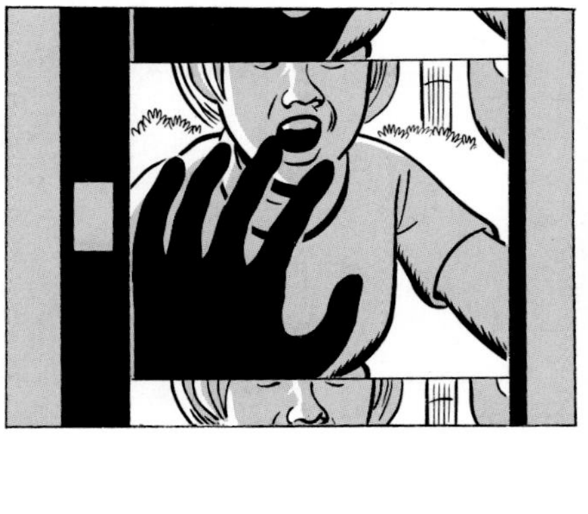

AFTER GRADUATION I DEVISED A PLAN TO ELUDE THE UMBILICAL CLUTCHES OF MY MONSTROUS MOTHER BY MOVING TO THE CITY (WHERE I COULD BE CERTAIN SHE WOULD NEVER VISIT) WITH DOT (HER ARCH-RIVAL WHO SHE HAD ACTUALLY MET ONLY TWICE AND PRETENDED TO LIKE).

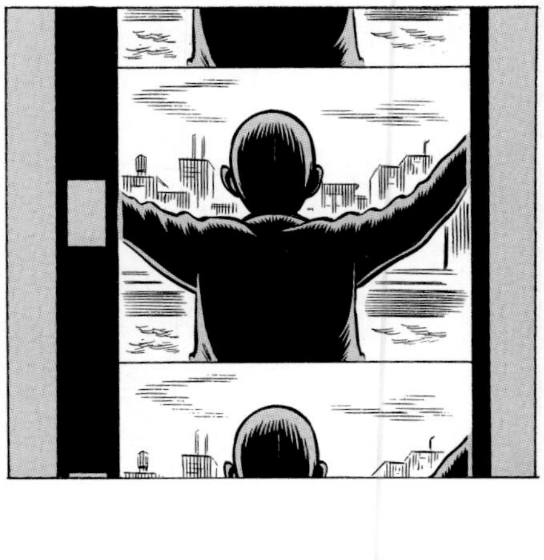

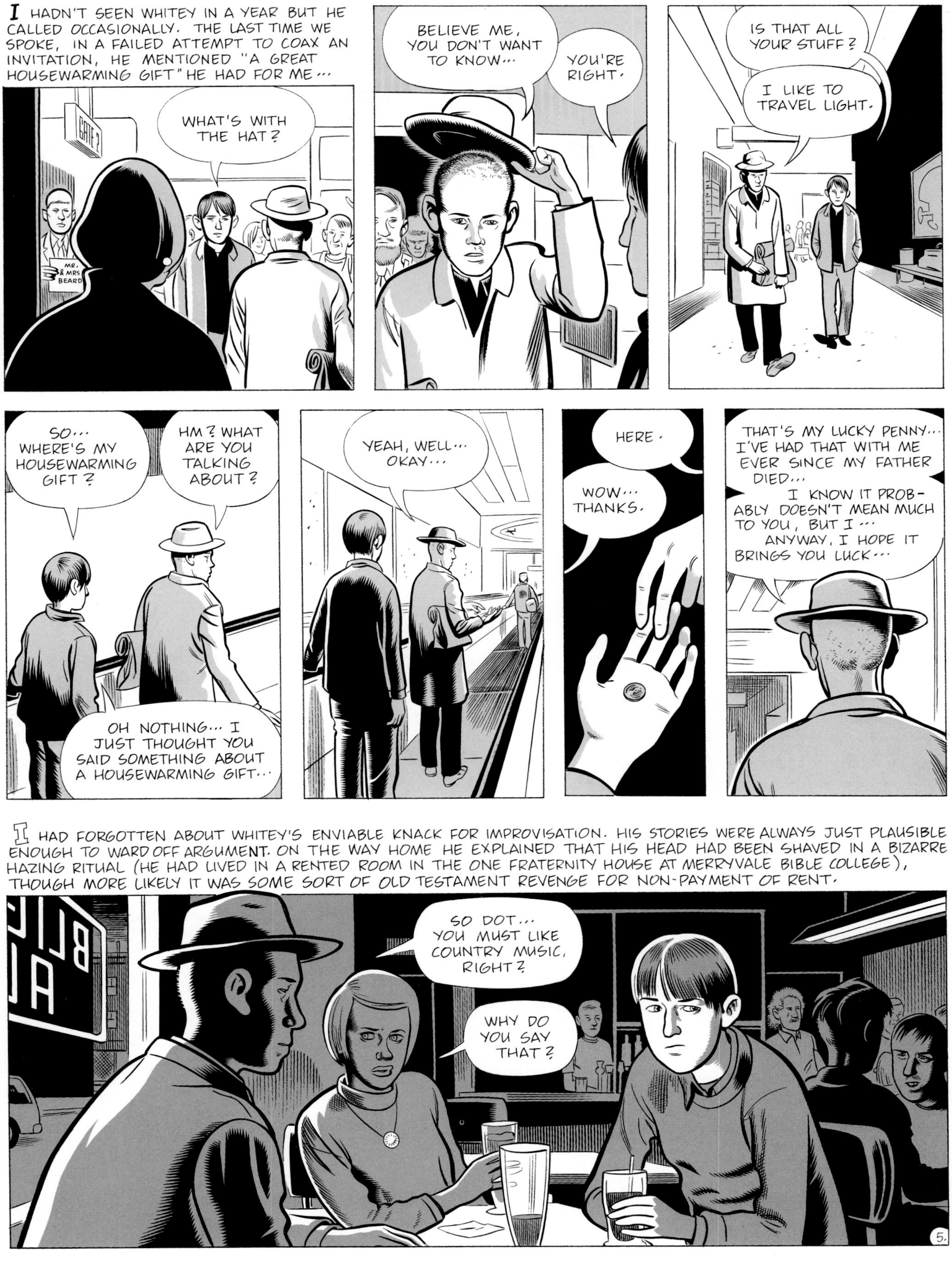
I HADN'T SEEN WHITEY IN A YEAR BUT HE CALLED OCCASIONALLY. THE LAST TIME WE SPOKE, IN A FAILED ATTEMPT TO COAX AN INVITATION, HE MENTIONED "A GREAT HOUSEWARMING GIFT" HE HAD FOR ME...
GATE 2
MR. & MRS. BEARD
WHAT'S WITH THE HAT?
BELIEVE ME, YOU DON'T WANT TO KNOW...
YOU'RE RIGHT.
IS THAT ALL YOUR STUFF?
I LIKE TO TRAVEL LIGHT.
SO... WHERE'S MY HOUSEWARMING GIFT?
HM? WHAT ARE YOU TALKING ABOUT?
OH NOTHING... I JUST THOUGHT YOU SAID SOMETHING ABOUT A HOUSEWARMING GIFT...
YEAH, WELL... OKAY...
HERE.
WOW... THANKS.
THAT'S MY LUCKY PENNY... I'VE HAD THAT WITH ME EVER SINCE MY FATHER DIED... I KNOW IT PROBABLY DOESN'T MEAN MUCH TO YOU, BUT I... ANYWAY, I HOPE IT BRINGS YOU LUCK...
I HAD FORGOTTEN ABOUT WHITEY'S ENVIABLE KNACK FOR IMPROVISATION. HIS STORIES WERE ALWAYS JUST PLAUSIBLE ENOUGH TO WARD OFF ARGUMENT. ON THE WAY HOME HE EXPLAINED THAT HIS HEAD HAD BEEN SHAVED IN A BIZARRE HAZING RITUAL (HE HAD LIVED IN A RENTED ROOM IN THE ONE FRATERNITY HOUSE AT MERRYVALE BIBLE COLLEGE), THOUGH MORE LIKELY IT WAS SOME SORT OF OLD TESTAMENT REVENGE FOR NON-PAYMENT OF RENT.
SO DOT... YOU MUST LIKE COUNTRY MUSIC, RIGHT?
WHY DO YOU SAY THAT?

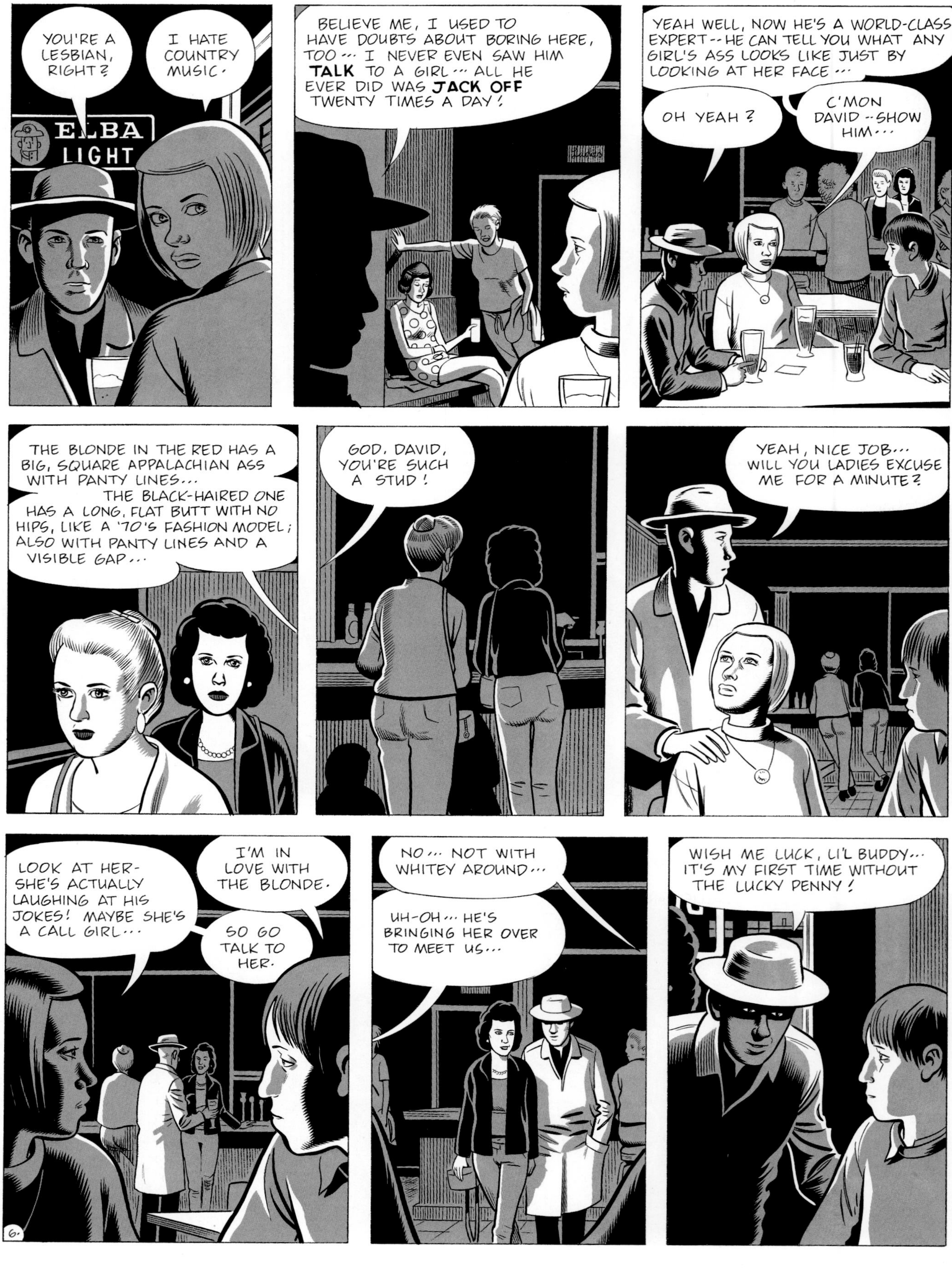

YOU'RE A LESBIAN, RIGHT?
I HATE COUNTRY MUSIC.
ELBA LIGHT
BELIEVE ME, I USED TO HAVE DOUBTS ABOUT BORING HERE, TOO... I NEVER EVEN SAW HIM **TALK** TO A GIRL... ALL HE EVER DID WAS **JACK OFF** TWENTY TIMES A DAY!
YEAH WELL, NOW HE'S A WORLD-CLASS EXPERT--HE CAN TELL YOU WHAT ANY GIRL'S ASS LOOKS LIKE JUST BY LOOKING AT HER FACE...
OH YEAH?
C'MON DAVID--SHOW HIM...
THE BLONDE IN THE RED HAS A BIG, SQUARE APPALACHIAN ASS WITH PANTY LINES... THE BLACK-HAIRED ONE HAS A LONG, FLAT BUTT WITH NO HIPS, LIKE A '70'S FASHION MODEL; ALSO WITH PANTY LINES AND A VISIBLE GAP...
GOD, DAVID, YOU'RE SUCH A STUD!
YEAH, NICE JOB... WILL YOU LADIES EXCUSE ME FOR A MINUTE?
LOOK AT HER-SHE'S ACTUALLY LAUGHING AT HIS JOKES! MAYBE SHE'S A CALL GIRL...
I'M IN LOVE WITH THE BLONDE.
SO GO TALK TO HER.
NO... NOT WITH WHITEY AROUND...
UH-OH... HE'S BRINGING HER OVER TO MEET US...
WISH ME LUCK, LI'L BUDDY... IT'S MY FIRST TIME WITHOUT THE LUCKY PENNY!

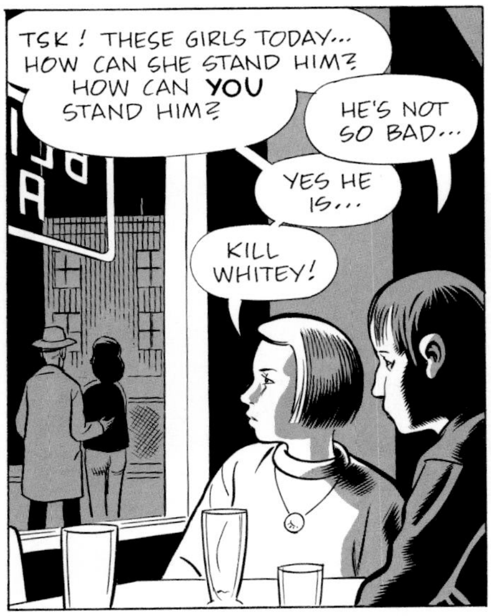
TSK! THESE GIRLS TODAY... HOW CAN SHE STAND HIM? HOW CAN **YOU** STAND HIM?
HE'S NOT SO BAD...
YES HE IS...
KILL WHITEY!

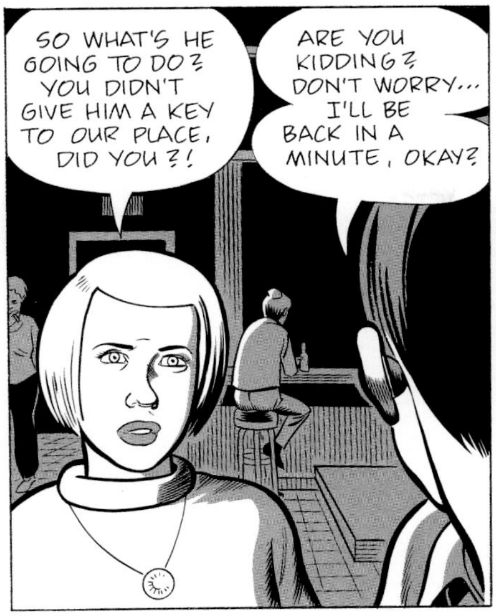
SO WHAT'S HE GOING TO DO? YOU DIDN'T GIVE HIM A KEY TO OUR PLACE, DID YOU?!
ARE YOU KIDDING? DON'T WORRY... I'LL BE BACK IN A MINUTE, OKAY?

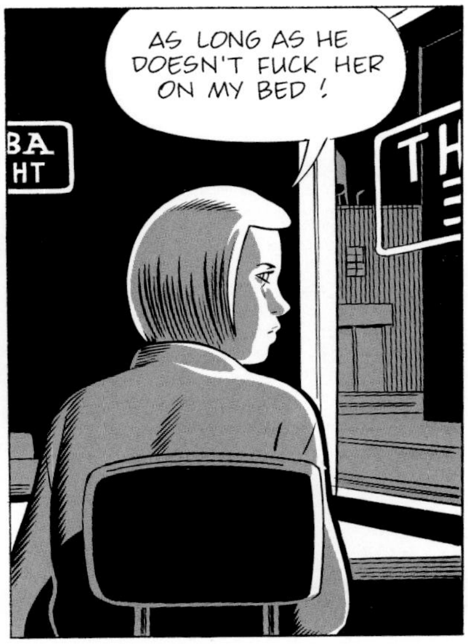
AS LONG AS HE DOESN'T FUCK HER ON MY BED!

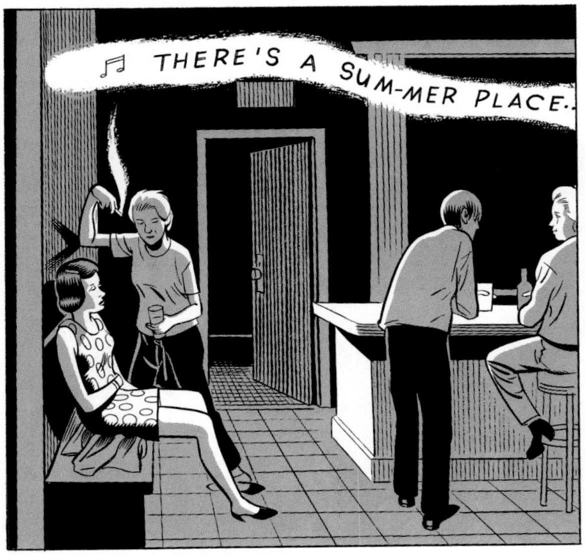
♫ THERE'S A SUM-MER PLACE..

THE FACT IS, I'VE ALWAYS BEEN EMBARRASSED TO TALK TO GIRLS IN FRONT OF WHITEY. HE HAS A WAY OF MAKING YOU FEEL SUBNORMAL IF YOU'RE NOT ATTRACTED TO HIS TYPE (GAUNT, FASHIONABLE AND DUMB). I'VE PURSUED SEVERAL WOMEN (THE "ACTRESS" IN SC. 1, FOR EXAMPLE) BECAUSE I KNEW, ON SOME LEVEL, THAT WHITEY WOULD BE IMPRESSED.

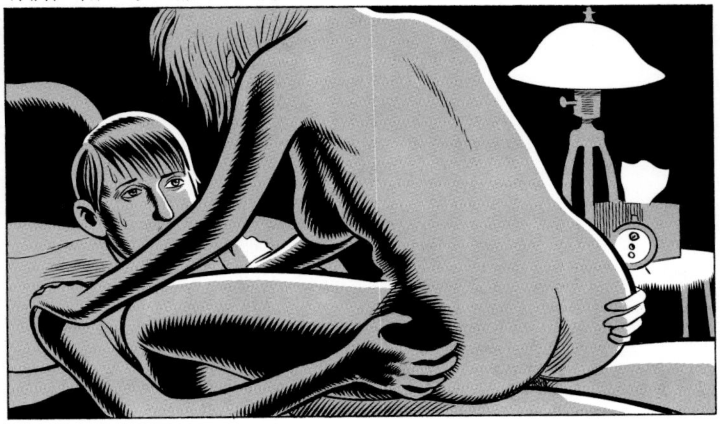

I AM CURSED BY TWO THINGS: AN UNSYMPATHETIC EYE FOR PERFECTION AND A BLOSSOMING KNOWLEDGE OF MY OWN FEMININE IDEAL, SPECIFICALLY: THE HEAD (ROUND EYES AND MOUTH, A JAUNTY ARC TO THE NOSE BRIDGE), SMALLISH AND OVOID, LEADING WITH A PARTICULAR TILT TO AN EXTENDED NECK, SWOOPING OUTWARD AT THE SHOULDERS...

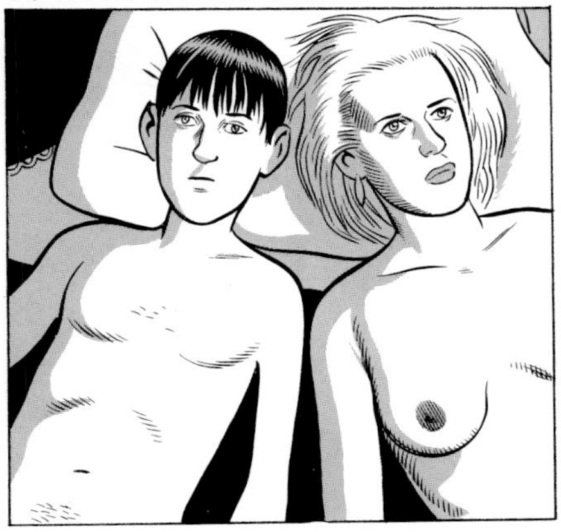

A SUBSTANTIAL CARRIAGE AND ARMS; SMALLISH ROUND BREASTS; A CONVEX STOMACH DIVIDING POWERFUL HIPS WHICH, FROM SIDE TO BACK, DESCRIBE A MEATY SEMI-CIRCLE; PROCEEDING DOWNWARD TO THICK, GIRLISH LEGS AND INSIGNIFICANT FEET.

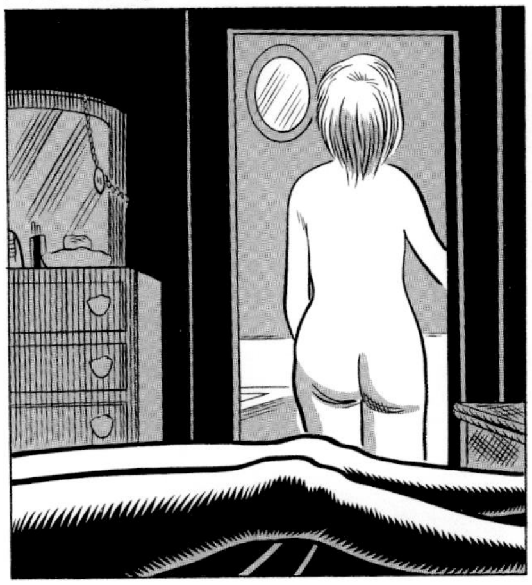

IN SOME WAYS, I LONG FOR THE "OLD DAYS," WHEN FETISHES WERE APPLIED TO HANDKERCHIEFS AND PETTICOATS, RATHER THAN DIRECTLY TO FRAIL PHYSICAL FORMS THAT CAN NEVER LIVE UP TO THE EMBELLISHED PERFECTION OF OUR (WE PERVERTS) IDEALS.

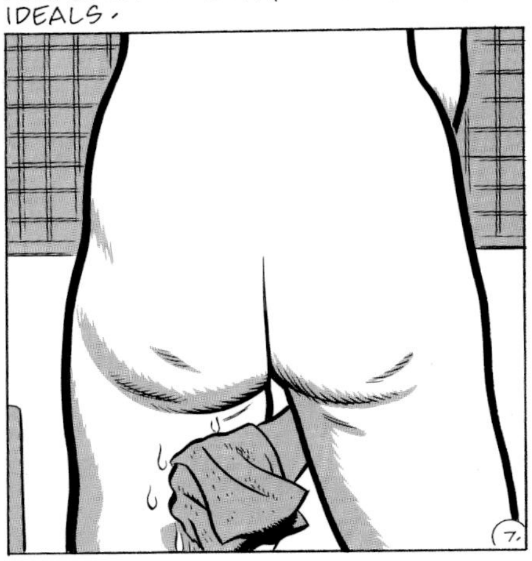

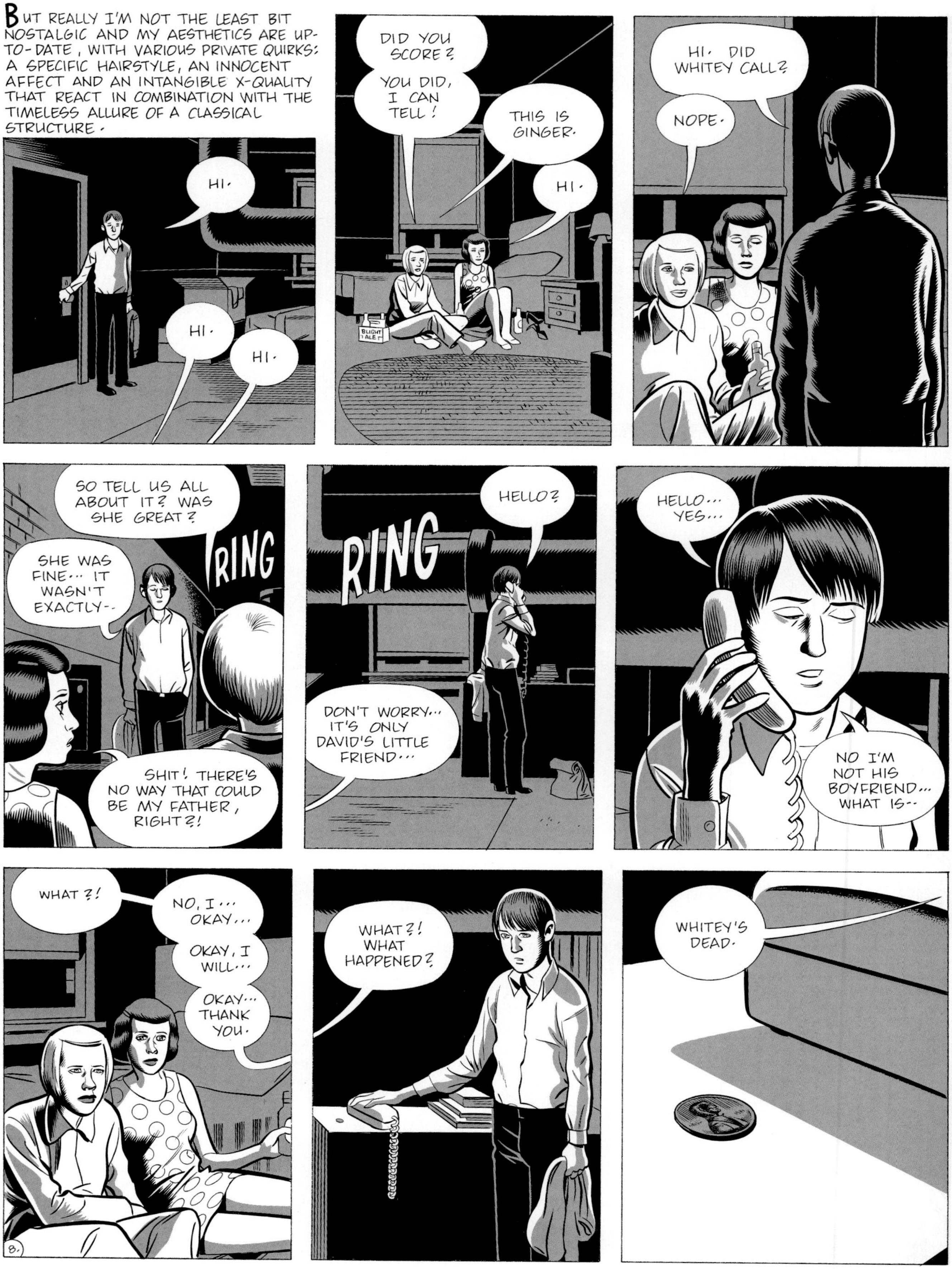
BUT REALLY I'M NOT THE LEAST BIT NOSTALGIC AND MY AESTHETICS ARE UP-TO-DATE, WITH VARIOUS PRIVATE QUIRKS: A SPECIFIC HAIRSTYLE, AN INNOCENT AFFECT AND AN INTANGIBLE X-QUALITY THAT REACT IN COMBINATION WITH THE TIMELESS ALLURE OF A CLASSICAL STRUCTURE.
HI.
HI.
HI.
DID YOU SCORE?
YOU DID, I CAN TELL!
THIS IS GINGER.
HI.
HI. DID WHITEY CALL?
NOPE.
SO TELL US ALL ABOUT IT? WAS SHE GREAT?
SHE WAS FINE... IT WASN'T EXACTLY--
RING
SHIT! THERE'S NO WAY THAT COULD BE MY FATHER, RIGHT?!
RING
HELLO?
DON'T WORRY... IT'S ONLY DAVID'S LITTLE FRIEND...
HELLO... YES...
NO I'M NOT HIS BOYFRIEND... WHAT IS--
WHAT?!
NO, I... OKAY...
OKAY, I WILL...
OKAY... THANK YOU.
WHAT?! WHAT HAPPENED?
WHITEY'S DEAD.

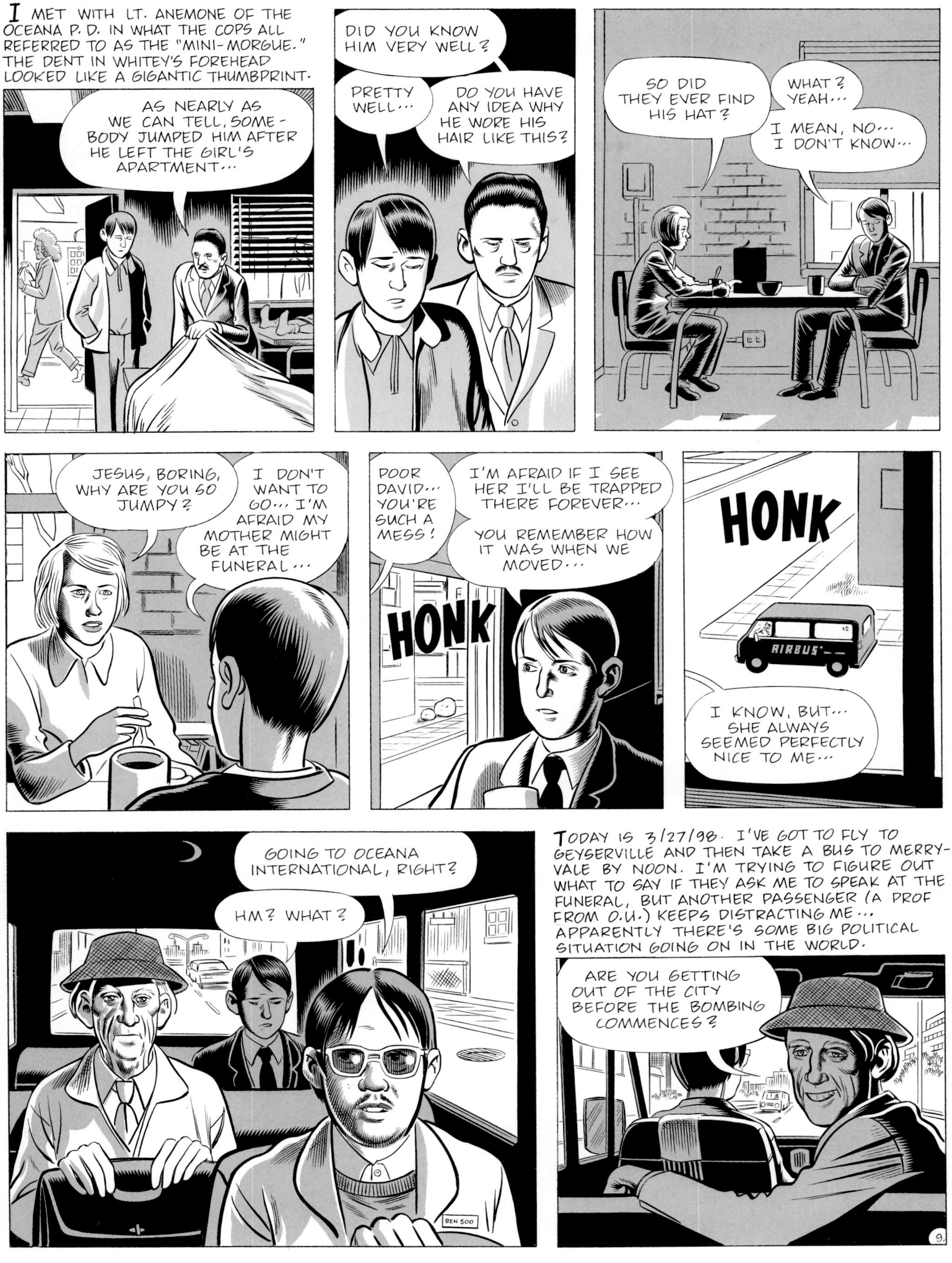

I MET WITH LT. ANEMONE OF THE OCEANA P. D. IN WHAT THE COPS ALL REFERRED TO AS THE "MINI-MORGUE." THE DENT IN WHITEY'S FOREHEAD LOOKED LIKE A GIGANTIC THUMBPRINT.
AS NEARLY AS WE CAN TELL, SOMEBODY JUMPED HIM AFTER HE LEFT THE GIRL'S APARTMENT...
DID YOU KNOW HIM VERY WELL?
PRETTY WELL...
DO YOU HAVE ANY IDEA WHY HE WORE HIS HAIR LIKE THIS?
SO DID THEY EVER FIND HIS HAT?
WHAT? YEAH...
I MEAN, NO... I DON'T KNOW...
JESUS, BORING, WHY ARE YOU SO JUMPY?
I DON'T WANT TO GO... I'M AFRAID MY MOTHER MIGHT BE AT THE FUNERAL...
POOR DAVID... YOU'RE SUCH A MESS!
I'M AFRAID IF I SEE HER I'LL BE TRAPPED THERE FOREVER...
YOU REMEMBER HOW IT WAS WHEN WE MOVED...
HONK
HONK
AIRBUS
I KNOW, BUT... SHE ALWAYS SEEMED PERFECTLY NICE TO ME...
GOING TO OCEANA INTERNATIONAL, RIGHT?
HM? WHAT?
BEN SOO
TODAY IS 3/27/98. I'VE GOT TO FLY TO GEYSERVILLE AND THEN TAKE A BUS TO MERRYVALE BY NOON. I'M TRYING TO FIGURE OUT WHAT TO SAY IF THEY ASK ME TO SPEAK AT THE FUNERAL, BUT ANOTHER PASSENGER (A PROF FROM O.U.) KEEPS DISTRACTING ME... APPARENTLY THERE'S SOME BIG POLITICAL SITUATION GOING ON IN THE WORLD.
ARE YOU GETTING OUT OF THE CITY BEFORE THE BOMBING COMMENCES?

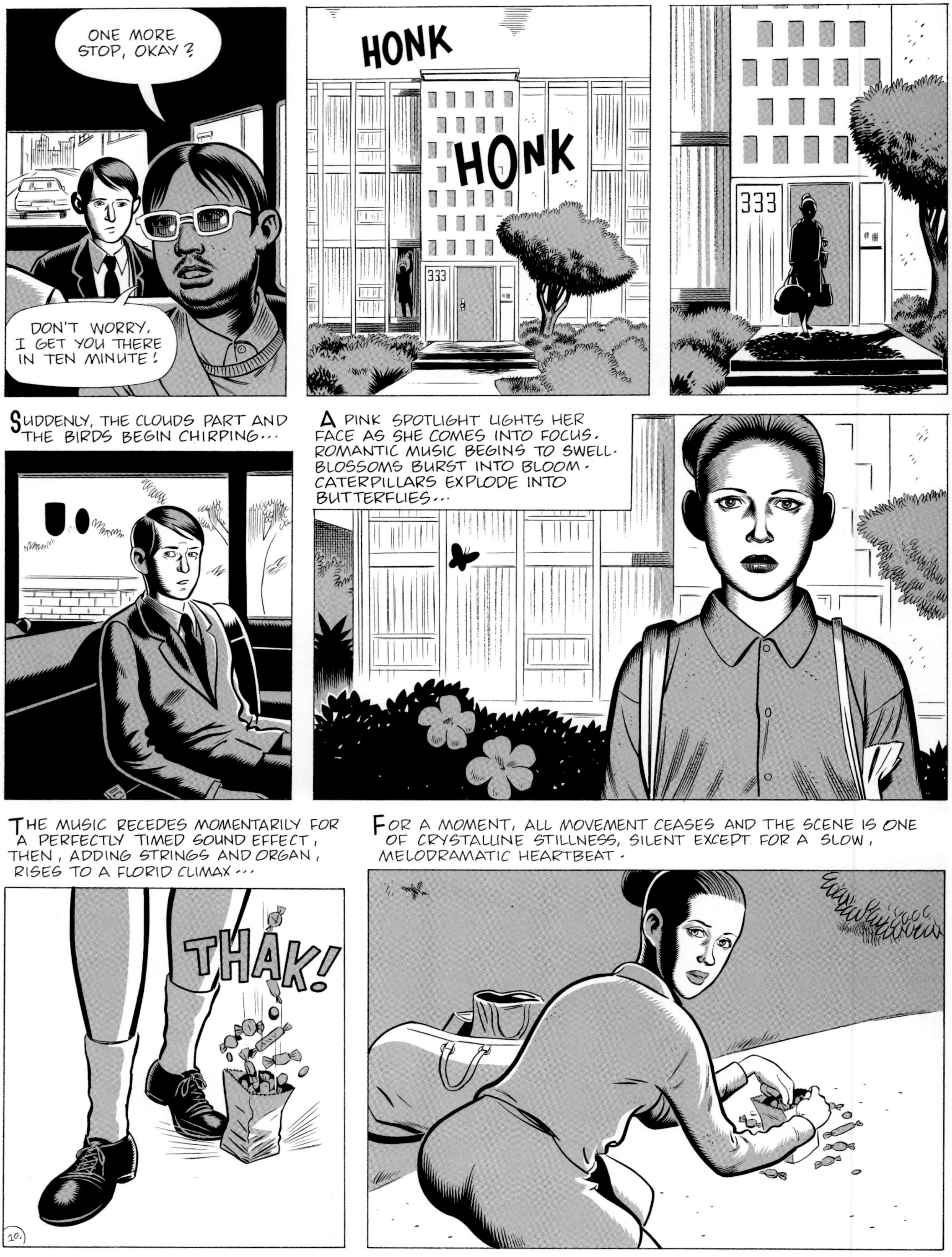
ONE MORE STOP, OKAY?
DON'T WORRY. I GET YOU THERE IN TEN MINUTE!
HONK
HONK
333
333
SUDDENLY, THE CLOUDS PART AND THE BIRDS BEGIN CHIRPING...
A PINK SPOTLIGHT LIGHTS HER FACE AS SHE COMES INTO FOCUS. ROMANTIC MUSIC BEGINS TO SWELL. BLOSSOMS BURST INTO BLOOM. CATERPILLARS EXPLODE INTO BUTTERFLIES...
THE MUSIC RECEDES MOMENTARILY FOR A PERFECTLY TIMED SOUND EFFECT, THEN, ADDING STRINGS AND ORGAN, RISES TO A FLORID CLIMAX...
THAK!
FOR A MOMENT, ALL MOVEMENT CEASES AND THE SCENE IS ONE OF CRYSTALLINE STILLNESS, SILENT EXCEPT FOR A SLOW, MELODRAMATIC HEARTBEAT.
10.

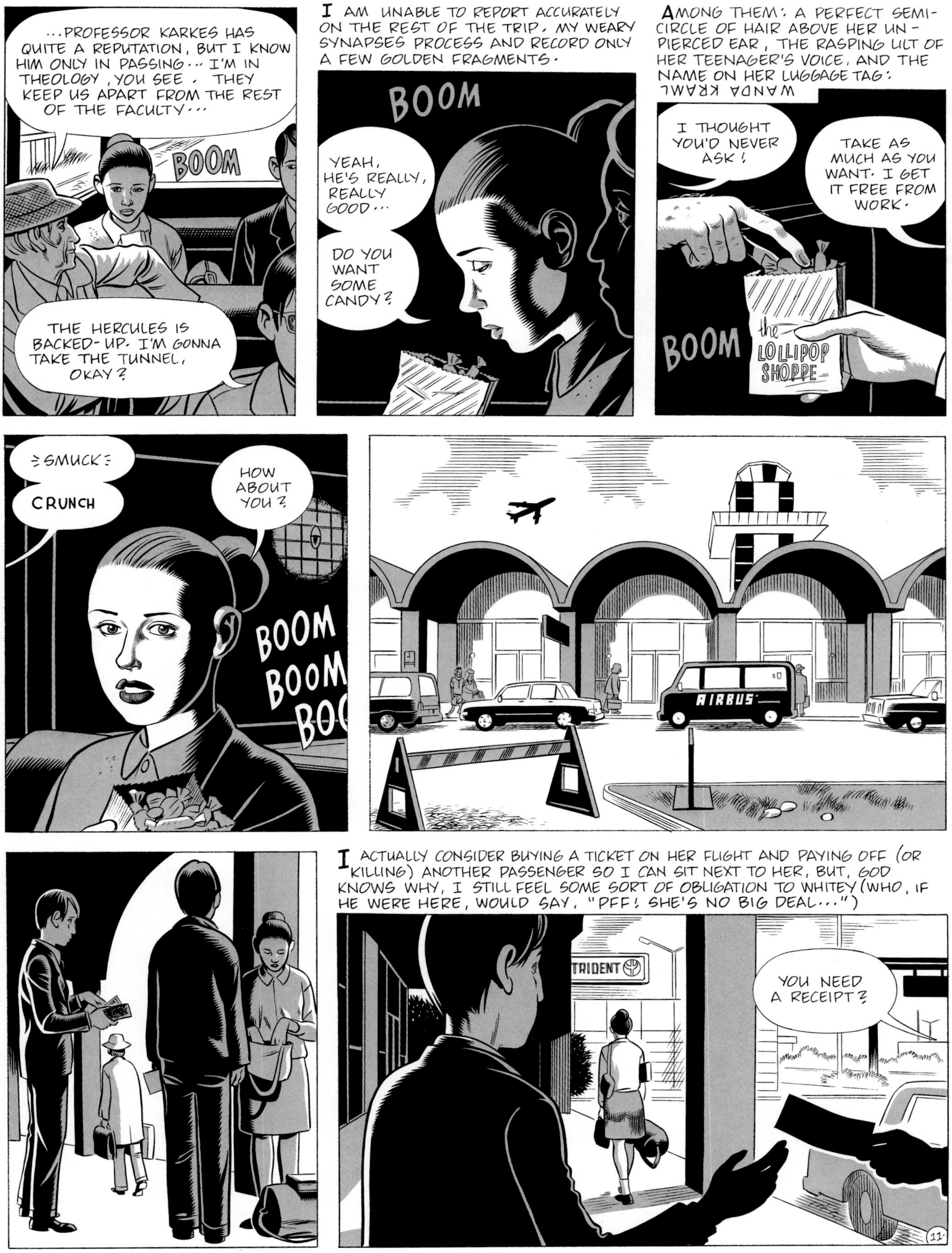
...PROFESSOR KARKES HAS QUITE A REPUTATION, BUT I KNOW HIM ONLY IN PASSING... I'M IN THEOLOGY, YOU SEE. THEY KEEP US APART FROM THE REST OF THE FACULTY...
BOOM
THE HERCULES IS BACKED-UP. I'M GONNA TAKE THE TUNNEL, OKAY?
I AM UNABLE TO REPORT ACCURATELY ON THE REST OF THE TRIP. MY WEARY SYNAPSES PROCESS AND RECORD ONLY A FEW GOLDEN FRAGMENTS.
BOOM
YEAH, HE'S REALLY, REALLY GOOD...
DO YOU WANT SOME CANDY?
AMONG THEM: A PERFECT SEMI-CIRCLE OF HAIR ABOVE HER UN-PIERCED EAR, THE RASPING LILT OF HER TEENAGER'S VOICE, AND THE NAME ON HER LUGGAGE TAG:
WANDA KRAWL
I THOUGHT YOU'D NEVER ASK!
TAKE AS MUCH AS YOU WANT. I GET IT FREE FROM WORK.
BOOM
the LOLLIPOP SHOPPE
=SMUCK=
CRUNCH
HOW ABOUT YOU?
BOOM
BOOM
BOO
AIRBUS
I ACTUALLY CONSIDER BUYING A TICKET ON HER FLIGHT AND PAYING OFF (OR KILLING) ANOTHER PASSENGER SO I CAN SIT NEXT TO HER, BUT, GOD KNOWS WHY, I STILL FEEL SOME SORT OF OBLIGATION TO WHITEY (WHO, IF HE WERE HERE, WOULD SAY, "PFF! SHE'S NO BIG DEAL...")
TRIDENT
YOU NEED A RECEIPT?
11.

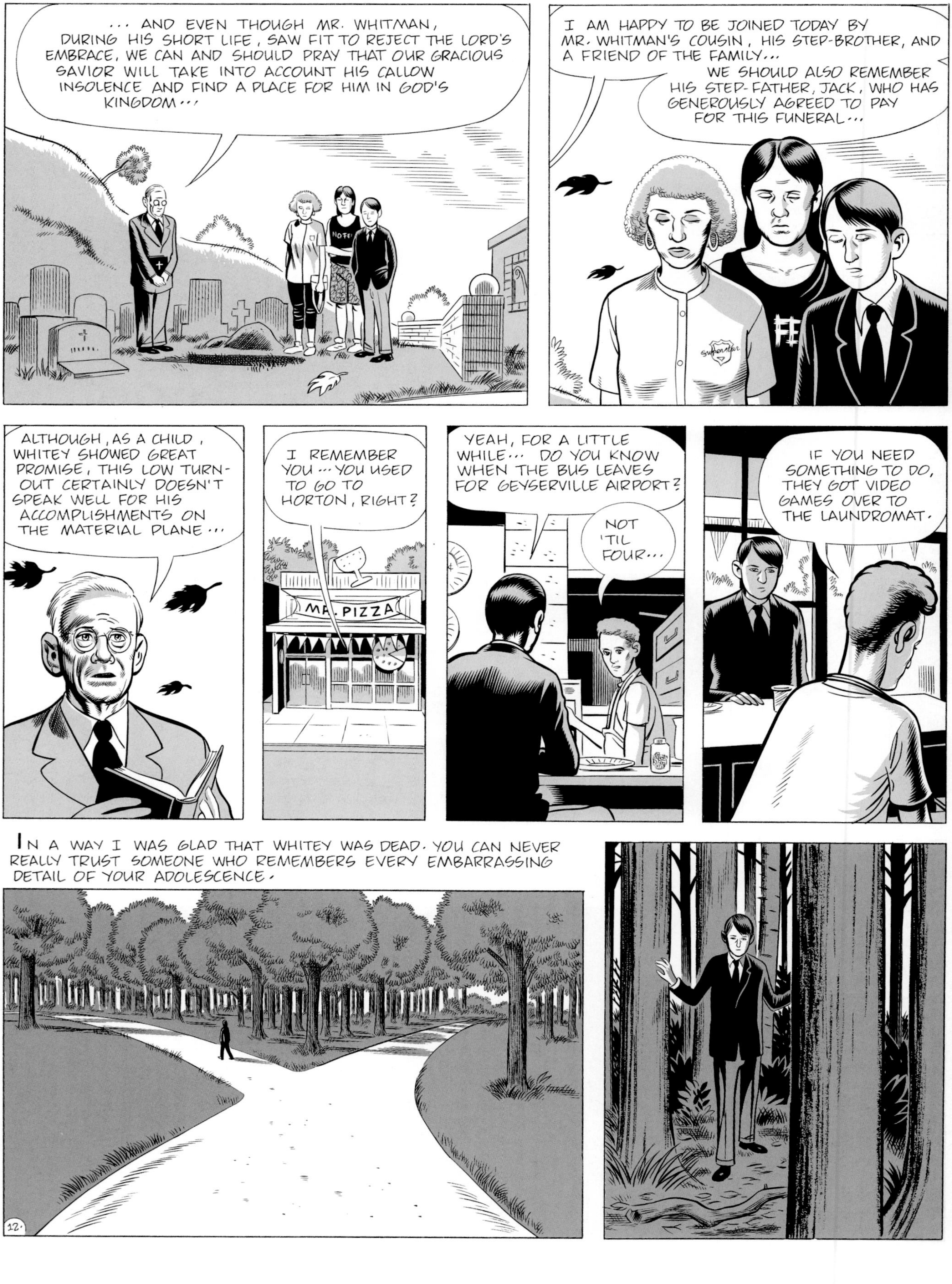
... AND EVEN THOUGH MR. WHITMAN, DURING HIS SHORT LIFE, SAW FIT TO REJECT THE LORD'S EMBRACE, WE CAN AND SHOULD PRAY THAT OUR GRACIOUS SAVIOR WILL TAKE INTO ACCOUNT HIS CALLOW INSOLENCE AND FIND A PLACE FOR HIM IN GOD'S KINGDOM...
I AM HAPPY TO BE JOINED TODAY BY MR. WHITMAN'S COUSIN, HIS STEP-BROTHER, AND A FRIEND OF THE FAMILY...
WE SHOULD ALSO REMEMBER HIS STEP-FATHER, JACK, WHO HAS GENEROUSLY AGREED TO PAY FOR THIS FUNERAL...
ALTHOUGH, AS A CHILD, WHITEY SHOWED GREAT PROMISE, THIS LOW TURN-OUT CERTAINLY DOESN'T SPEAK WELL FOR HIS ACCOMPLISHMENTS ON THE MATERIAL PLANE...
I REMEMBER YOU... YOU USED TO GO TO HORTON, RIGHT?
MR. PIZZA
YEAH, FOR A LITTLE WHILE... DO YOU KNOW WHEN THE BUS LEAVES FOR GEYSERVILLE AIRPORT?
NOT 'TIL FOUR...
IF YOU NEED SOMETHING TO DO, THEY GOT VIDEO GAMES OVER TO THE LAUNDROMAT.
IN A WAY I WAS GLAD THAT WHITEY WAS DEAD. YOU CAN NEVER REALLY TRUST SOMEONE WHO REMEMBERS EVERY EMBARRASSING DETAIL OF YOUR ADOLESCENCE.
12.

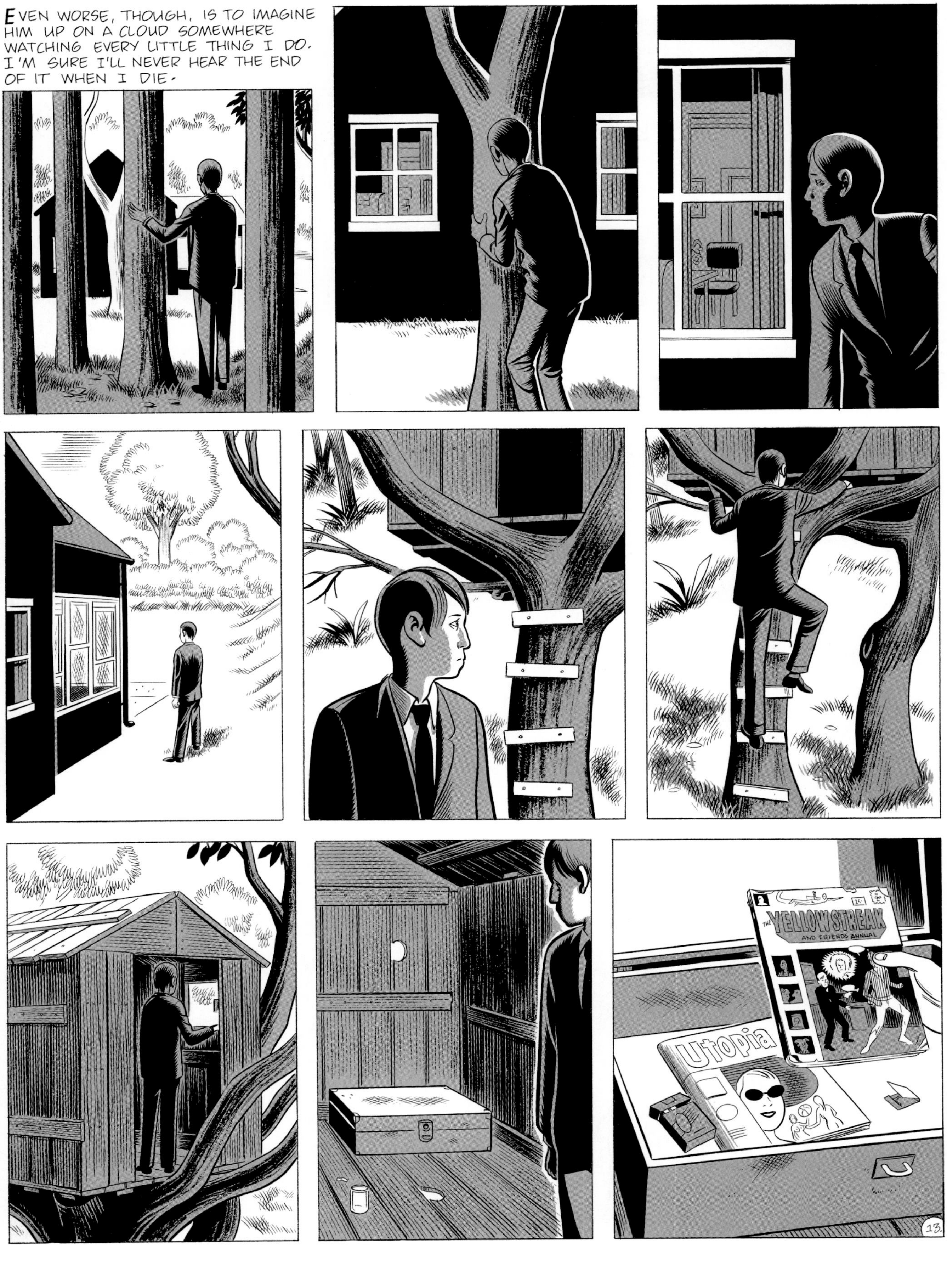
EVEN WORSE, THOUGH, IS TO IMAGINE HIM UP ON A CLOUD SOMEWHERE WATCHING EVERY LITTLE THING I DO. I'M SURE I'LL NEVER HEAR THE END OF IT WHEN I DIE.
THE YELLOW STREAK AND FRIENDS ANNUAL
Utopia

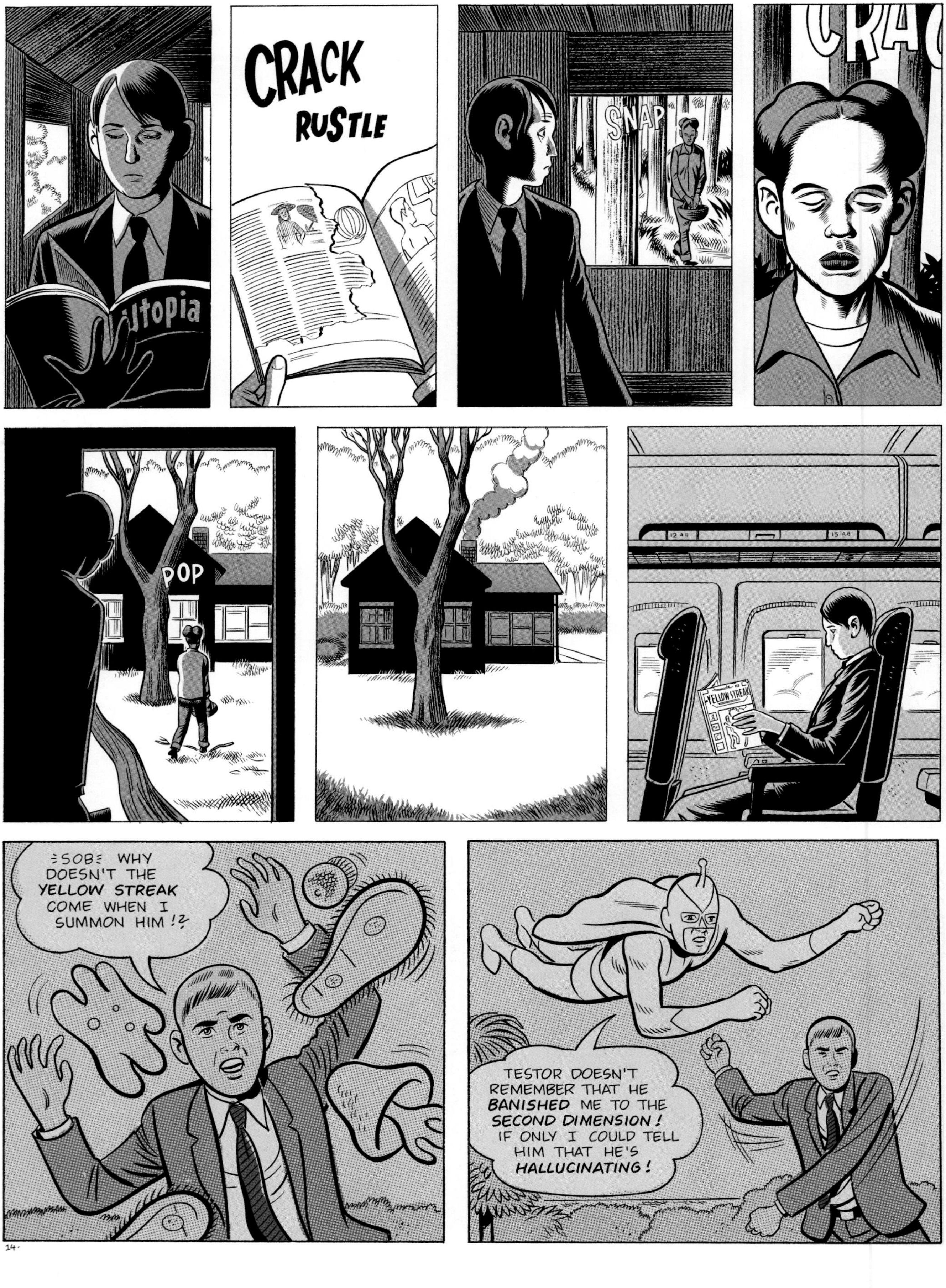
Utopia
CRACK
RUSTLE
SNAP
CRAC
POP
YELLOW STREAK
12 AB
13 AB
SOB WHY DOESN'T THE YELLOW STREAK COME WHEN I SUMMON HIM!?
TESTOR DOESN'T REMEMBER THAT HE BANISHED ME TO THE SECOND DIMENSION! IF ONLY I COULD TELL HIM THAT HE'S HALLUCINATING!

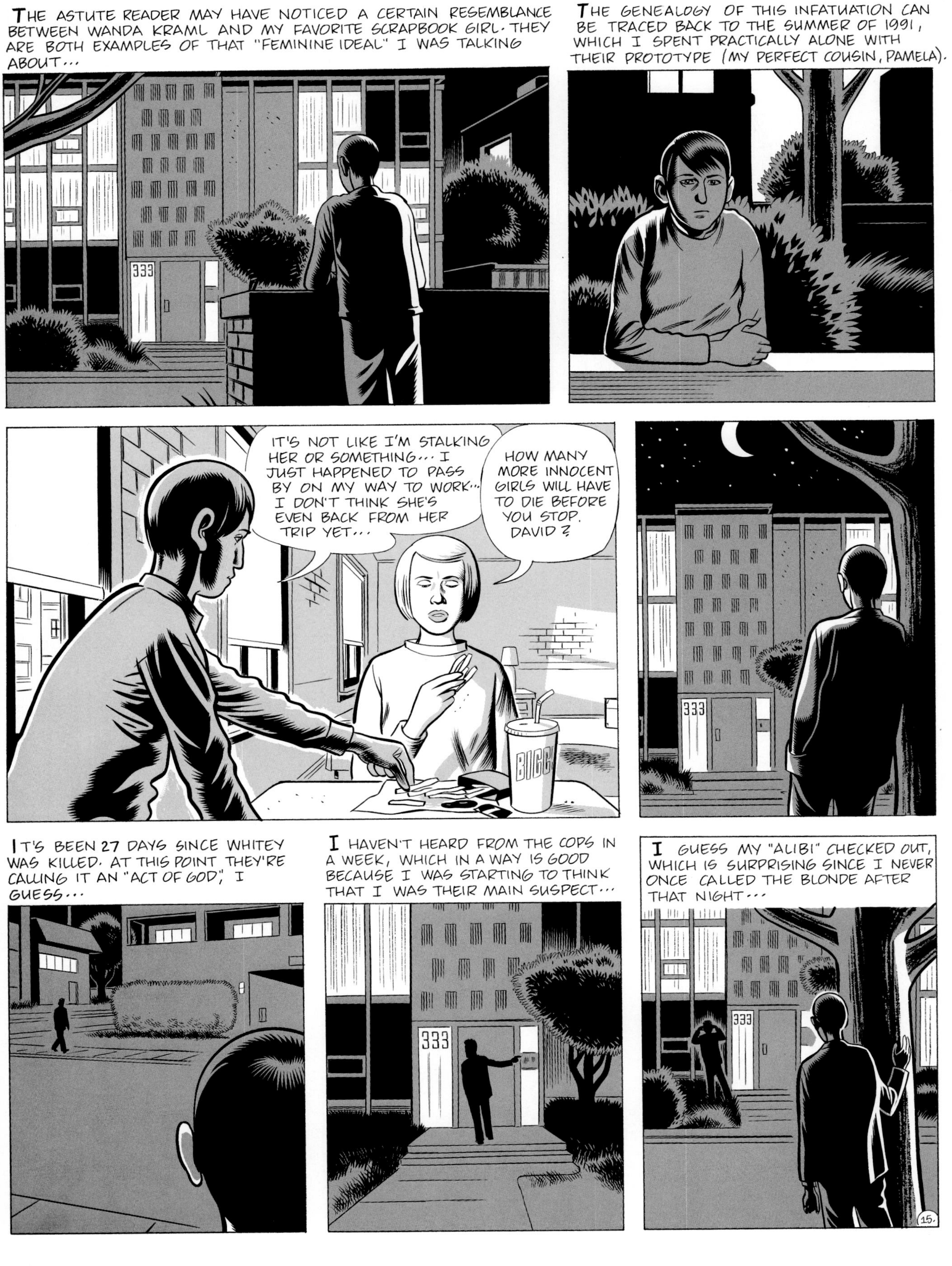

THE ASTUTE READER MAY HAVE NOTICED A CERTAIN RESEMBLANCE BETWEEN WANDA KRAML AND MY FAVORITE SCRAPBOOK GIRL. THEY ARE BOTH EXAMPLES OF THAT "FEMININE IDEAL" I WAS TALKING ABOUT...
333
THE GENEALOGY OF THIS INFATUATION CAN BE TRACED BACK TO THE SUMMER OF 1991, WHICH I SPENT PRACTICALLY ALONE WITH THEIR PROTOTYPE (MY PERFECT COUSIN, PAMELA).
IT'S NOT LIKE I'M STALKING HER OR SOMETHING... I JUST HAPPENED TO PASS BY ON MY WAY TO WORK... I DON'T THINK SHE'S EVEN BACK FROM HER TRIP YET...
HOW MANY MORE INNOCENT GIRLS WILL HAVE TO DIE BEFORE YOU STOP, DAVID ?
333
IT'S BEEN 27 DAYS SINCE WHITEY WAS KILLED. AT THIS POINT THEY'RE CALLING IT AN "ACT OF GOD," I GUESS...
I HAVEN'T HEARD FROM THE COPS IN A WEEK, WHICH IN A WAY IS GOOD BECAUSE I WAS STARTING TO THINK THAT I WAS THEIR MAIN SUSPECT...
333
I GUESS MY "ALIBI" CHECKED OUT, WHICH IS SURPRISING SINCE I NEVER ONCE CALLED THE BLONDE AFTER THAT NIGHT...
333
15.

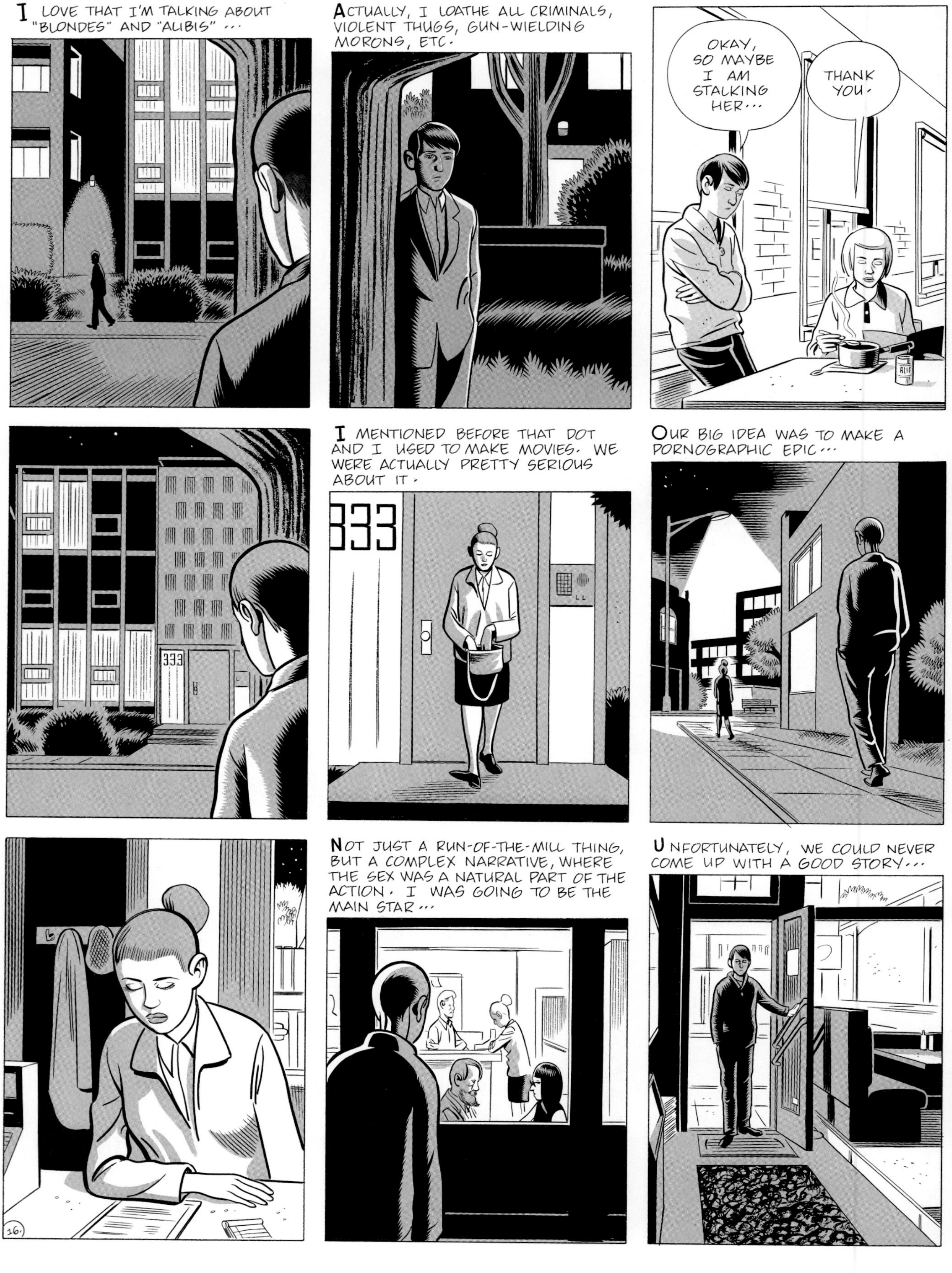
I LOVE THAT I'M TALKING ABOUT "BLONDES" AND "ALIBIS"...
ACTUALLY, I LOATHE ALL CRIMINALS, VIOLENT THUGS, GUN-WIELDING MORONS, ETC.
OKAY, SO MAYBE I AM STALKING HER...
THANK YOU.
333
I MENTIONED BEFORE THAT DOT AND I USED TO MAKE MOVIES. WE WERE ACTUALLY PRETTY SERIOUS ABOUT IT.
333
OUR BIG IDEA WAS TO MAKE A PORNOGRAPHIC EPIC...
NOT JUST A RUN-OF-THE-MILL THING, BUT A COMPLEX NARRATIVE, WHERE THE SEX WAS A NATURAL PART OF THE ACTION. I WAS GOING TO BE THE MAIN STAR...
UNFORTUNATELY, WE COULD NEVER COME UP WITH A GOOD STORY...

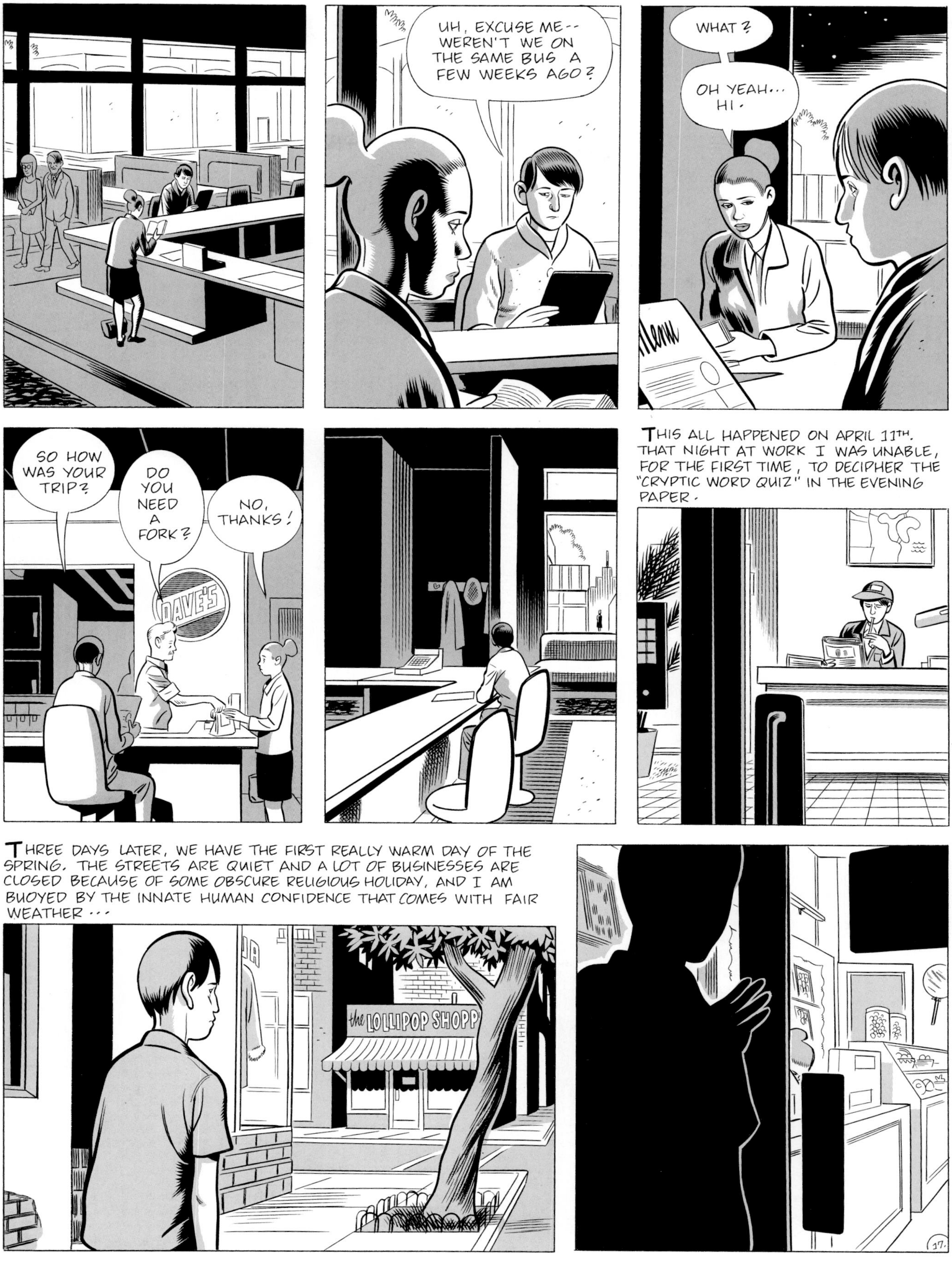

UH, EXCUSE ME--
WEREN'T WE ON THE SAME BUS A FEW WEEKS AGO?
WHAT?
OH YEAH... HI.
SO HOW WAS YOUR TRIP?
DO YOU NEED A FORK?
NO, THANKS!
DAVE'S
THIS ALL HAPPENED ON APRIL 11TH. THAT NIGHT AT WORK I WAS UNABLE, FOR THE FIRST TIME, TO DECIPHER THE "CRYPTIC WORD QUIZ" IN THE EVENING PAPER.
THREE DAYS LATER, WE HAVE THE FIRST REALLY WARM DAY OF THE SPRING. THE STREETS ARE QUIET AND A LOT OF BUSINESSES ARE CLOSED BECAUSE OF SOME OBSCURE RELIGIOUS HOLIDAY, AND I AM BUOYED BY THE INNATE HUMAN CONFIDENCE THAT COMES WITH FAIR WEATHER...
the LOLLIPOP SHOPP

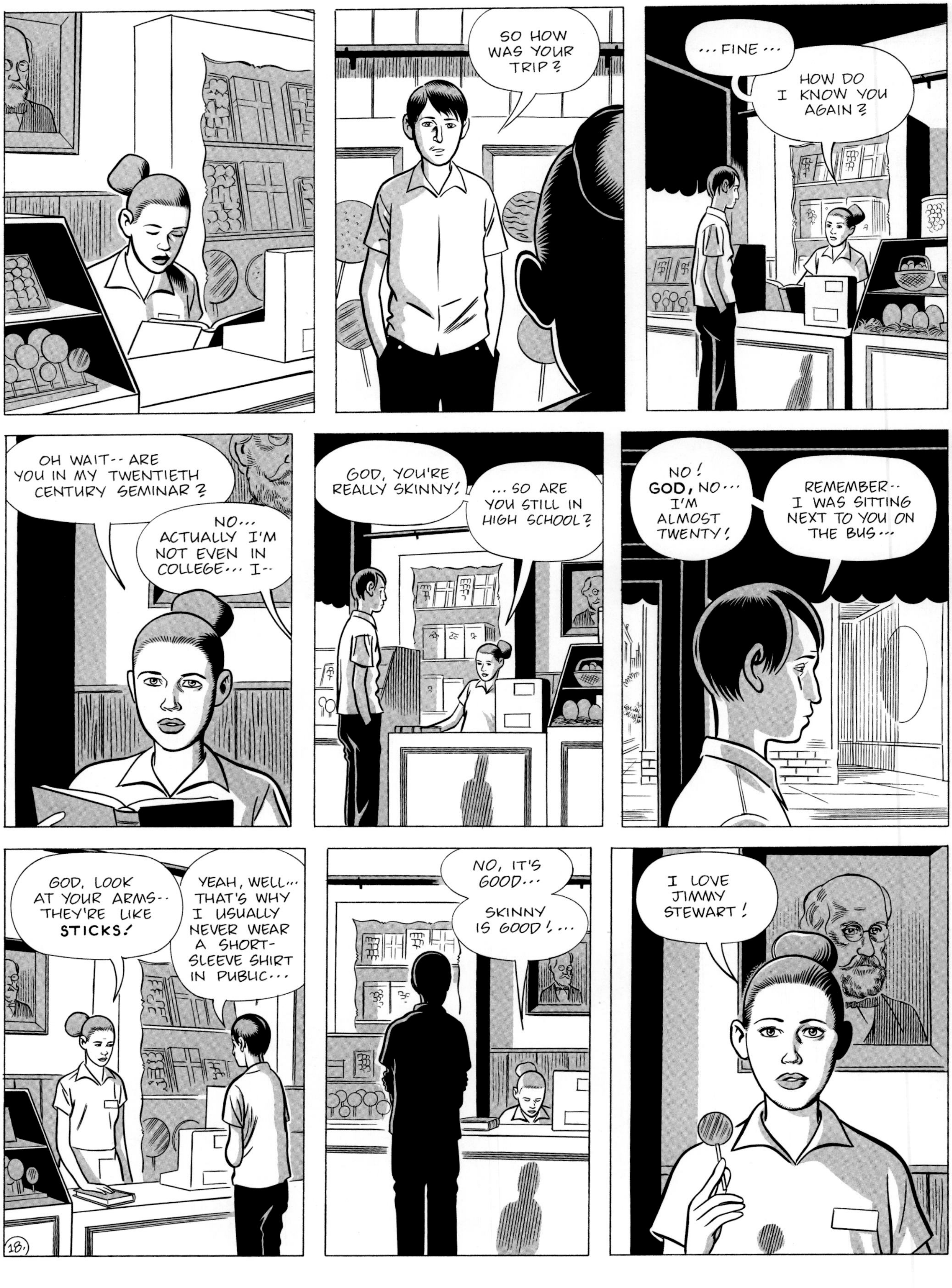

SO HOW WAS YOUR TRIP?
...FINE...
HOW DO I KNOW YOU AGAIN?
OH WAIT-- ARE YOU IN MY TWENTIETH CENTURY SEMINAR?
NO... ACTUALLY I'M NOT EVEN IN COLLEGE... I--
GOD, YOU'RE REALLY SKINNY!
...SO ARE YOU STILL IN HIGH SCHOOL?
NO! GOD, NO... I'M ALMOST TWENTY!
REMEMBER-- I WAS SITTING NEXT TO YOU ON THE BUS...
GOD, LOOK AT YOUR ARMS-- THEY'RE LIKE STICKS!
YEAH, WELL... THAT'S WHY I USUALLY NEVER WEAR A SHORT-SLEEVE SHIRT IN PUBLIC...
NO, IT'S GOOD...
SKINNY IS GOOD!...
I LOVE JIMMY STEWART!

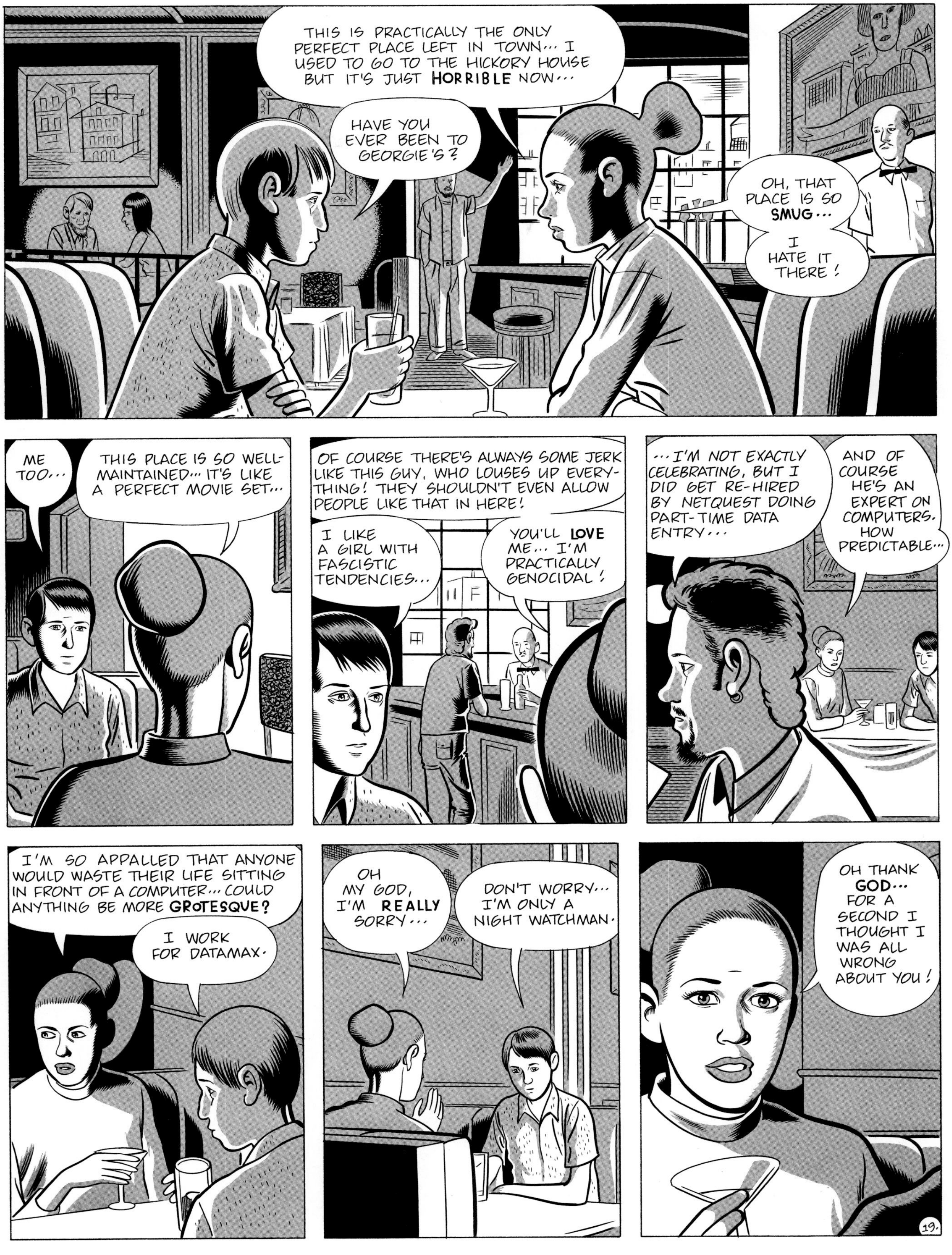
THIS IS PRACTICALLY THE ONLY PERFECT PLACE LEFT IN TOWN... I USED TO GO TO THE HICKORY HOUSE BUT IT'S JUST **HORRIBLE** NOW...
HAVE YOU EVER BEEN TO GEORGIE'S?
OH, THAT PLACE IS SO **SMUG**...
I HATE IT THERE!
ME TOO...
THIS PLACE IS SO WELL-MAINTAINED... IT'S LIKE A PERFECT MOVIE SET...
OF COURSE THERE'S ALWAYS SOME JERK LIKE THIS GUY, WHO LOUSES UP EVERYTHING! THEY SHOULDN'T EVEN ALLOW PEOPLE LIKE THAT IN HERE!
I LIKE A GIRL WITH FASCISTIC TENDENCIES...
YOU'LL **LOVE** ME... I'M PRACTICALLY GENOCIDAL!
...I'M NOT EXACTLY CELEBRATING, BUT I DID GET RE-HIRED BY NETQUEST DOING PART-TIME DATA ENTRY...
AND OF COURSE HE'S AN EXPERT ON COMPUTERS. HOW PREDICTABLE...
I'M SO APPALLED THAT ANYONE WOULD WASTE THEIR LIFE SITTING IN FRONT OF A COMPUTER... COULD ANYTHING BE MORE **GROTESQUE?**
I WORK FOR DATAMAX.
OH MY GOD, I'M **REALLY** SORRY...
DON'T WORRY... I'M ONLY A NIGHT WATCHMAN.
OH THANK **GOD**... FOR A SECOND I THOUGHT I WAS ALL WRONG ABOUT YOU!

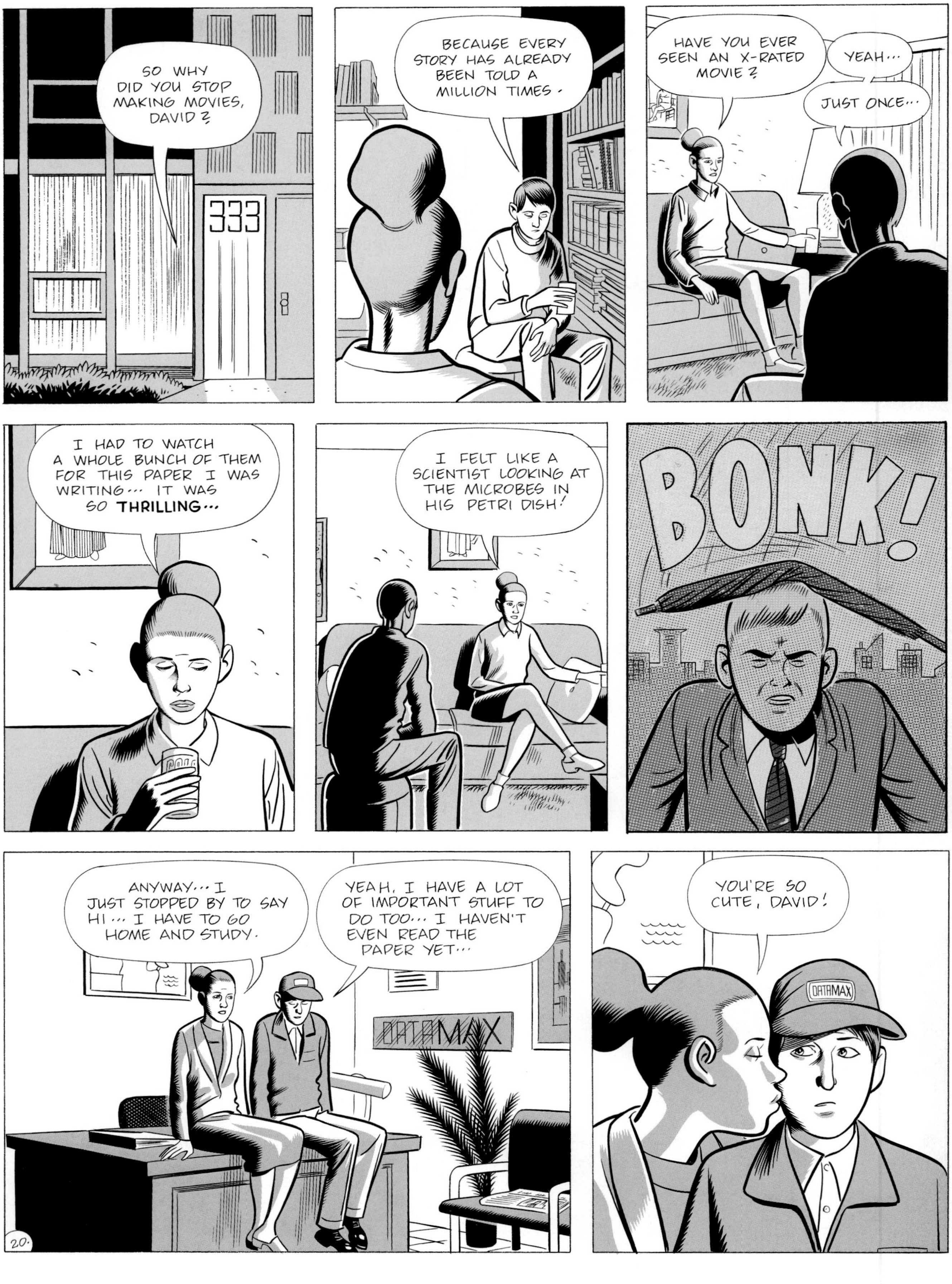
SO WHY DID YOU STOP MAKING MOVIES, DAVID?
333
BECAUSE EVERY STORY HAS ALREADY BEEN TOLD A MILLION TIMES.
HAVE YOU EVER SEEN AN X-RATED MOVIE?
YEAH...
JUST ONCE...
I HAD TO WATCH A WHOLE BUNCH OF THEM FOR THIS PAPER I WAS WRITING... IT WAS SO THRILLING...
I FELT LIKE A SCIENTIST LOOKING AT THE MICROBES IN HIS PETRI DISH!
BONK!
ANYWAY... I JUST STOPPED BY TO SAY HI... I HAVE TO GO HOME AND STUDY.
YEAH, I HAVE A LOT OF IMPORTANT STUFF TO DO TOO... I HAVEN'T EVEN READ THE PAPER YET...
DATAMAX
YOU'RE SO CUTE, DAVID!
DATAMAX

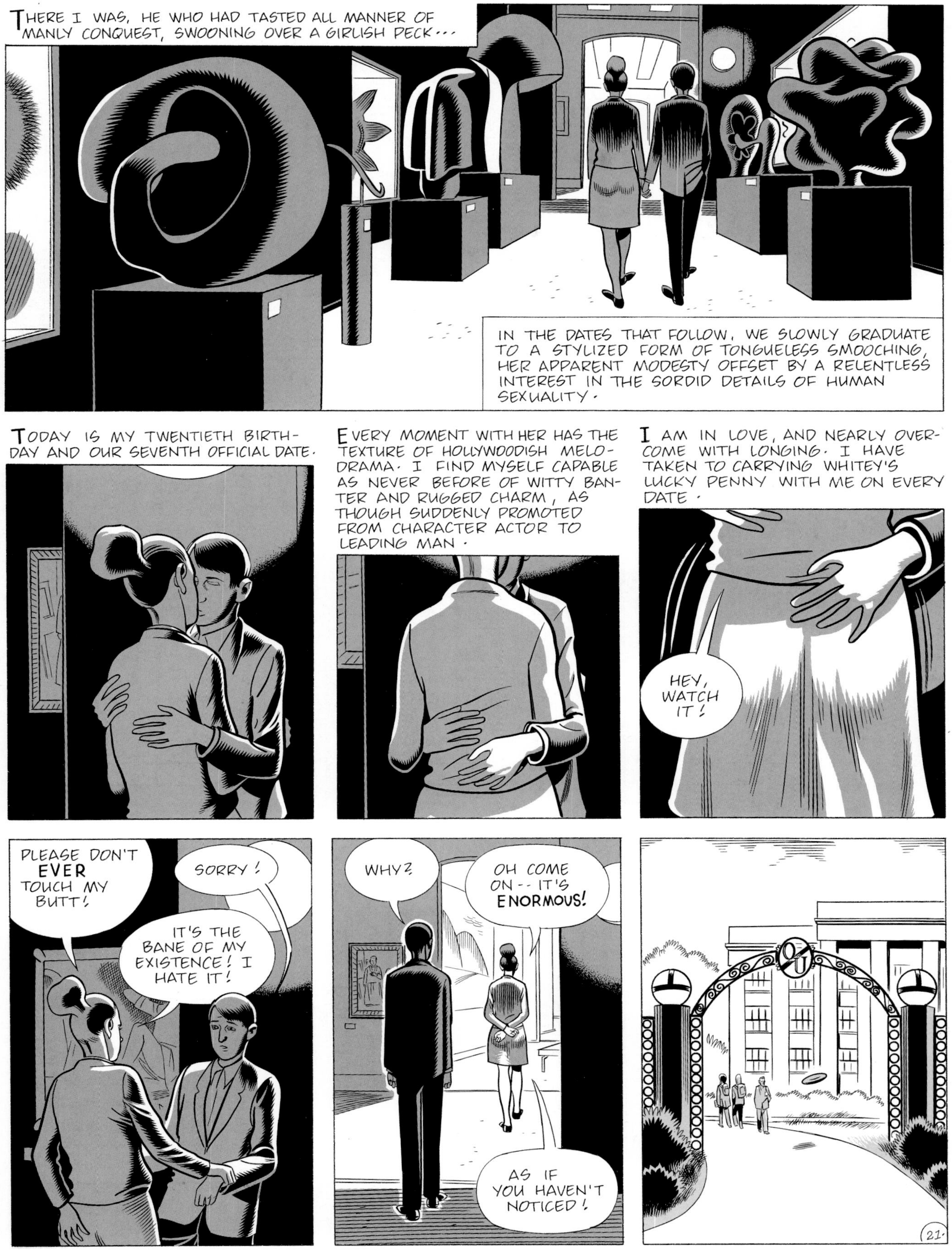
THERE I WAS, HE WHO HAD TASTED ALL MANNER OF MANLY CONQUEST, SWOONING OVER A GIRLISH PECK...
IN THE DATES THAT FOLLOW, WE SLOWLY GRADUATE TO A STYLIZED FORM OF TONGUELESS SMOOCHING, HER APPARENT MODESTY OFFSET BY A RELENTLESS INTEREST IN THE SORDID DETAILS OF HUMAN SEXUALITY.
TODAY IS MY TWENTIETH BIRTHDAY AND OUR SEVENTH OFFICIAL DATE.
EVERY MOMENT WITH HER HAS THE TEXTURE OF HOLLYWOODISH MELODRAMA. I FIND MYSELF CAPABLE AS NEVER BEFORE OF WITTY BANTER AND RUGGED CHARM, AS THOUGH SUDDENLY PROMOTED FROM CHARACTER ACTOR TO LEADING MAN.
I AM IN LOVE, AND NEARLY OVERCOME WITH LONGING. I HAVE TAKEN TO CARRYING WHITEY'S LUCKY PENNY WITH ME ON EVERY DATE.
HEY, WATCH IT!
PLEASE DON'T **EVER** TOUCH MY BUTT!
SORRY!
IT'S THE BANE OF MY EXISTENCE! I HATE IT!
WHY?
OH COME ON -- IT'S **ENORMOUS!**
AS IF YOU HAVEN'T NOTICED!

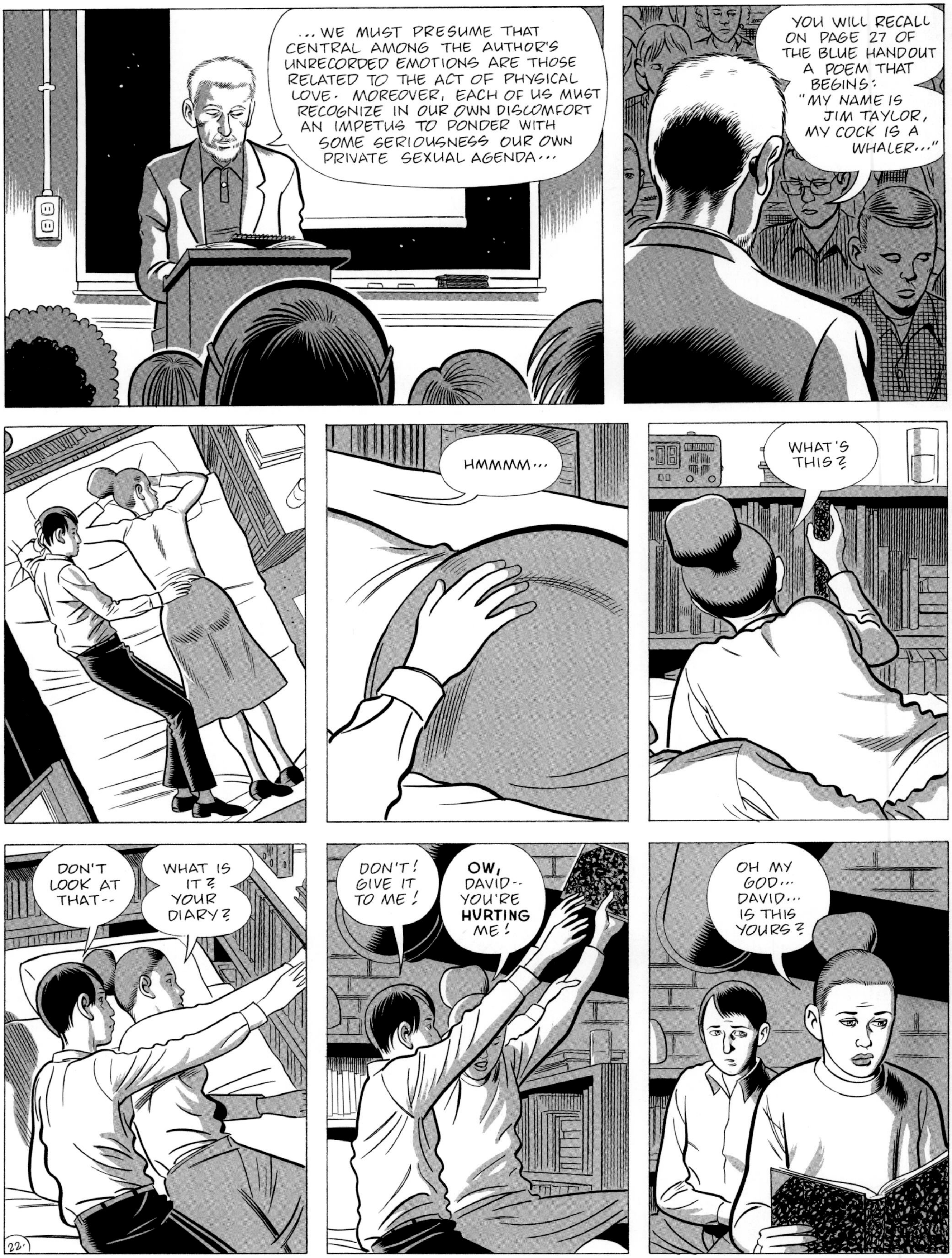
...WE MUST PRESUME THAT CENTRAL AMONG THE AUTHOR'S UNRECORDED EMOTIONS ARE THOSE RELATED TO THE ACT OF PHYSICAL LOVE. MOREOVER, EACH OF US MUST RECOGNIZE IN OUR OWN DISCOMFORT AN IMPETUS TO PONDER WITH SOME SERIOUSNESS OUR OWN PRIVATE SEXUAL AGENDA...
YOU WILL RECALL ON PAGE 27 OF THE BLUE HANDOUT A POEM THAT BEGINS: "MY NAME IS JIM TAYLOR, MY COCK IS A WHALER..."
HMMMM...
WHAT'S THIS?
DON'T LOOK AT THAT--
WHAT IS IT? YOUR DIARY?
DON'T! GIVE IT TO ME!
OW, DAVID-- YOU'RE HURTING ME!
OH MY GOD... DAVID... IS THIS YOURS?
22.

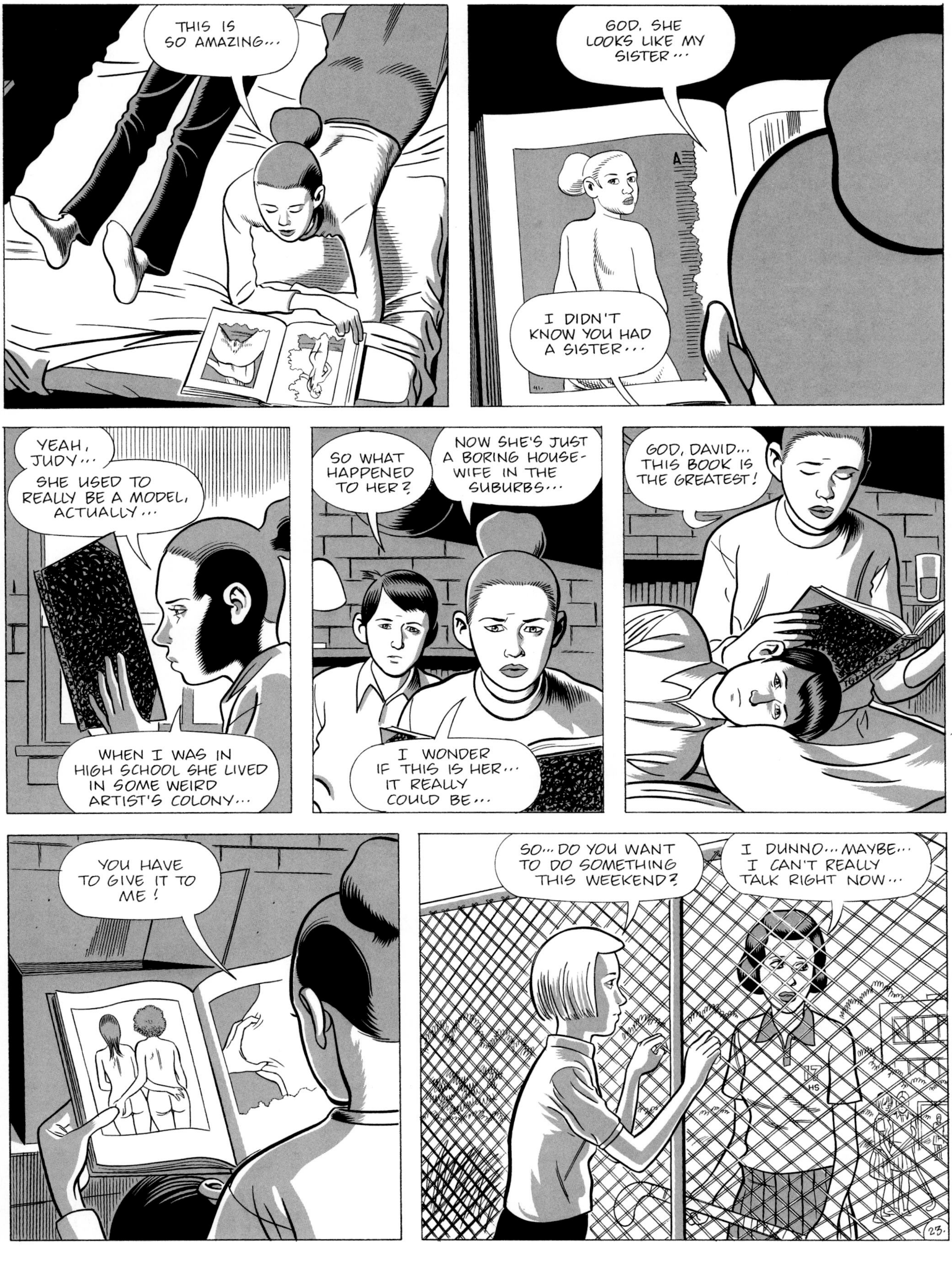
THIS IS SO AMAZING...
GOD, SHE LOOKS LIKE MY SISTER...
I DIDN'T KNOW YOU HAD A SISTER...
YEAH, JUDY...
SHE USED TO REALLY BE A MODEL, ACTUALLY...
WHEN I WAS IN HIGH SCHOOL SHE LIVED IN SOME WEIRD ARTIST'S COLONY...
SO WHAT HAPPENED TO HER?
NOW SHE'S JUST A BORING HOUSE-WIFE IN THE SUBURBS...
I WONDER IF THIS IS HER... IT REALLY COULD BE...
GOD, DAVID... THIS BOOK IS THE GREATEST!
YOU HAVE TO GIVE IT TO ME!
SO... DO YOU WANT TO DO SOMETHING THIS WEEKEND?
I DUNNO... MAYBE... I CAN'T REALLY TALK RIGHT NOW...
23.

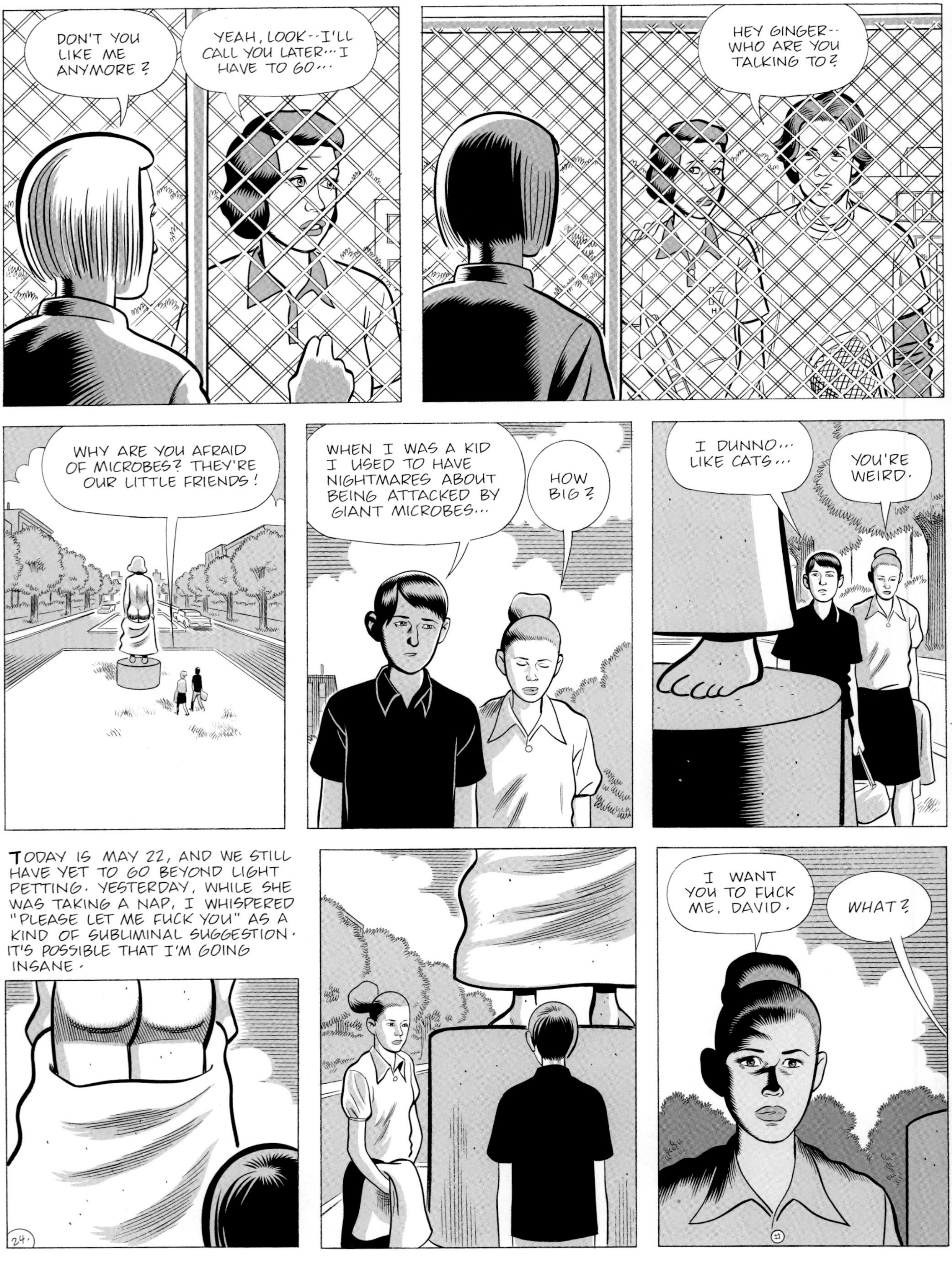
DON'T YOU LIKE ME ANYMORE?
YEAH, LOOK--I'LL CALL YOU LATER... I HAVE TO GO...
HEY GINGER-- WHO ARE YOU TALKING TO?
WHY ARE YOU AFRAID OF MICROBES? THEY'RE OUR LITTLE FRIENDS!
WHEN I WAS A KID I USED TO HAVE NIGHTMARES ABOUT BEING ATTACKED BY GIANT MICROBES...
HOW BIG?
I DUNNO... LIKE CATS...
YOU'RE WEIRD.
TODAY IS MAY 22, AND WE STILL HAVE YET TO GO BEYOND LIGHT PETTING. YESTERDAY, WHILE SHE WAS TAKING A NAP, I WHISPERED "PLEASE LET ME FUCK YOU" AS A KIND OF SUBLIMINAL SUGGESTION. IT'S POSSIBLE THAT I'M GOING INSANE.
I WANT YOU TO FUCK ME, DAVID.
WHAT?

WHAT WHAT? I DIDN'T SAY ANYTHING.

MY **POINT** IS THAT IF A STUDENT WERE TO UNDERSTAND **DEEPLY** AND **TRUTHFULLY** THE MATERIAL, HE WOULD **NEVER HESITATE** TO ACT PASSIONATELY, TO PUT HIS SEXUAL APPETITE ON EQUAL FOOTING WITH--

BUT ISN'T THAT IRRESPONSIBLE?...

CERTAINLY YOU DON'T HAVE TO BE A **RAKE** TO ENJOY FIELDING...

WHAT COULD YOU POSSIBLY KNOW ABOUT IT, EDWARDS? WHEN HAVE YOU EVER HAD A PASSIONATE IMPULSE IN YOUR LIFE?

STEADY, KARKES... THAT'S UNCALLED FOR!

I-I'M SORRY...

HAVING A FLARE-UP OF THE MID-LIFE CRISIS, FERDINAND?

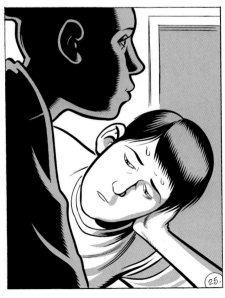

25.

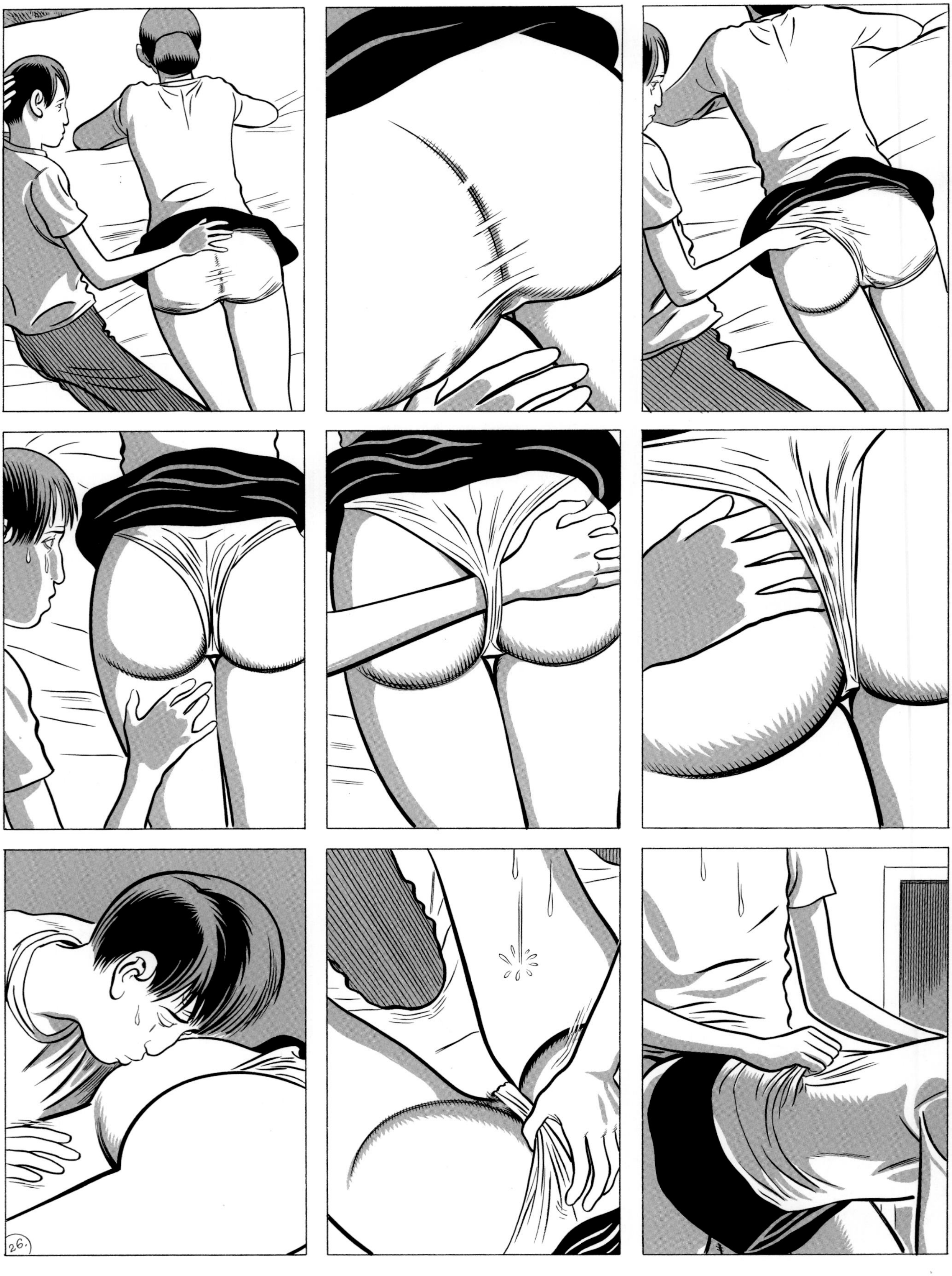

YES, MY FRIENDS, IT WAS ABSOLUTELY REAL ; THE ACT HAVING TAKEN PLACE BETWEEN 3:30 AND 4:00 PM ON MEMORIAL DAY, 1998 DURING WHAT MY RECORDS INDICATE TO HAVE BEEN OUR 13TH DATE.

NO PRECAUTIONS OF ANY KIND WERE TAKEN AND UNFATHOMABLE HEIGHTS OF ECSTASY, ETC. WERE REACHED.

...THAT'S IT! SHE DOESN'T WANT ANY OF YOUR DYKE BULLSHIT!

THAT'S NOT WHAT SHE SAID BEFORE!

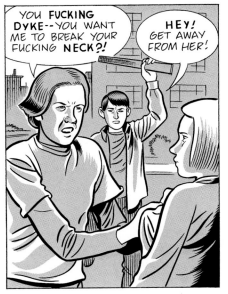

YOU FUCKING DYKE-- YOU WANT ME TO BREAK YOUR FUCKING NECK?!

HEY! GET AWAY FROM HER!

YOU HEARD ME!

YOU WANNA FUCK WITH ME, TOUGH GUY?

I'LL KILL YOU, MOTHER-FUCKER!

FUCKING FAGGOT!

YOUR GIRLFRIEND'S A RUG-MUNCHER, MAN!

LIMP-DICK ASSHOLE!

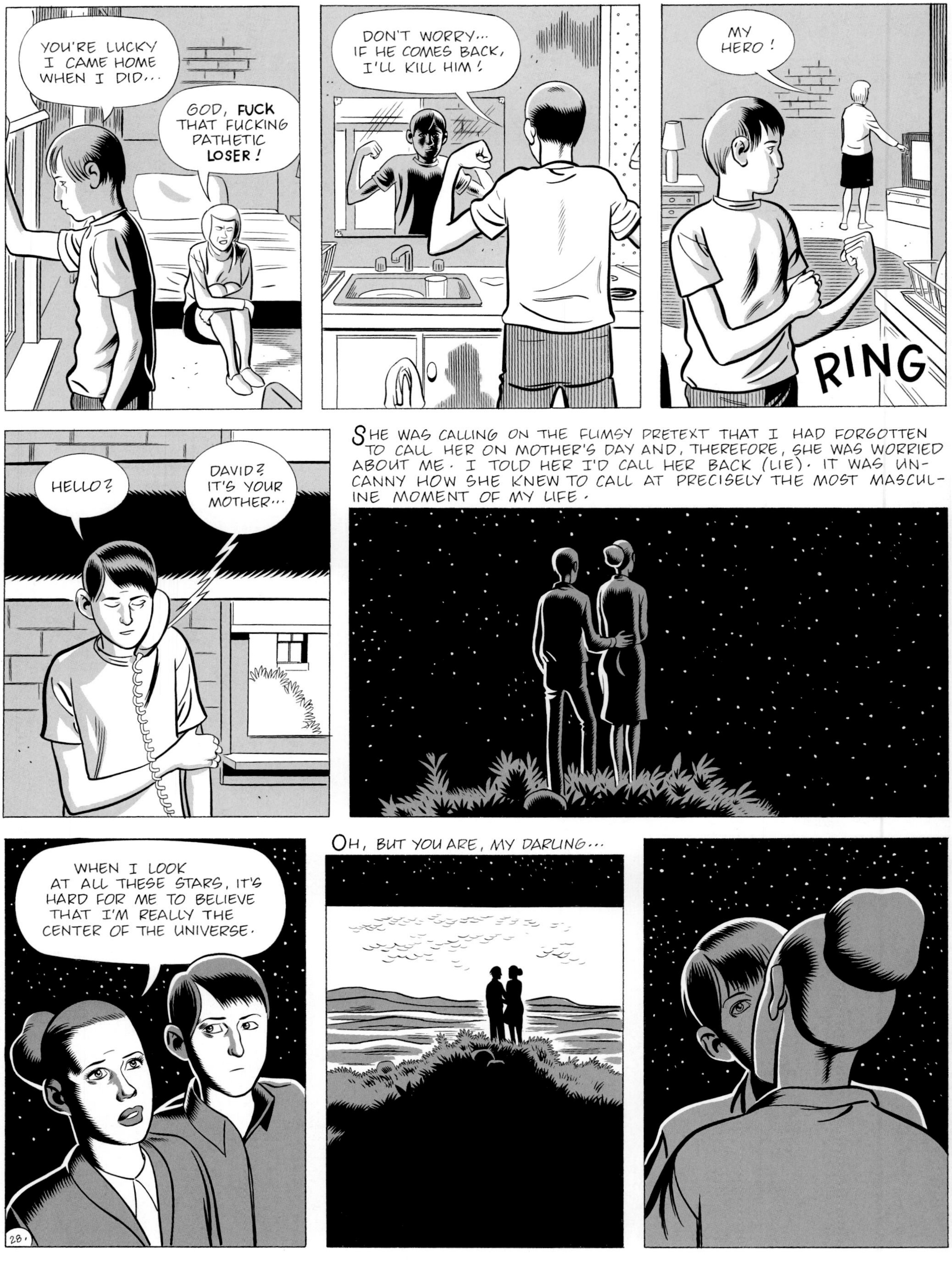
YOU'RE LUCKY I CAME HOME WHEN I DID...
GOD, FUCK THAT FUCKING PATHETIC LOSER!
DON'T WORRY... IF HE COMES BACK, I'LL KILL HIM!
MY HERO!
RING
HELLO?
DAVID? IT'S YOUR MOTHER...
SHE WAS CALLING ON THE FLIMSY PRETEXT THAT I HAD FORGOTTEN TO CALL HER ON MOTHER'S DAY AND, THEREFORE, SHE WAS WORRIED ABOUT ME. I TOLD HER I'D CALL HER BACK (LIE). IT WAS UNCANNY HOW SHE KNEW TO CALL AT PRECISELY THE MOST MASCULINE MOMENT OF MY LIFE.
WHEN I LOOK AT ALL THESE STARS, IT'S HARD FOR ME TO BELIEVE THAT I'M REALLY THE CENTER OF THE UNIVERSE.
OH, BUT YOU ARE, MY DARLING...

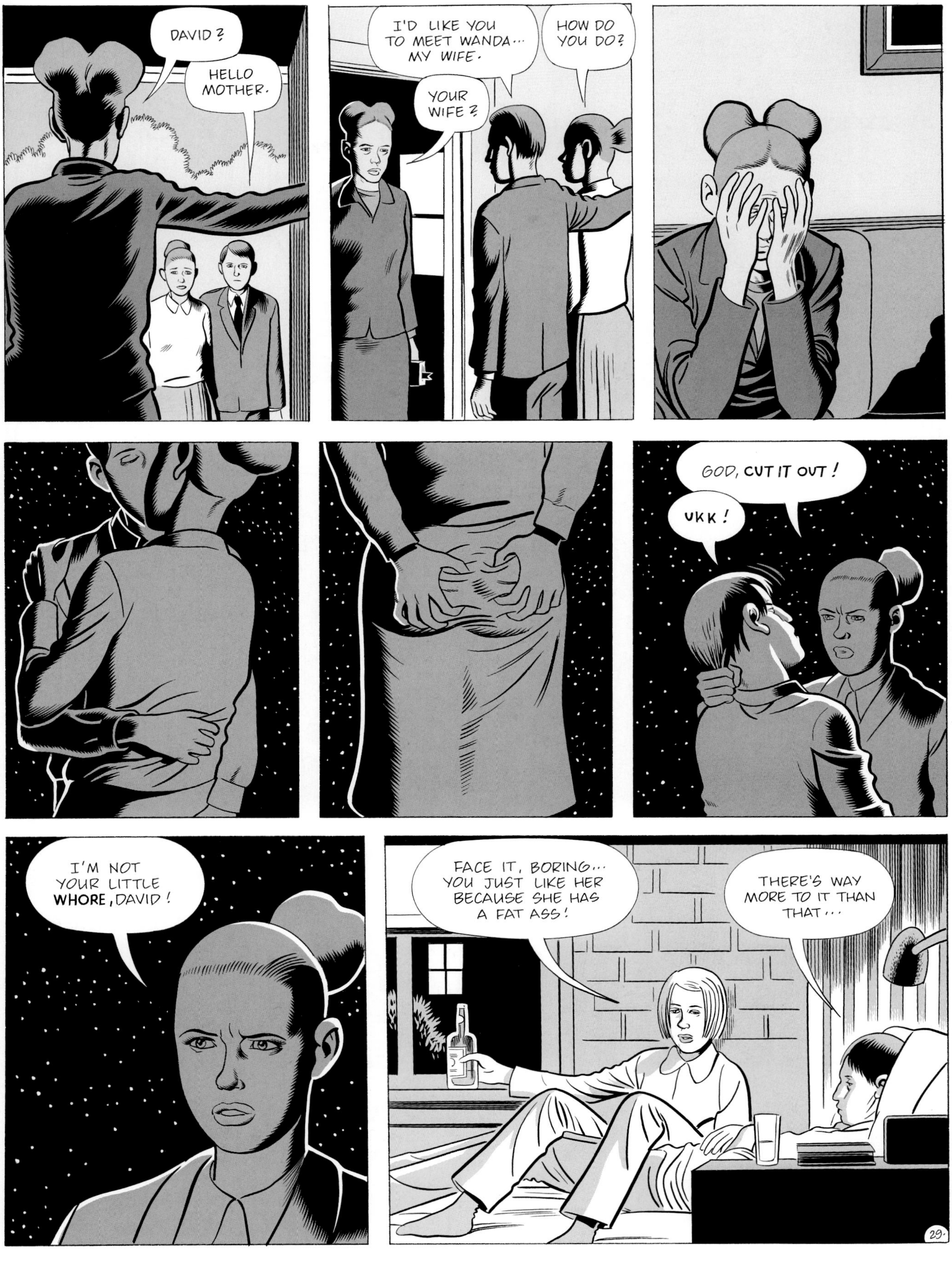
DAVID?
HELLO MOTHER.
I'D LIKE YOU TO MEET WANDA... MY WIFE.
HOW DO YOU DO?
YOUR WIFE?
GOD, CUT IT OUT!
UKK!
I'M NOT YOUR LITTLE WHORE, DAVID!
FACE IT, BORING... YOU JUST LIKE HER BECAUSE SHE HAS A FAT ASS!
THERE'S WAY MORE TO IT THAN THAT...

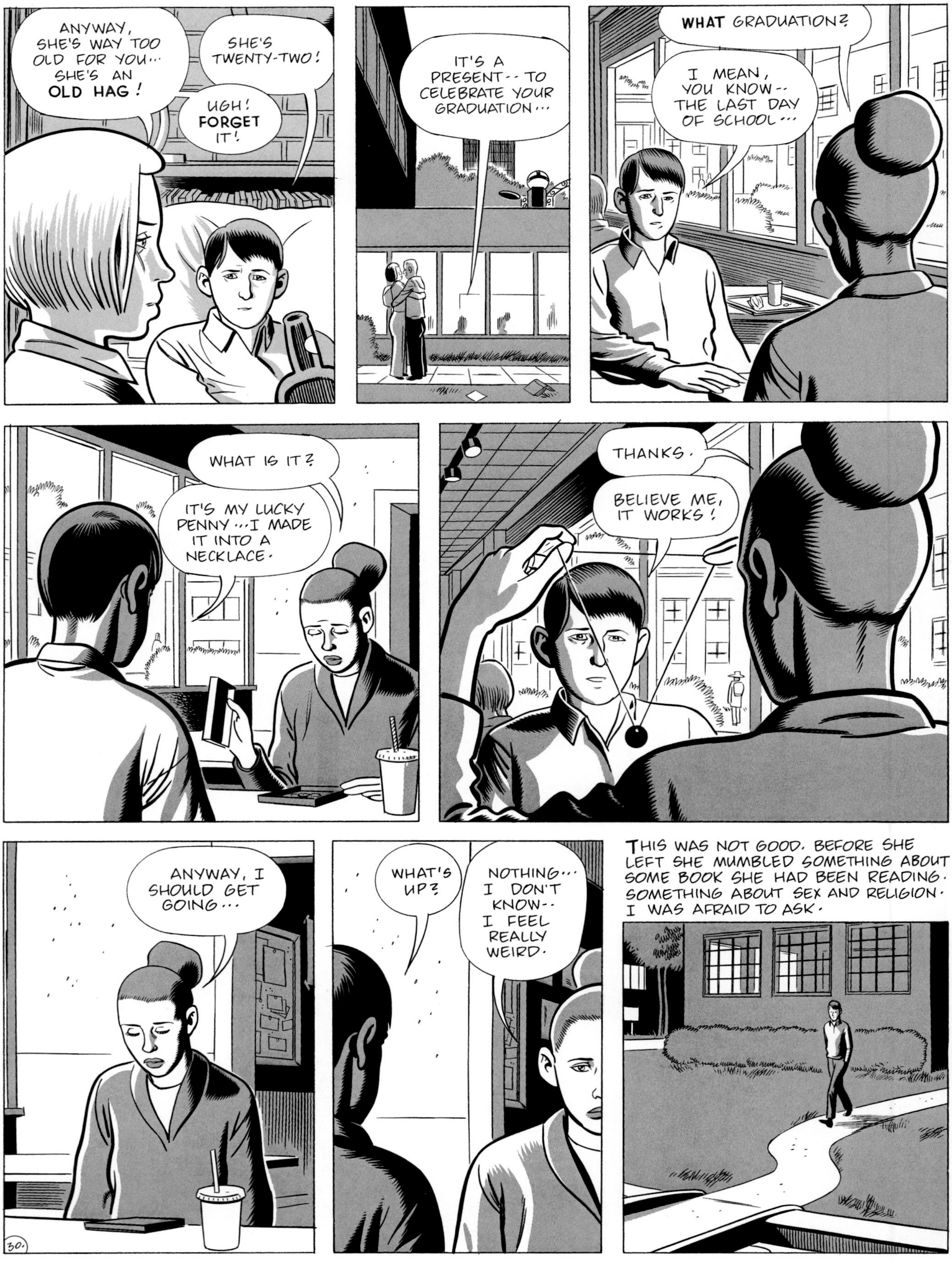
ANYWAY, SHE'S WAY TOO OLD FOR YOU... SHE'S AN OLD HAG!
SHE'S TWENTY-TWO!
UGH! FORGET IT!
IT'S A PRESENT-- TO CELEBRATE YOUR GRADUATION...
WHAT GRADUATION?
I MEAN, YOU KNOW-- THE LAST DAY OF SCHOOL...
WHAT IS IT?
IT'S MY LUCKY PENNY...I MADE IT INTO A NECKLACE.
THANKS.
BELIEVE ME, IT WORKS!
ANYWAY, I SHOULD GET GOING...
WHAT'S UP?
NOTHING... I DON'T KNOW-- I FEEL REALLY WEIRD.
THIS WAS NOT GOOD. BEFORE SHE LEFT SHE MUMBLED SOMETHING ABOUT SOME BOOK SHE HAD BEEN READING. SOMETHING ABOUT SEX AND RELIGION. I WAS AFRAID TO ASK.

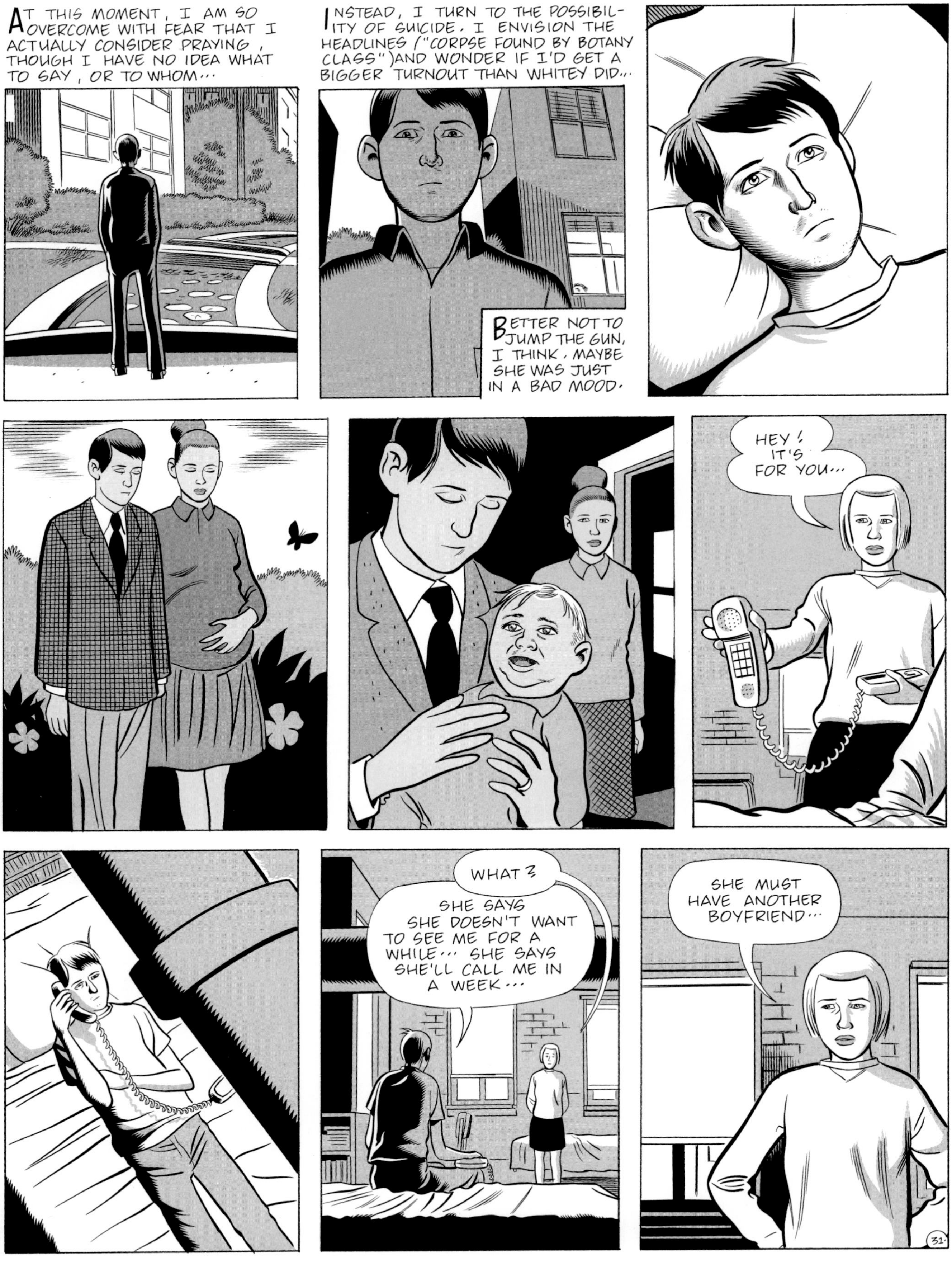

AT THIS MOMENT, I AM SO OVERCOME WITH FEAR THAT I ACTUALLY CONSIDER PRAYING, THOUGH I HAVE NO IDEA WHAT TO SAY, OR TO WHOM...
INSTEAD, I TURN TO THE POSSIBILITY OF SUICIDE. I ENVISION THE HEADLINES ("CORPSE FOUND BY BOTANY CLASS") AND WONDER IF I'D GET A BIGGER TURNOUT THAN WHITEY DID...
BETTER NOT TO JUMP THE GUN, I THINK. MAYBE SHE WAS JUST IN A BAD MOOD.
HEY! IT'S FOR YOU...
WHAT?
SHE SAYS SHE DOESN'T WANT TO SEE ME FOR A WHILE... SHE SAYS SHE'LL CALL ME IN A WEEK...
SHE MUST HAVE ANOTHER BOYFRIEND...

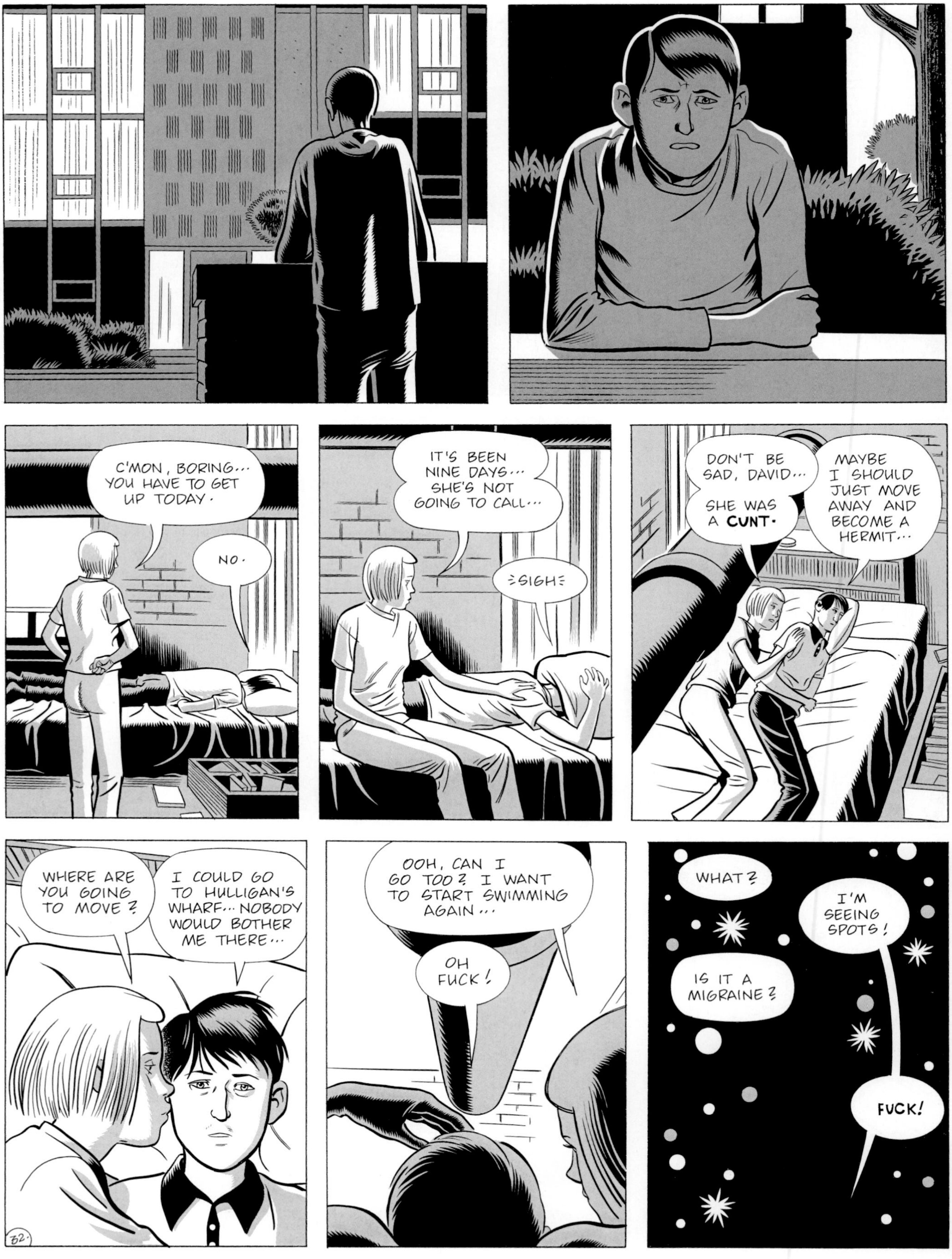

C'MON, BORING... YOU HAVE TO GET UP TODAY.
NO.
IT'S BEEN NINE DAYS... SHE'S NOT GOING TO CALL...
SIGH
DON'T BE SAD, DAVID...
SHE WAS A **CUNT**.
MAYBE I SHOULD JUST MOVE AWAY AND BECOME A HERMIT...
WHERE ARE YOU GOING TO MOVE?
I COULD GO TO HULLIGAN'S WHARF... NOBODY WOULD BOTHER ME THERE...
OOH, CAN I GO TOO? I WANT TO START SWIMMING AGAIN...
OH FUCK!
WHAT?
I'M SEEING SPOTS!
IS IT A MIGRAINE?
FUCK!

POOR BABY... WHAT CAN I DO?

NOT SO LOUD!

THIS IS THE WORST HEADACHE OF MY LIFE, AN UNBEARABLE KNOT OF PAIN ABOVE MY RIGHT EYE.

I CAN'T SLEEP OR EAT FOR TWO DAYS.

"IS IT AN ANEURISM? DO YOU WANT ME TO CALL AN AMBULANCE OR SOMETHING?"

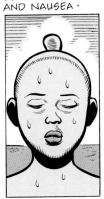

I BANG MY HEAD AGAINST THE WALL IN A FUTILE ATTEMPT TO DERAIL THE MADDENING TORRENT OF HALLUCINATIONS AND NAUSEA.

"you must have very potent sperm"

IS IT EVEN POSSIBLE TO DERAIL A TORRENT? DOES ANYTHING I SAY MAKE SENSE?

SOMEBODY PLEASE KILL ME PLEASE KILL ME PLEASE PLEASE PLEASE KILL ME

(AGONIZED MOAN).

33.

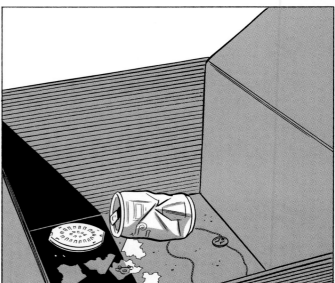

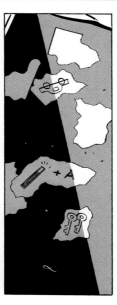

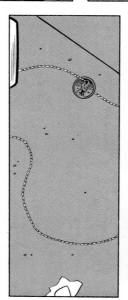

I GUESS SHE DECIDED TO KEEP MY SCRAPBOOK; THAT WAS SOMETHING··· AND AT LEAST MY EMBARRASSING LOVE LETTER OF MAY 27 WASN'T IN THE BOX···

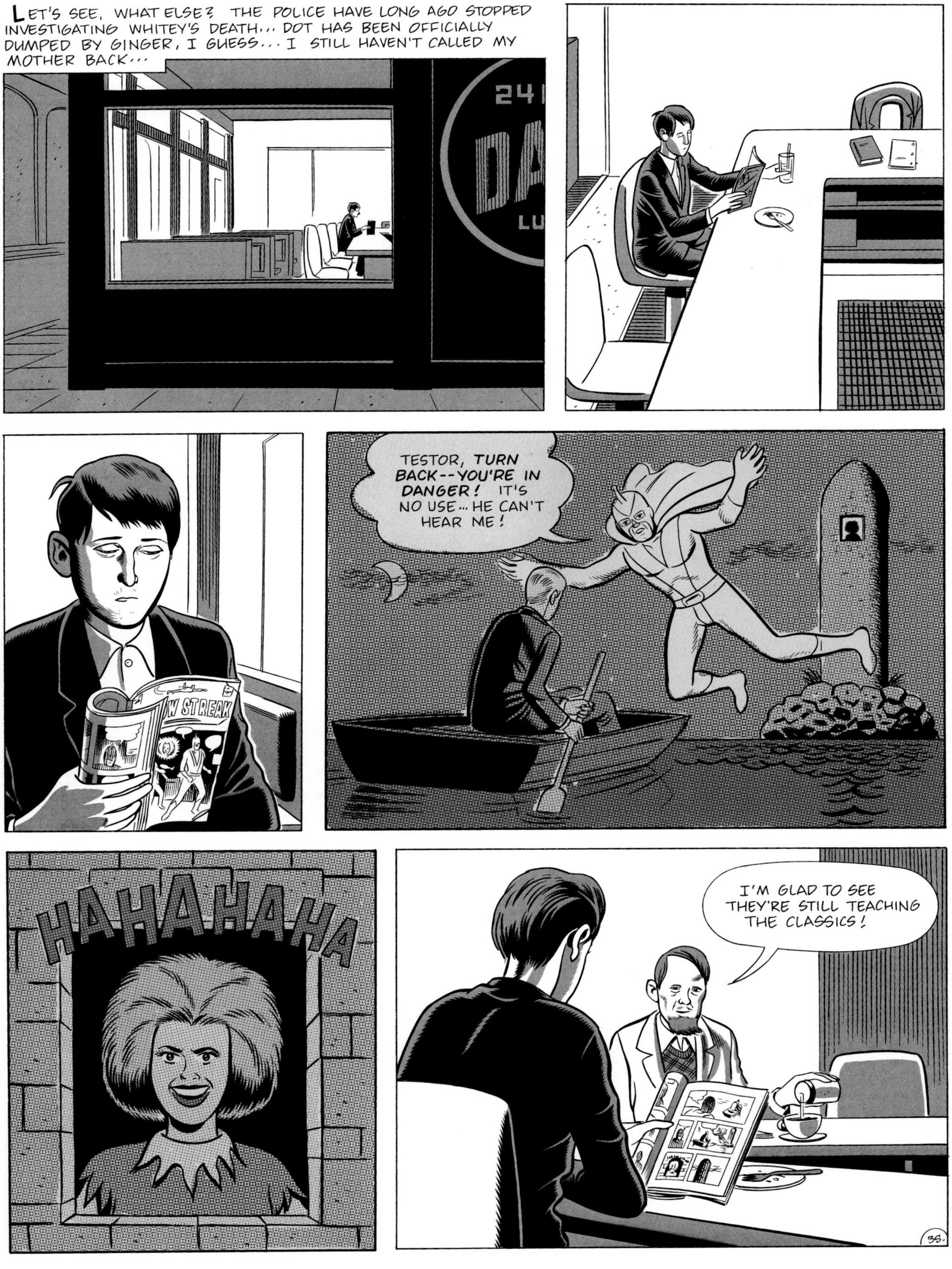
LET'S SEE, WHAT ELSE? THE POLICE HAVE LONG AGO STOPPED INVESTIGATING WHITEY'S DEATH... DOT HAS BEEN OFFICIALLY DUMPED BY GINGER, I GUESS... I STILL HAVEN'T CALLED MY MOTHER BACK...
TESTOR, **TURN BACK--YOU'RE IN DANGER!** IT'S NO USE... HE CAN'T HEAR ME!
HAHAHAHA
I'M GLAD TO SEE THEY'RE STILL TEACHING THE CLASSICS!

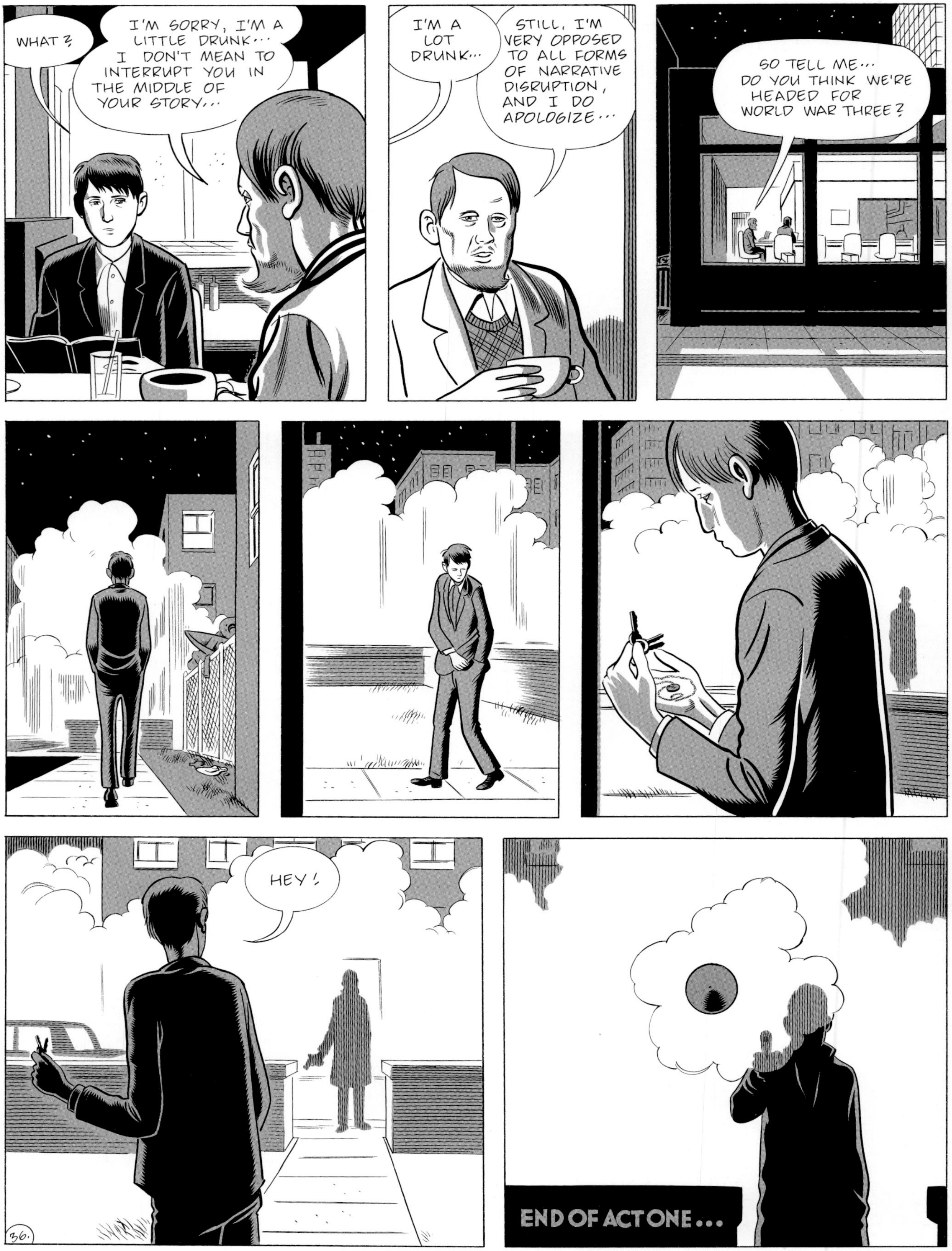
WHAT?
I'M SORRY, I'M A LITTLE DRUNK... I DON'T MEAN TO INTERRUPT YOU IN THE MIDDLE OF YOUR STORY...
I'M A LOT DRUNK...
STILL, I'M VERY OPPOSED TO ALL FORMS OF NARRATIVE DISRUPTION, AND I DO APOLOGIZE...
SO TELL ME... DO YOU THINK WE'RE HEADED FOR WORLD WAR THREE?
HEY!
36.
END OF ACT ONE...

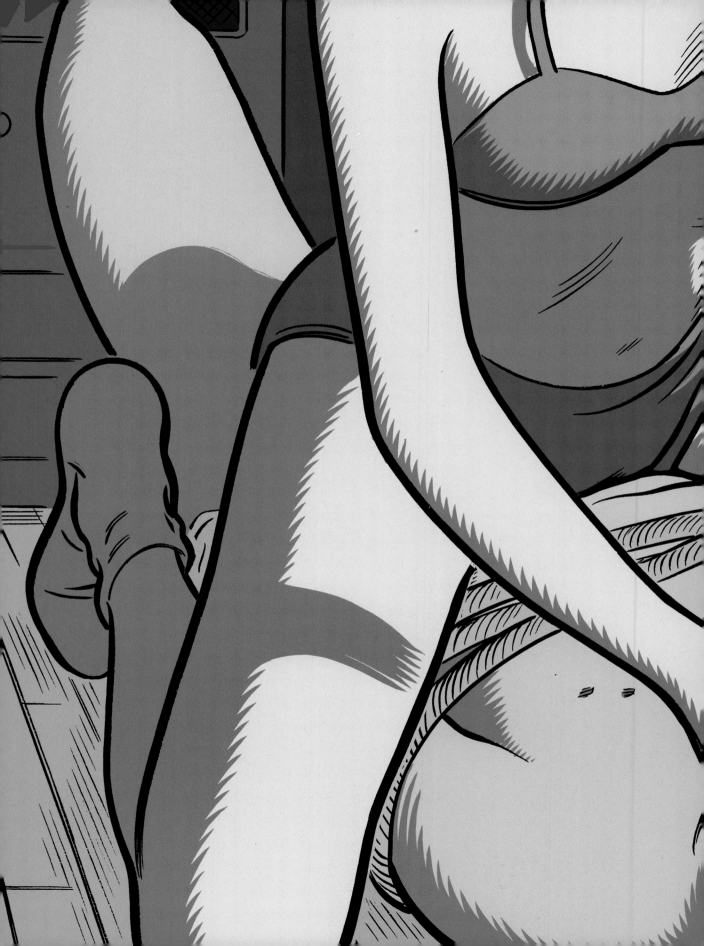

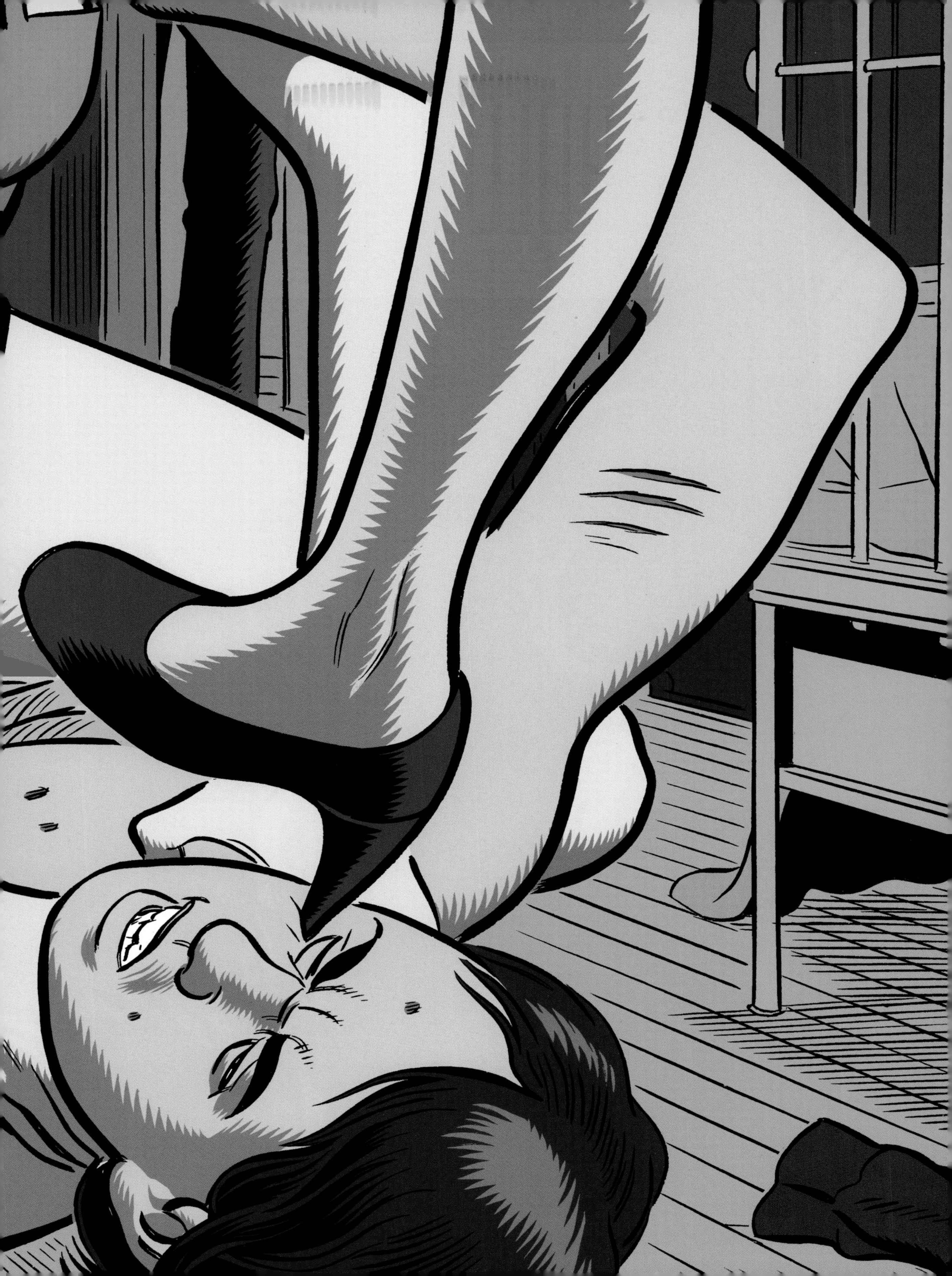

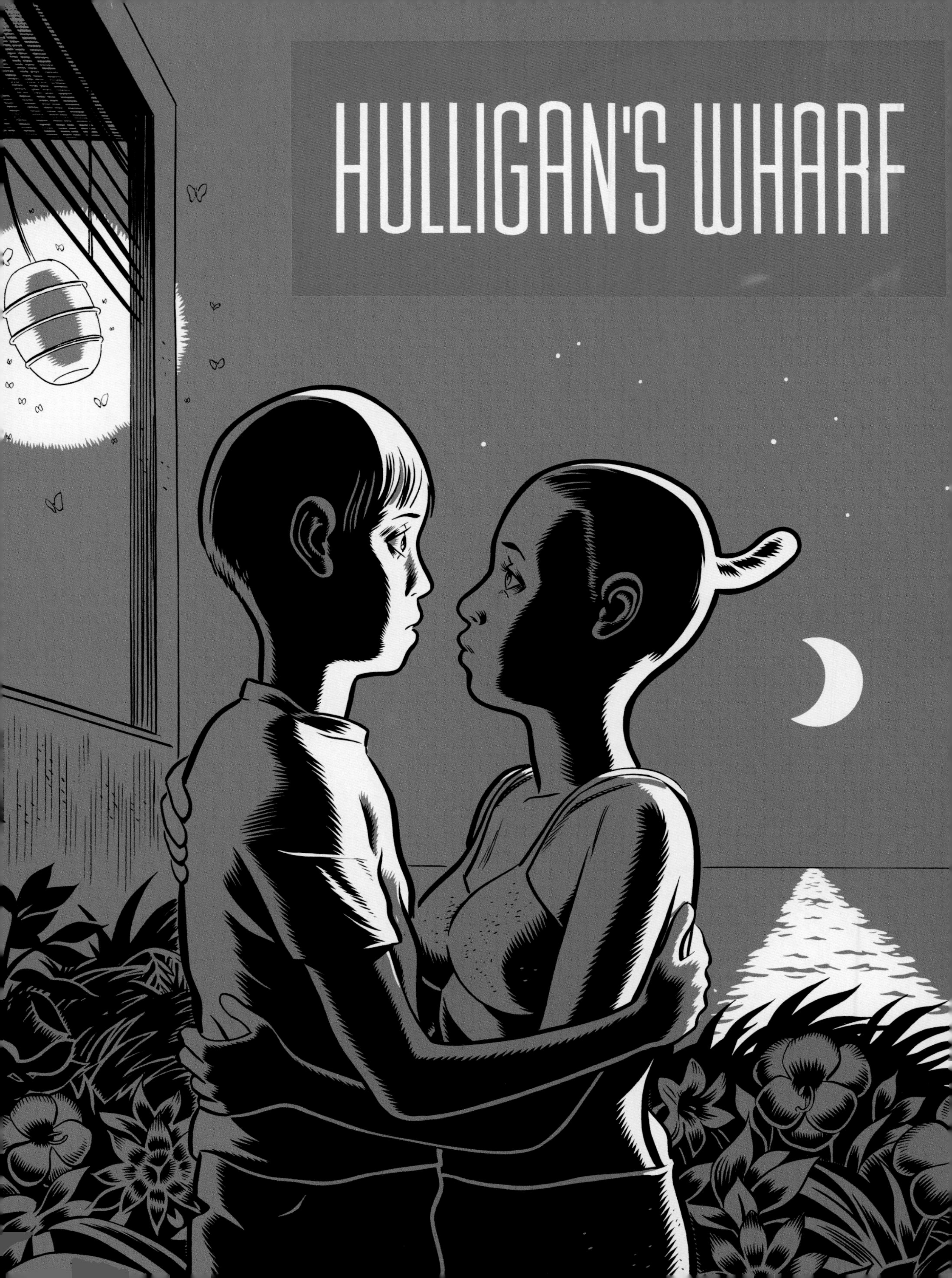
HULLIGAN'S WHARF

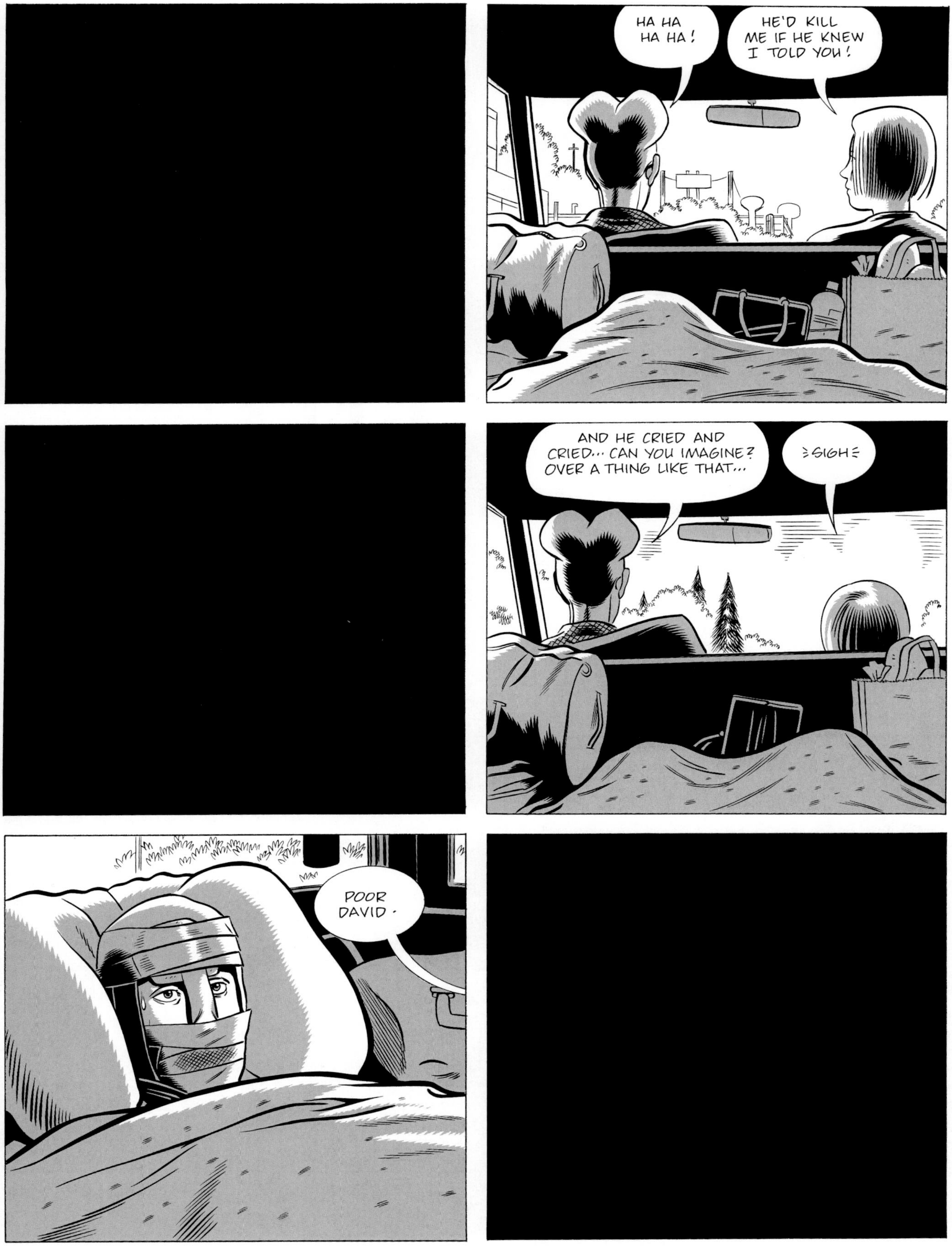
HA HA
HA HA!
HE'D KILL
ME IF HE KNEW
I TOLD YOU!
AND HE CRIED AND
CRIED... CAN YOU IMAGINE?
OVER A THING LIKE THAT...
SIGH
POOR
DAVID.

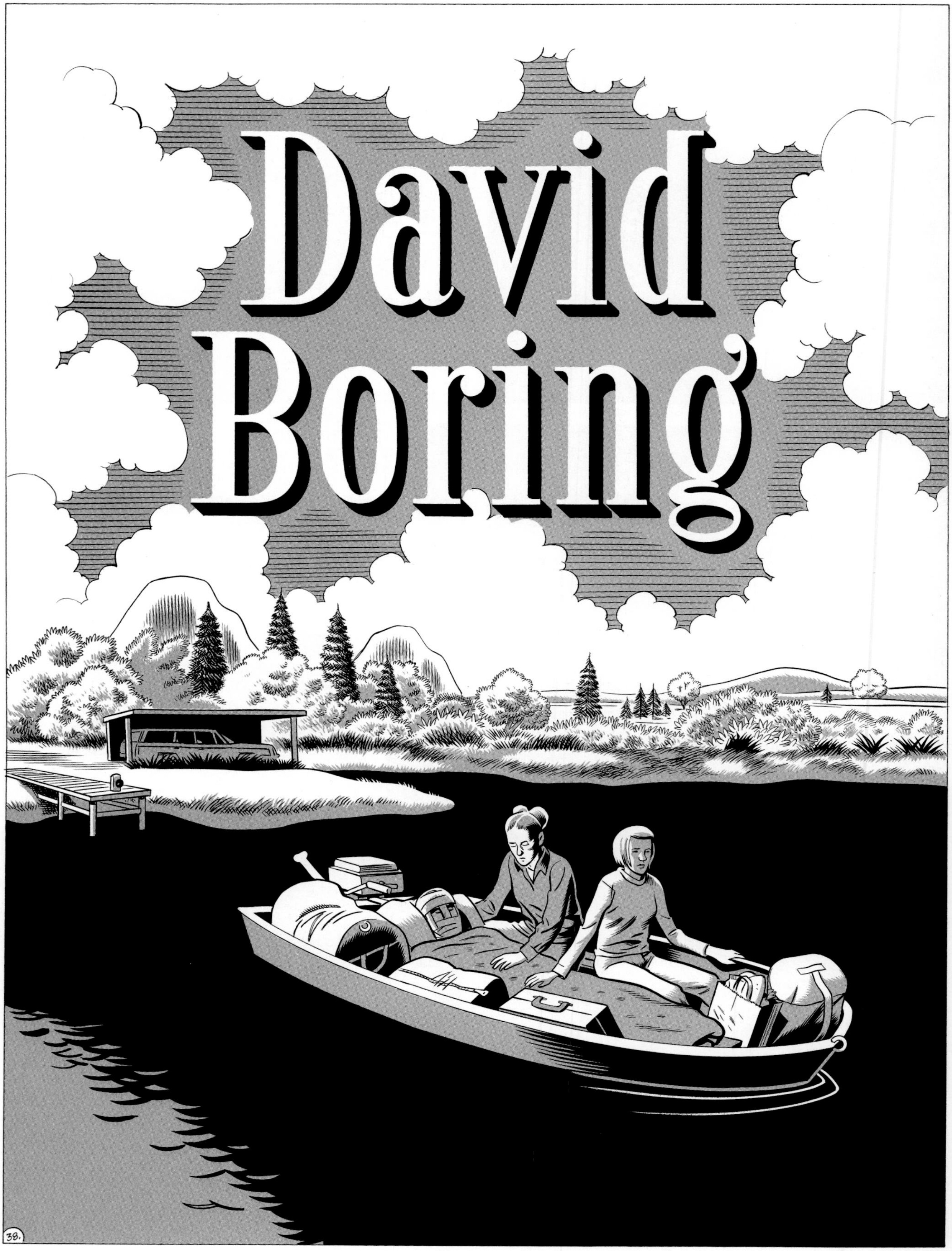
David
Boring
38.

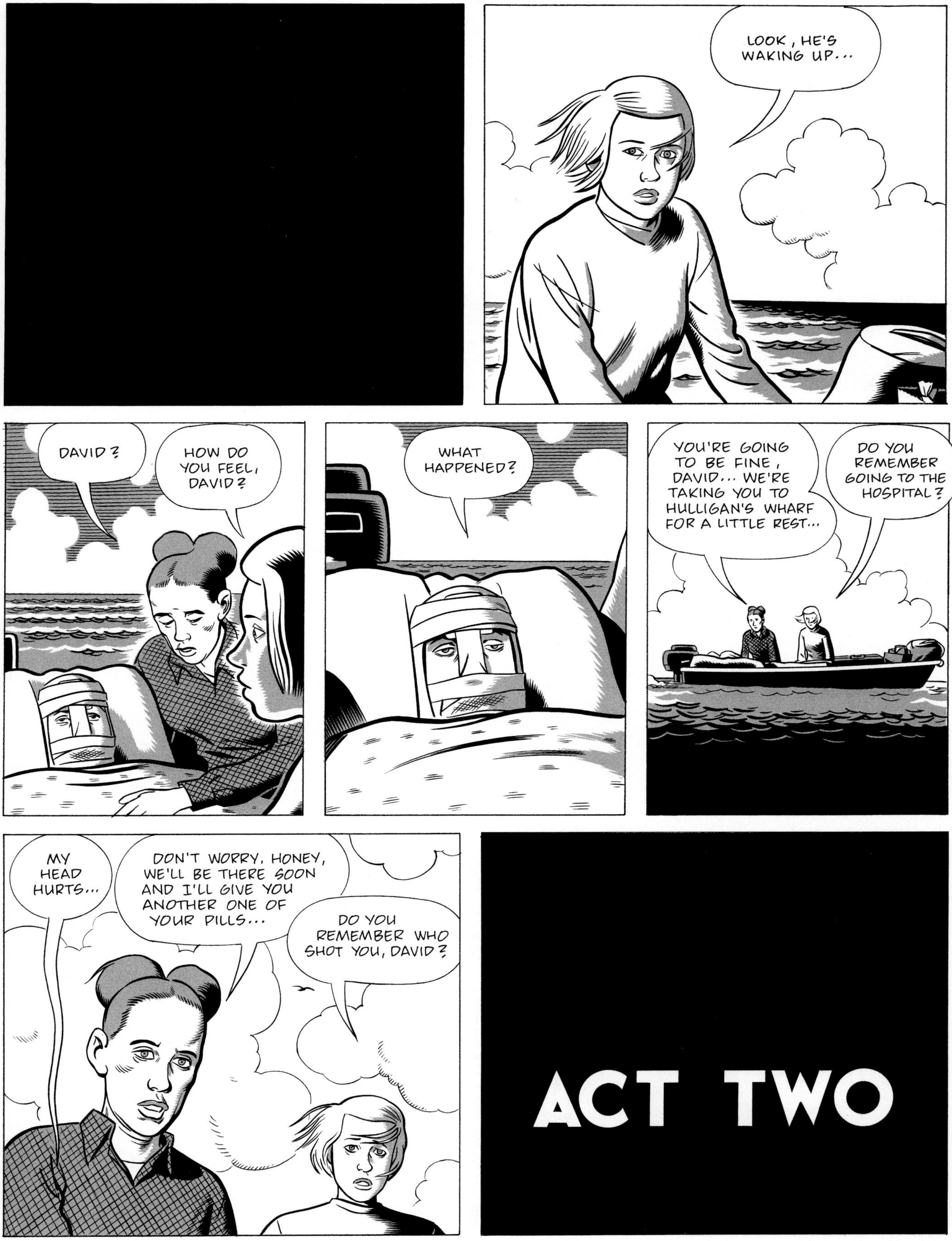
LOOK, HE'S WAKING UP...
DAVID?
HOW DO YOU FEEL, DAVID?
WHAT HAPPENED?
YOU'RE GOING TO BE FINE, DAVID... WE'RE TAKING YOU TO HULLIGAN'S WHARF FOR A LITTLE REST...
DO YOU REMEMBER GOING TO THE HOSPITAL?
MY HEAD HURTS...
DON'T WORRY, HONEY, WE'LL BE THERE SOON AND I'LL GIVE YOU ANOTHER ONE OF YOUR PILLS...
DO YOU REMEMBER WHO SHOT YOU, DAVID?
ACT TWO

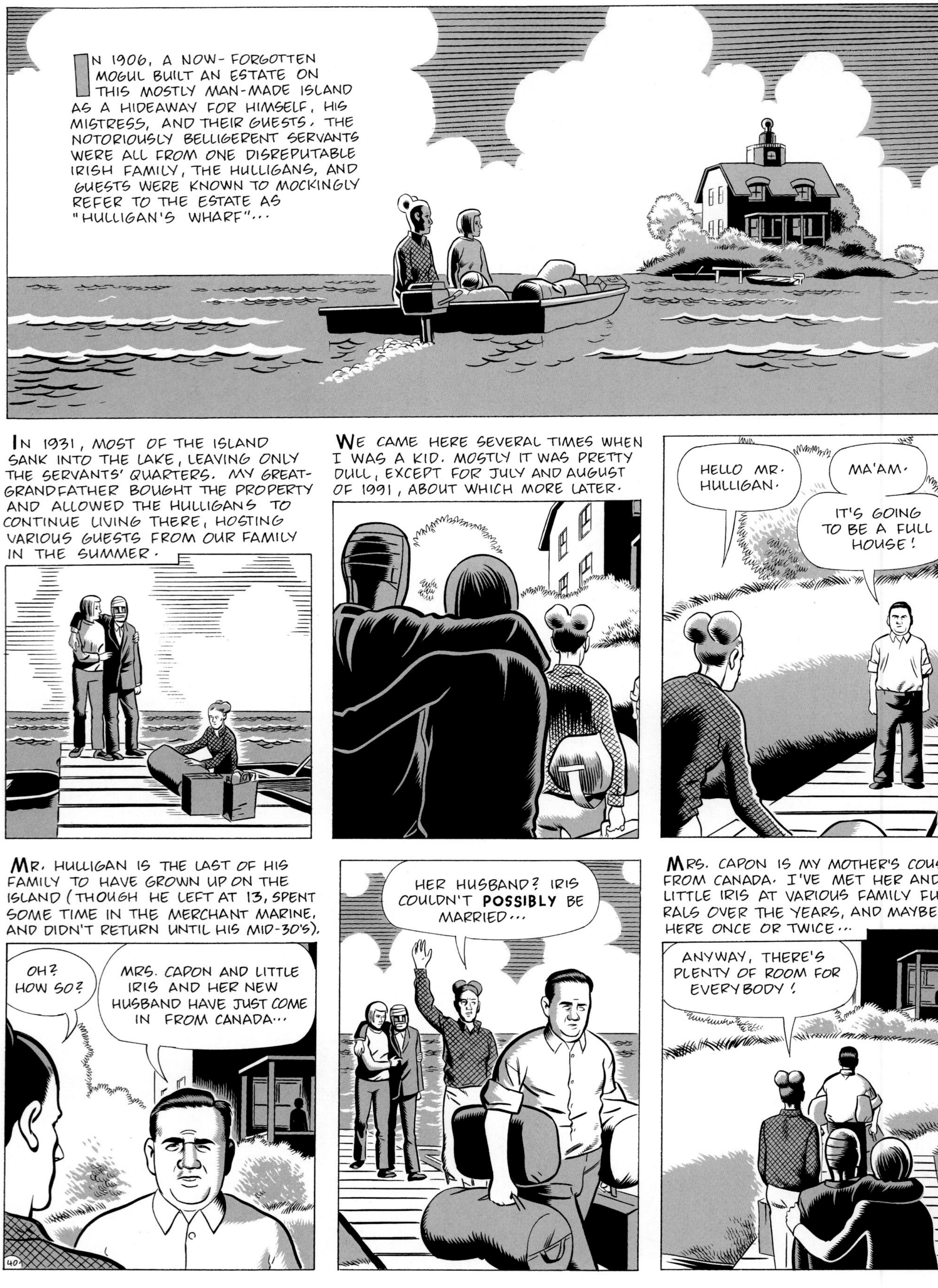
IN 1906, A NOW-FORGOTTEN MOGUL BUILT AN ESTATE ON THIS MOSTLY MAN-MADE ISLAND AS A HIDEAWAY FOR HIMSELF, HIS MISTRESS, AND THEIR GUESTS. THE NOTORIOUSLY BELLIGERENT SERVANTS WERE ALL FROM ONE DISREPUTABLE IRISH FAMILY, THE HULLIGANS, AND GUESTS WERE KNOWN TO MOCKINGLY REFER TO THE ESTATE AS "HULLIGAN'S WHARF"...
IN 1931, MOST OF THE ISLAND SANK INTO THE LAKE, LEAVING ONLY THE SERVANTS' QUARTERS. MY GREAT-GRANDFATHER BOUGHT THE PROPERTY AND ALLOWED THE HULLIGANS TO CONTINUE LIVING THERE, HOSTING VARIOUS GUESTS FROM OUR FAMILY IN THE SUMMER.
WE CAME HERE SEVERAL TIMES WHEN I WAS A KID. MOSTLY IT WAS PRETTY DULL, EXCEPT FOR JULY AND AUGUST OF 1991, ABOUT WHICH MORE LATER.
HELLO MR. HULLIGAN.
MA'AM.
IT'S GOING TO BE A FULL HOUSE!
MR. HULLIGAN IS THE LAST OF HIS FAMILY TO HAVE GROWN UP ON THE ISLAND (THOUGH HE LEFT AT 13, SPENT SOME TIME IN THE MERCHANT MARINE, AND DIDN'T RETURN UNTIL HIS MID-30'S).
OH? HOW SO?
MRS. CAPON AND LITTLE IRIS AND HER NEW HUSBAND HAVE JUST COME IN FROM CANADA...
HER HUSBAND? IRIS COULDN'T **POSSIBLY** BE MARRIED...
MRS. CAPON IS MY MOTHER'S COUSIN FROM CANADA. I'VE MET HER AND LITTLE IRIS AT VARIOUS FAMILY FUNERALS OVER THE YEARS, AND MAYBE HERE ONCE OR TWICE...
ANYWAY, THERE'S PLENTY OF ROOM FOR EVERYBODY!
40

IN KEEPING WITH THE ORIGINAL DICTATES OF THE ISLAND, NO COMMUNICATION WITH THE MAINLAND IS ALLOWED. THERE ARE NO PHONES, RADIOS, ETC., AND ALL POWER IS SELF-GENERATED.

MR. HULLIGAN GOES FOR SUPPLIES EVERY 3 OR 4 WEEKS, BUT THERE IS ENOUGH FOOD IN DRY STORAGE TO FEED 10 PEOPLE FOR 3 MONTHS.

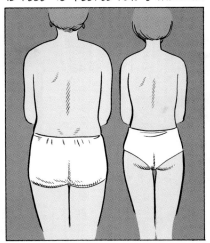

HE'S NOT **CONTAGIOUS**, IS HE?

NOW THAT WE'VE ESTABLISHED OUR SETTING, LET ME TAKE THIS OPPORTUNITY TO RE-INTRODUCE OUR VARIOUS PLAYERS. STARTING TO MY RIGHT WE HAVE **DOT**, WHO YOU KNOW; **MRS. CAPON**; HER 16-YEAR-OLD DAUGHTER **IRIS ROLAND** (NÉE CAPON); IRIS'S HUSBAND **MAN** (SHORT FOR MANFRED, HE SAYS); MY **MOTHER**; AND (STANDING) **HULLIGAN**. IF YOU GET CONFUSED, YOU MAY WANT TO REFER BACK TO THIS SCENE.

SO WHAT HAPPENED TO **HIM**?

HE LOOKS LIKE HE'S BEEN IN A HOCKEY FIGHT!

SOMEBODY SHOT HIM.

HOW AWFUL... WHY DID THEY SHOOT HIM?

HE DOESN'T REMEMBER ANYTHING ABOUT IT...

YOU AMERICANS AND YOUR GUNS!

I THINK IT'S PRETTY COOL!

IRIS!

HEY MULLIGAN! CAN YOU HURRY IT UP WITH THE RICE!

41.

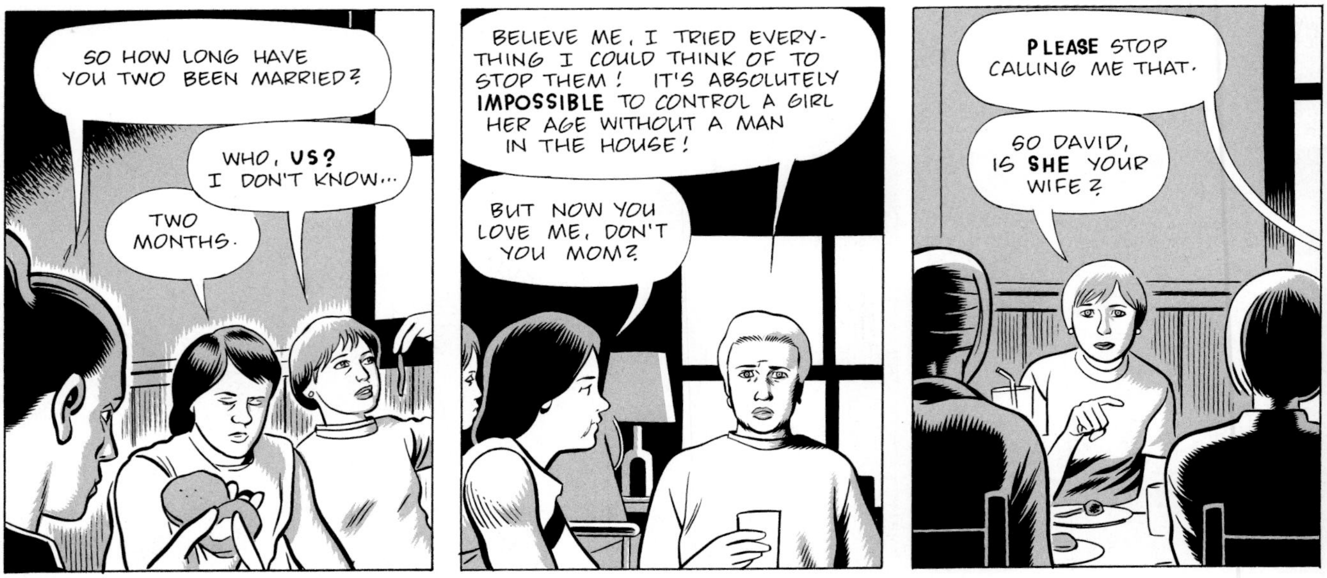
SO HOW LONG HAVE YOU TWO BEEN MARRIED?
WHO, US? I DON'T KNOW...
TWO MONTHS.
BELIEVE ME, I TRIED EVERYTHING I COULD THINK OF TO STOP THEM! IT'S ABSOLUTELY IMPOSSIBLE TO CONTROL A GIRL HER AGE WITHOUT A MAN IN THE HOUSE!
BUT NOW YOU LOVE ME, DON'T YOU MOM?
PLEASE STOP CALLING ME THAT.
SO DAVID, IS SHE YOUR WIFE?

LATER THAT NIGHT THERE IS A TERRIBLE STORM. THE PAIN-KILLERS HAVE ME VEERING FROM NEAR-UNCONSCIOUSNESS TO A STATE OF LUCID REVELATION IN WHICH IT BECOMES CLEAR THAT WHAT I HAD ONCE THOUGHT WAS A ROMANTIC *COMEDY* IS ACTUALLY A *HORROR STORY*, COMPLETE WITH GOTHIC EFFECTS AND EERIE LIGHTING.

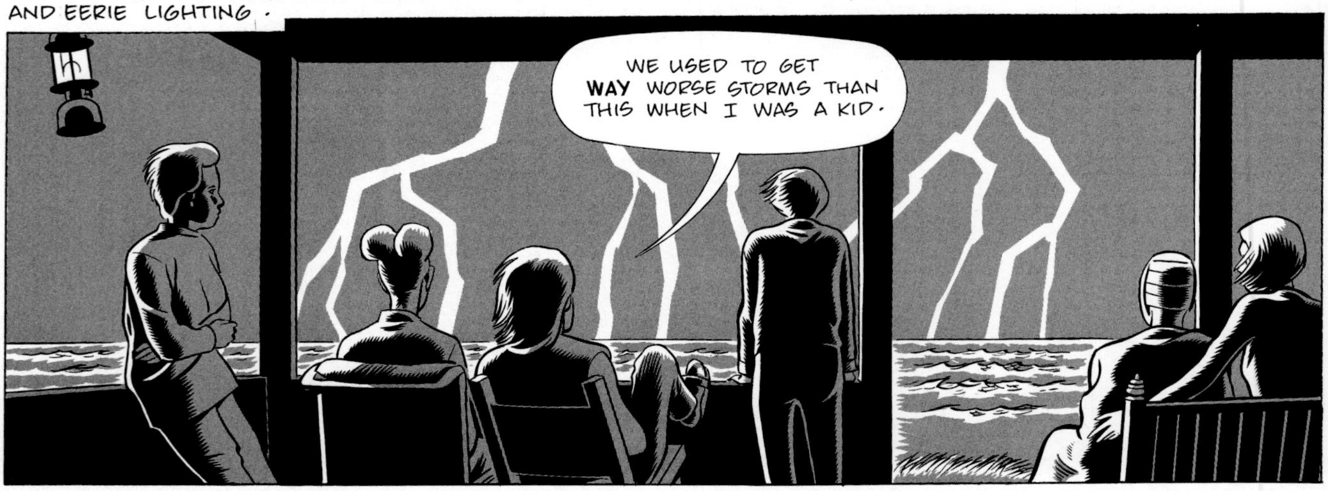
WE USED TO GET WAY WORSE STORMS THAN THIS WHEN I WAS A KID.

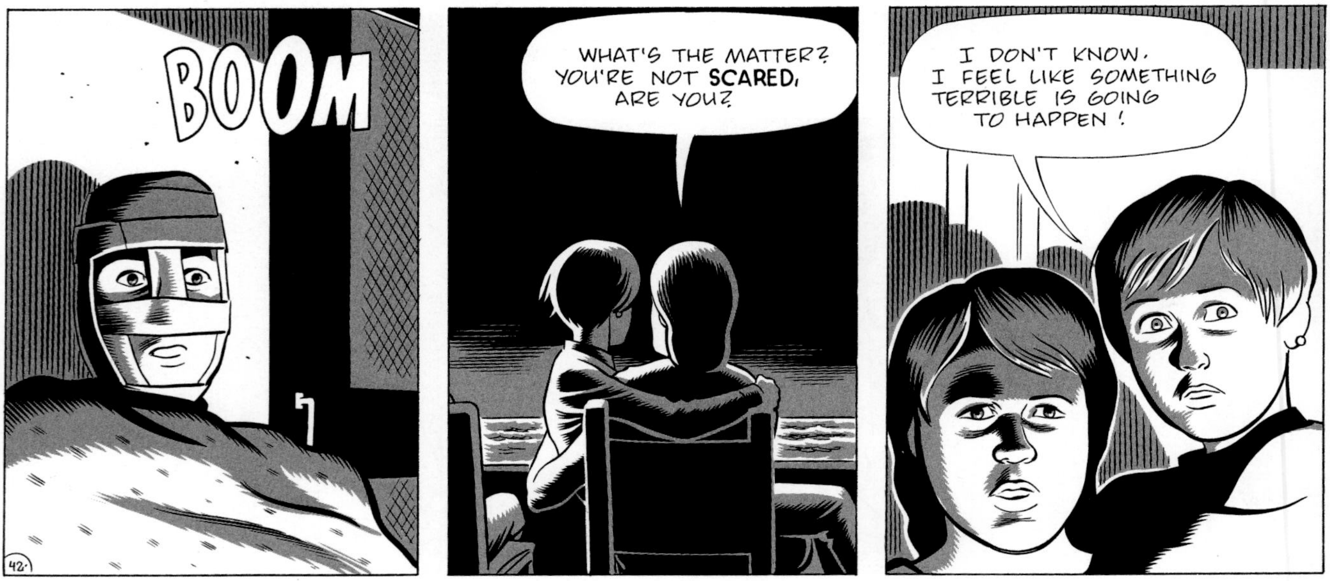
BOOM
WHAT'S THE MATTER? YOU'RE NOT SCARED, ARE YOU?
I DON'T KNOW. I FEEL LIKE SOMETHING TERRIBLE IS GOING TO HAPPEN!

APPARENTLY MY MOTHER DROVE STRAIGHT TO THE HOSPITAL WHEN SHE HEARD THE NEWS ABOUT MY SHOOTING.

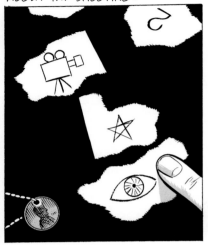

NOW SHE'S BACK IN CONTROL AND I'M IN NO POSITION TO RESIST; EVEN AT FULL STRENGTH IT'S A HARROWING STRUGGLE. I MUST SECRETLY DEVELOP AN IRON CONSTITUTION IF I AM TO THWART HER.

I DON'T ESPECIALLY CARE TO FIGURE OUT WHO SHOT ME, THOUGH THE THOUGHT THAT IT MIGHT HAVE BEEN WANDA IS CERTAINLY A THRILLING FANTASY.

WOULD YOU EVER KILL ME IN THE HEAT OF PASSION?

I DOUBT IT... I DON'T EVEN LIKE TO KILL ANTS.

SINCE WHEN AM I AN ANT?

WHEN I WAS A KID I ONCE CRIED FOR TWO HOURS BECAUSE MY MOTHER STEPPED ON AN ANTHILL.

MY PROFESSOR SAYS IT'S NOT LOVE IF YOU'RE NOT WILLING TO KILL FOR IT.

DOT THINKS THAT WANDA HAD A JEALOUS BOYFRIEND ON THE SIDE. WHO KNOWS? WHY WASTE TIME THINKING ABOUT IT? THIS ISN'T A MURDER MYSTERY...

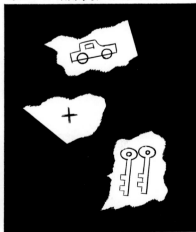

HELEN... COULD YOU GO GET MR. HULLIGAN?

43.

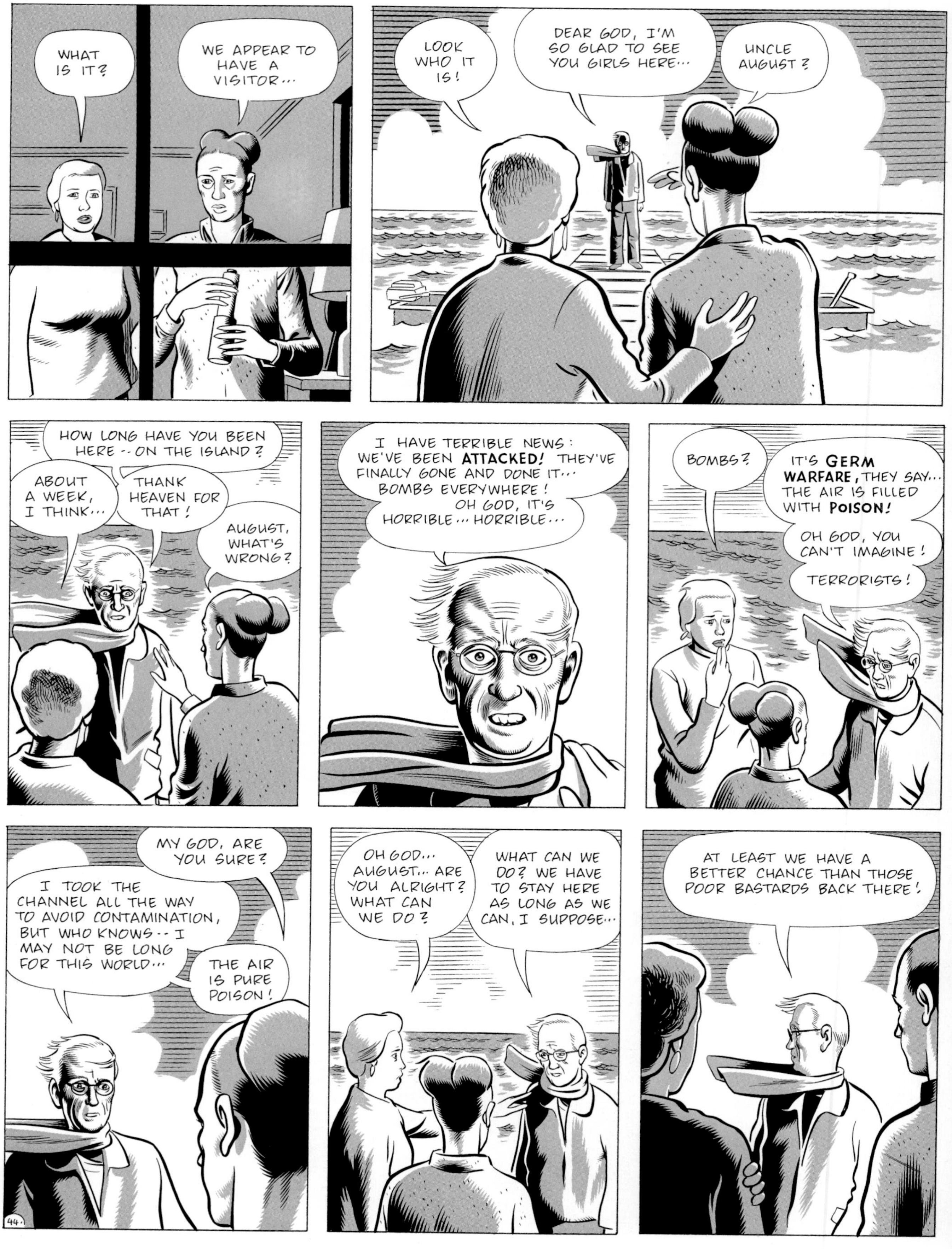
WHAT IS IT?
WE APPEAR TO HAVE A VISITOR...
LOOK WHO IT IS!
DEAR GOD, I'M SO GLAD TO SEE YOU GIRLS HERE...
UNCLE AUGUST?
HOW LONG HAVE YOU BEEN HERE -- ON THE ISLAND?
ABOUT A WEEK, I THINK...
THANK HEAVEN FOR THAT!
AUGUST, WHAT'S WRONG?
I HAVE TERRIBLE NEWS: WE'VE BEEN **ATTACKED!** THEY'VE FINALLY GONE AND DONE IT... BOMBS EVERYWHERE!
OH GOD, IT'S HORRIBLE... HORRIBLE...
BOMBS?
IT'S **GERM WARFARE,** THEY SAY... THE AIR IS FILLED WITH **POISON!**
OH GOD, YOU CAN'T IMAGINE!
TERRORISTS!
MY GOD, ARE YOU SURE?
I TOOK THE CHANNEL ALL THE WAY TO AVOID CONTAMINATION, BUT WHO KNOWS -- I MAY NOT BE LONG FOR THIS WORLD...
THE AIR IS PURE POISON!
OH GOD... AUGUST... ARE YOU ALRIGHT? WHAT CAN WE DO?
WHAT CAN WE DO? WE HAVE TO STAY HERE AS LONG AS WE CAN, I SUPPOSE...
AT LEAST WE HAVE A BETTER CHANCE THAN THOSE POOR BASTARDS BACK THERE!
44

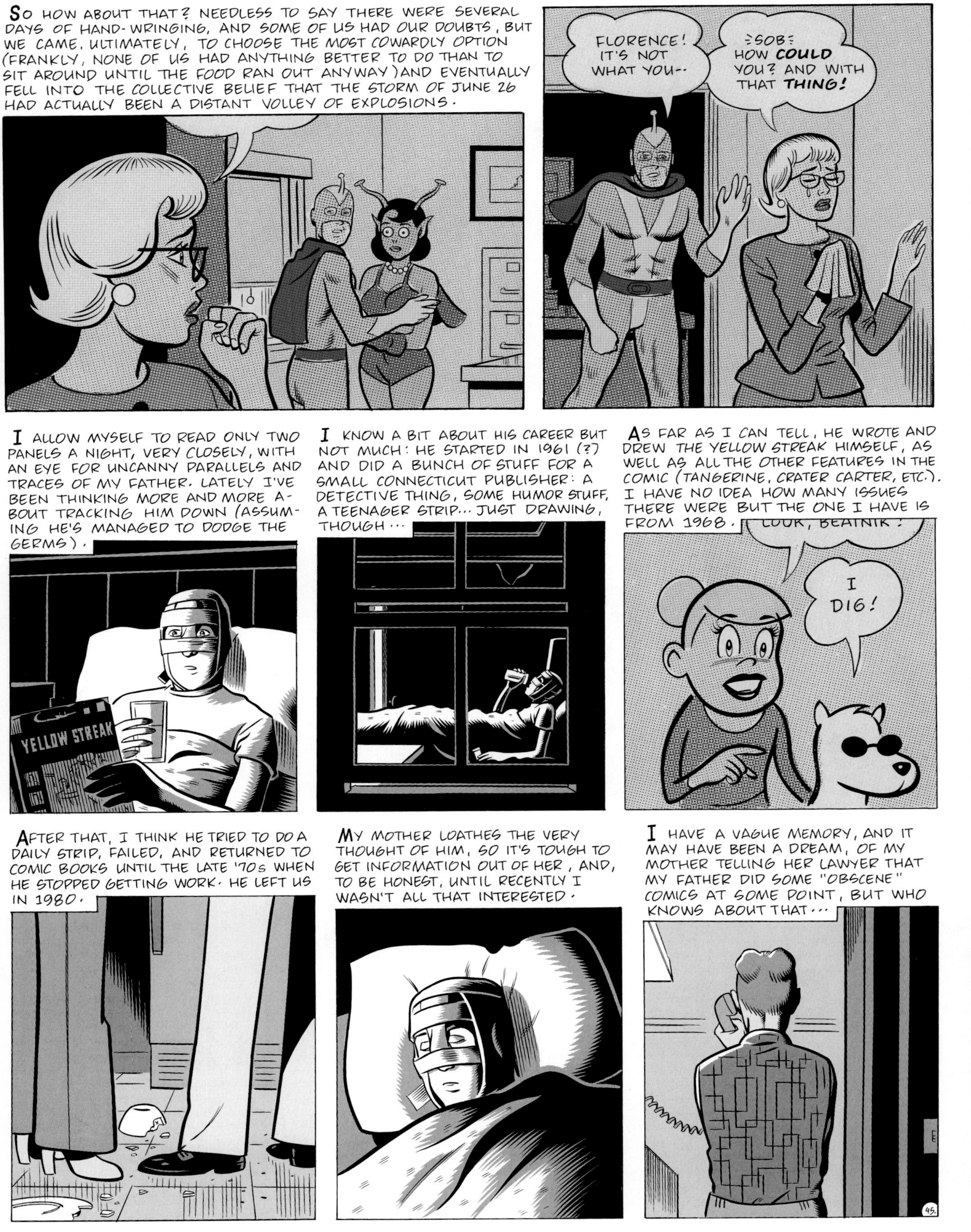
SO HOW ABOUT THAT? NEEDLESS TO SAY THERE WERE SEVERAL DAYS OF HAND-WRINGING, AND SOME OF US HAD OUR DOUBTS, BUT WE CAME, ULTIMATELY, TO CHOOSE THE MOST COWARDLY OPTION (FRANKLY, NONE OF US HAD ANYTHING BETTER TO DO THAN TO SIT AROUND UNTIL THE FOOD RAN OUT ANYWAY) AND EVENTUALLY FELL INTO THE COLLECTIVE BELIEF THAT THE STORM OF JUNE 26 HAD ACTUALLY BEEN A DISTANT VOLLEY OF EXPLOSIONS.
FLORENCE! IT'S NOT WHAT YOU--
=SOB= HOW **COULD** YOU? AND WITH THAT **THING!**
I ALLOW MYSELF TO READ ONLY TWO PANELS A NIGHT, VERY CLOSELY, WITH AN EYE FOR UNCANNY PARALLELS AND TRACES OF MY FATHER. LATELY I'VE BEEN THINKING MORE AND MORE ABOUT TRACKING HIM DOWN (ASSUMING HE'S MANAGED TO DODGE THE GERMS).
YELLOW STREAK
I KNOW A BIT ABOUT HIS CAREER BUT NOT MUCH: HE STARTED IN 1961 (?) AND DID A BUNCH OF STUFF FOR A SMALL CONNECTICUT PUBLISHER: A DETECTIVE THING, SOME HUMOR STUFF, A TEENAGER STRIP... JUST DRAWING, THOUGH...
AS FAR AS I CAN TELL, HE WROTE AND DREW THE YELLOW STREAK HIMSELF, AS WELL AS ALL THE OTHER FEATURES IN THE COMIC (TANGERINE, CRATER CARTER, ETC.). I HAVE NO IDEA HOW MANY ISSUES THERE WERE BUT THE ONE I HAVE IS FROM 1968.
LOOK, BEATNIK!
I DIG!
AFTER THAT, I THINK HE TRIED TO DO A DAILY STRIP, FAILED, AND RETURNED TO COMIC BOOKS UNTIL THE LATE '70s WHEN HE STOPPED GETTING WORK. HE LEFT US IN 1980.
MY MOTHER LOATHES THE VERY THOUGHT OF HIM, SO IT'S TOUGH TO GET INFORMATION OUT OF HER, AND, TO BE HONEST, UNTIL RECENTLY I WASN'T ALL THAT INTERESTED.
I HAVE A VAGUE MEMORY, AND IT MAY HAVE BEEN A DREAM, OF MY MOTHER TELLING HER LAWYER THAT MY FATHER DID SOME "OBSCENE" COMICS AT SOME POINT, BUT WHO KNOWS ABOUT THAT...

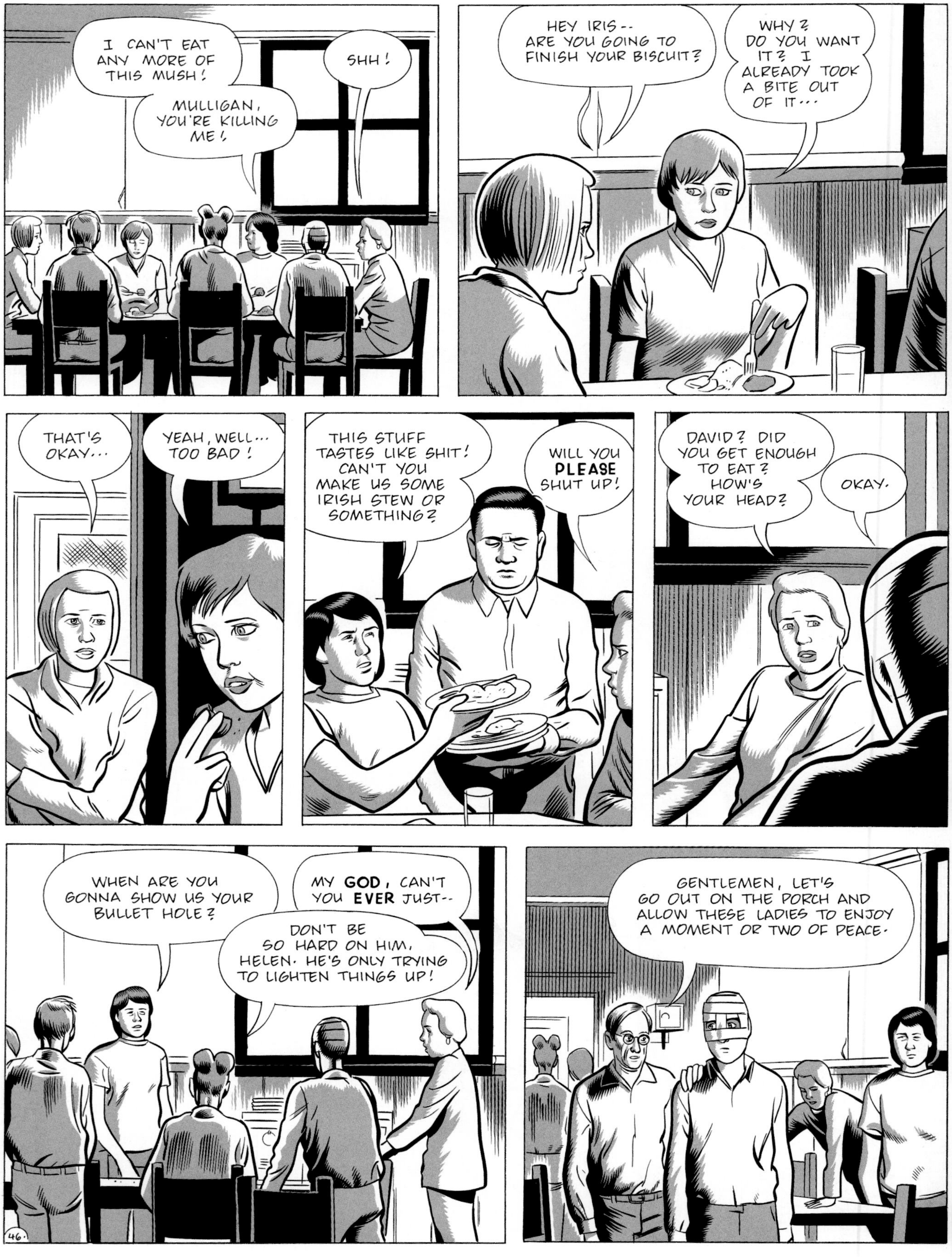
I CAN'T EAT ANY MORE OF THIS MUSH!
MULLIGAN, YOU'RE KILLING ME!
SHH!
HEY IRIS-- ARE YOU GOING TO FINISH YOUR BISCUIT?
WHY? DO YOU WANT IT? I ALREADY TOOK A BITE OUT OF IT...
THAT'S OKAY...
YEAH, WELL... TOO BAD!
THIS STUFF TASTES LIKE SHIT! CAN'T YOU MAKE US SOME IRISH STEW OR SOMETHING?
WILL YOU **PLEASE** SHUT UP!
DAVID? DID YOU GET ENOUGH TO EAT? HOW'S YOUR HEAD?
OKAY.
WHEN ARE YOU GONNA SHOW US YOUR BULLET HOLE?
MY **GOD**, CAN'T YOU **EVER** JUST--
DON'T BE SO HARD ON HIM, HELEN. HE'S ONLY TRYING TO LIGHTEN THINGS UP!
GENTLEMEN, LET'S GO OUT ON THE PORCH AND ALLOW THESE LADIES TO ENJOY A MOMENT OR TWO OF PEACE.

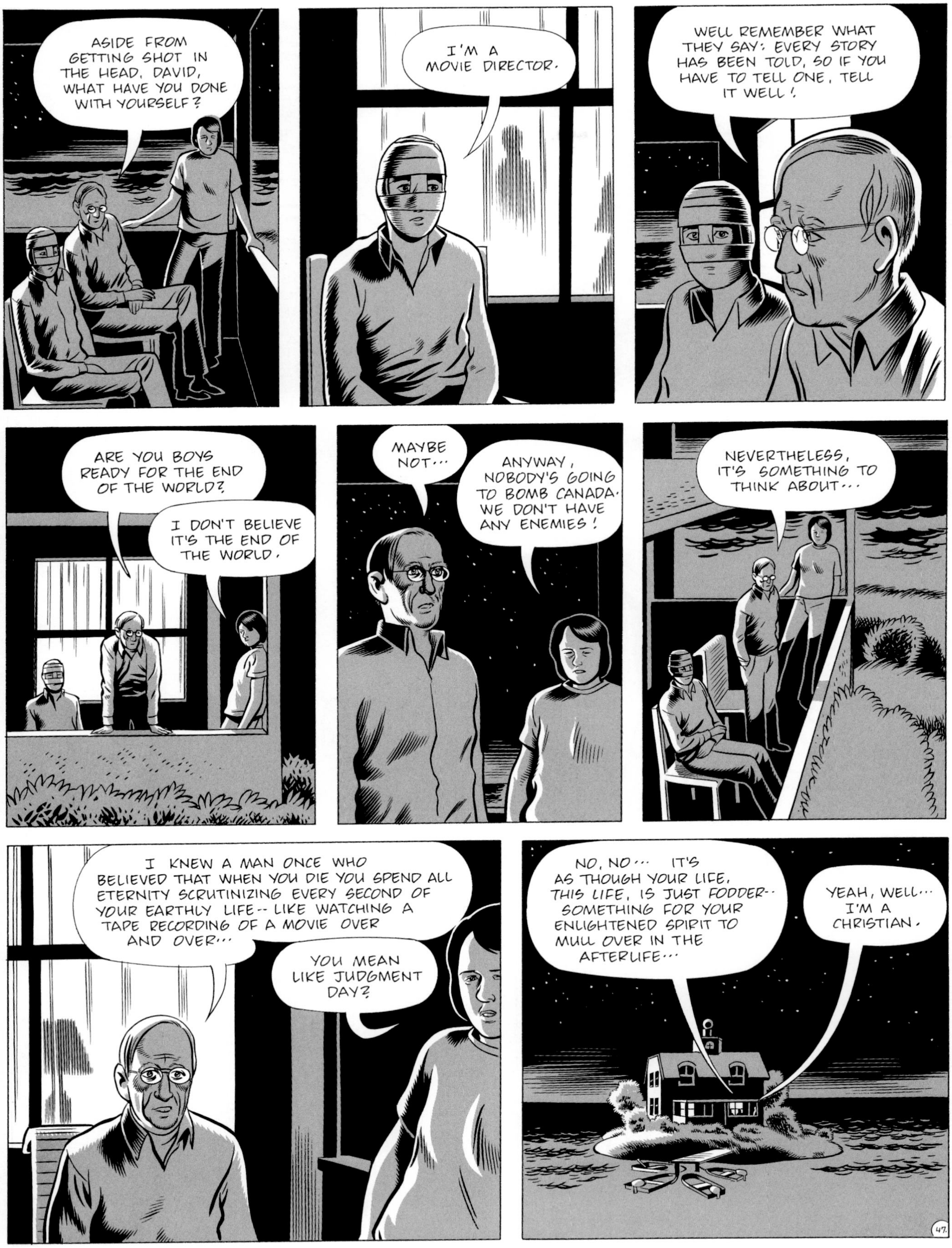
ASIDE FROM GETTING SHOT IN THE HEAD, DAVID, WHAT HAVE YOU DONE WITH YOURSELF?
I'M A MOVIE DIRECTOR.
WELL REMEMBER WHAT THEY SAY: EVERY STORY HAS BEEN TOLD, SO IF YOU HAVE TO TELL ONE, TELL IT WELL!
ARE YOU BOYS READY FOR THE END OF THE WORLD?
I DON'T BELIEVE IT'S THE END OF THE WORLD.
MAYBE NOT...
ANYWAY, NOBODY'S GOING TO BOMB CANADA. WE DON'T HAVE ANY ENEMIES!
NEVERTHELESS, IT'S SOMETHING TO THINK ABOUT...
I KNEW A MAN ONCE WHO BELIEVED THAT WHEN YOU DIE YOU SPEND ALL ETERNITY SCRUTINIZING EVERY SECOND OF YOUR EARTHLY LIFE-- LIKE WATCHING A TAPE RECORDING OF A MOVIE OVER AND OVER...
YOU MEAN LIKE JUDGMENT DAY?
NO, NO... IT'S AS THOUGH YOUR LIFE, THIS LIFE, IS JUST FODDER-- SOMETHING FOR YOUR ENLIGHTENED SPIRIT TO MULL OVER IN THE AFTERLIFE...
YEAH, WELL... I'M A CHRISTIAN.
47.

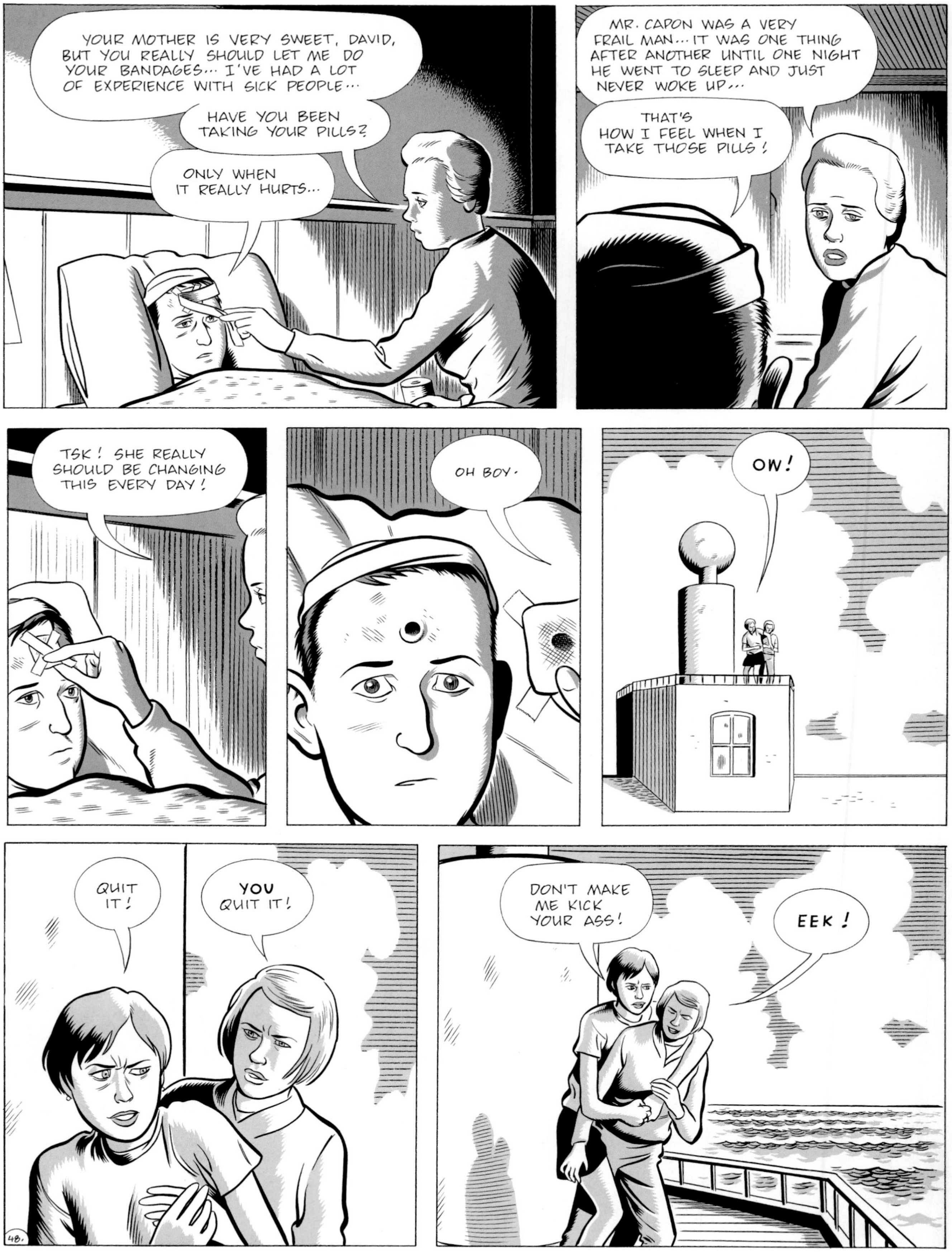
YOUR MOTHER IS VERY SWEET, DAVID, BUT YOU REALLY SHOULD LET ME DO YOUR BANDAGES... I'VE HAD A LOT OF EXPERIENCE WITH SICK PEOPLE...
HAVE YOU BEEN TAKING YOUR PILLS?
ONLY WHEN IT REALLY HURTS...
MR. CAPON WAS A VERY FRAIL MAN... IT WAS ONE THING AFTER ANOTHER UNTIL ONE NIGHT HE WENT TO SLEEP AND JUST NEVER WOKE UP...
THAT'S HOW I FEEL WHEN I TAKE THOSE PILLS!
TSK! SHE REALLY SHOULD BE CHANGING THIS EVERY DAY!
OH BOY.
OW!
QUIT IT!
YOU QUIT IT!
DON'T MAKE ME KICK YOUR ASS!
EEK!

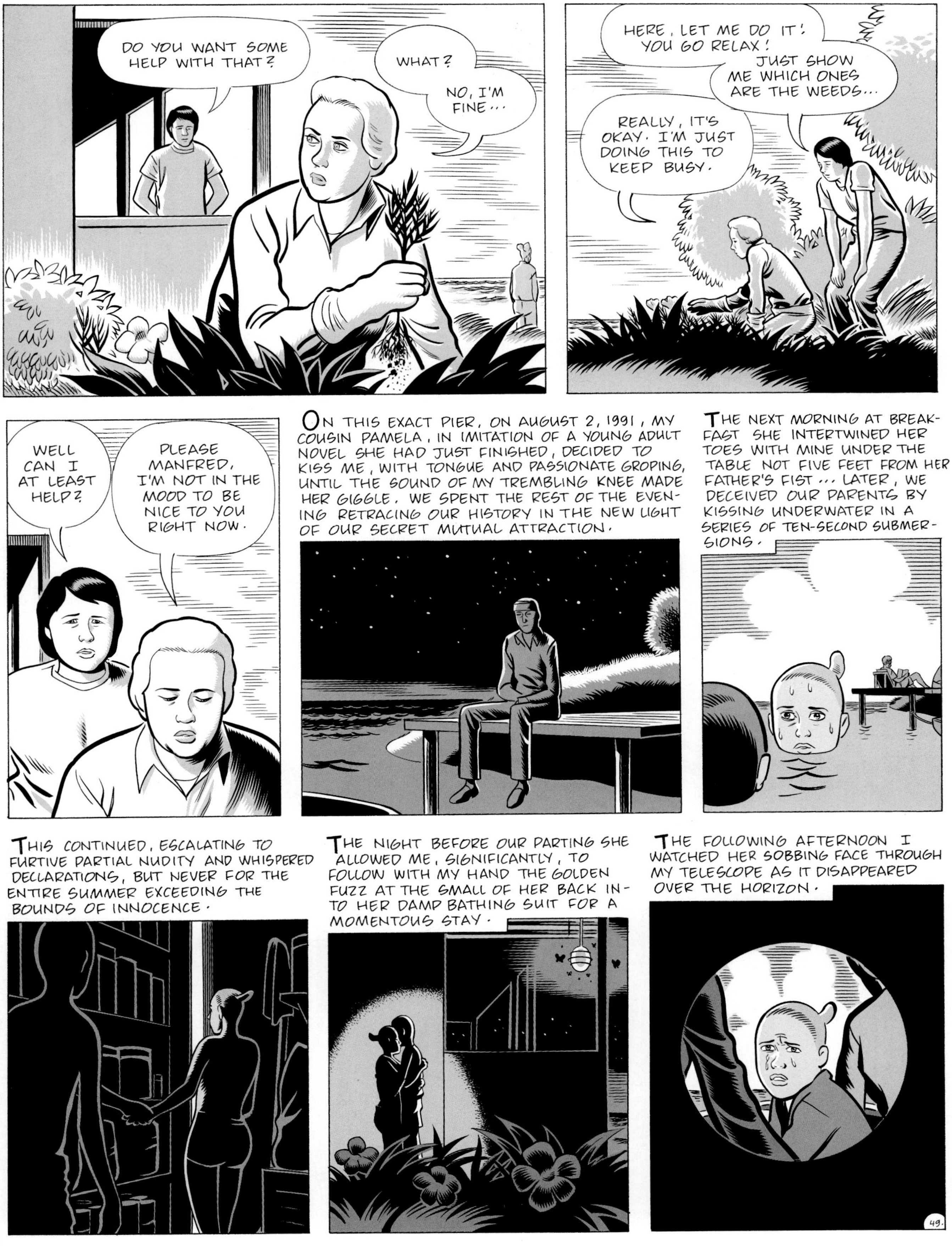

DO YOU WANT SOME HELP WITH THAT?
WHAT?
NO, I'M FINE...
HERE, LET ME DO IT! YOU GO RELAX!
JUST SHOW ME WHICH ONES ARE THE WEEDS...
REALLY, IT'S OKAY. I'M JUST DOING THIS TO KEEP BUSY.
WELL CAN I AT LEAST HELP?
PLEASE MANFRED, I'M NOT IN THE MOOD TO BE NICE TO YOU RIGHT NOW.
ON THIS EXACT PIER, ON AUGUST 2, 1991, MY COUSIN PAMELA, IN IMITATION OF A YOUNG ADULT NOVEL SHE HAD JUST FINISHED, DECIDED TO KISS ME, WITH TONGUE AND PASSIONATE GROPING, UNTIL THE SOUND OF MY TREMBLING KNEE MADE HER GIGGLE. WE SPENT THE REST OF THE EVENING RETRACING OUR HISTORY IN THE NEW LIGHT OF OUR SECRET MUTUAL ATTRACTION.
THE NEXT MORNING AT BREAKFAST SHE INTERTWINED HER TOES WITH MINE UNDER THE TABLE NOT FIVE FEET FROM HER FATHER'S FIST... LATER, WE DECEIVED OUR PARENTS BY KISSING UNDERWATER IN A SERIES OF TEN-SECOND SUBMERSIONS.
THIS CONTINUED, ESCALATING TO FURTIVE PARTIAL NUDITY AND WHISPERED DECLARATIONS, BUT NEVER FOR THE ENTIRE SUMMER EXCEEDING THE BOUNDS OF INNOCENCE.
THE NIGHT BEFORE OUR PARTING SHE ALLOWED ME, SIGNIFICANTLY, TO FOLLOW WITH MY HAND THE GOLDEN FUZZ AT THE SMALL OF HER BACK INTO HER DAMP BATHING SUIT FOR A MOMENTOUS STAY.
THE FOLLOWING AFTERNOON I WATCHED HER SOBBING FACE THROUGH MY TELESCOPE AS IT DISAPPEARED OVER THE HORIZON.

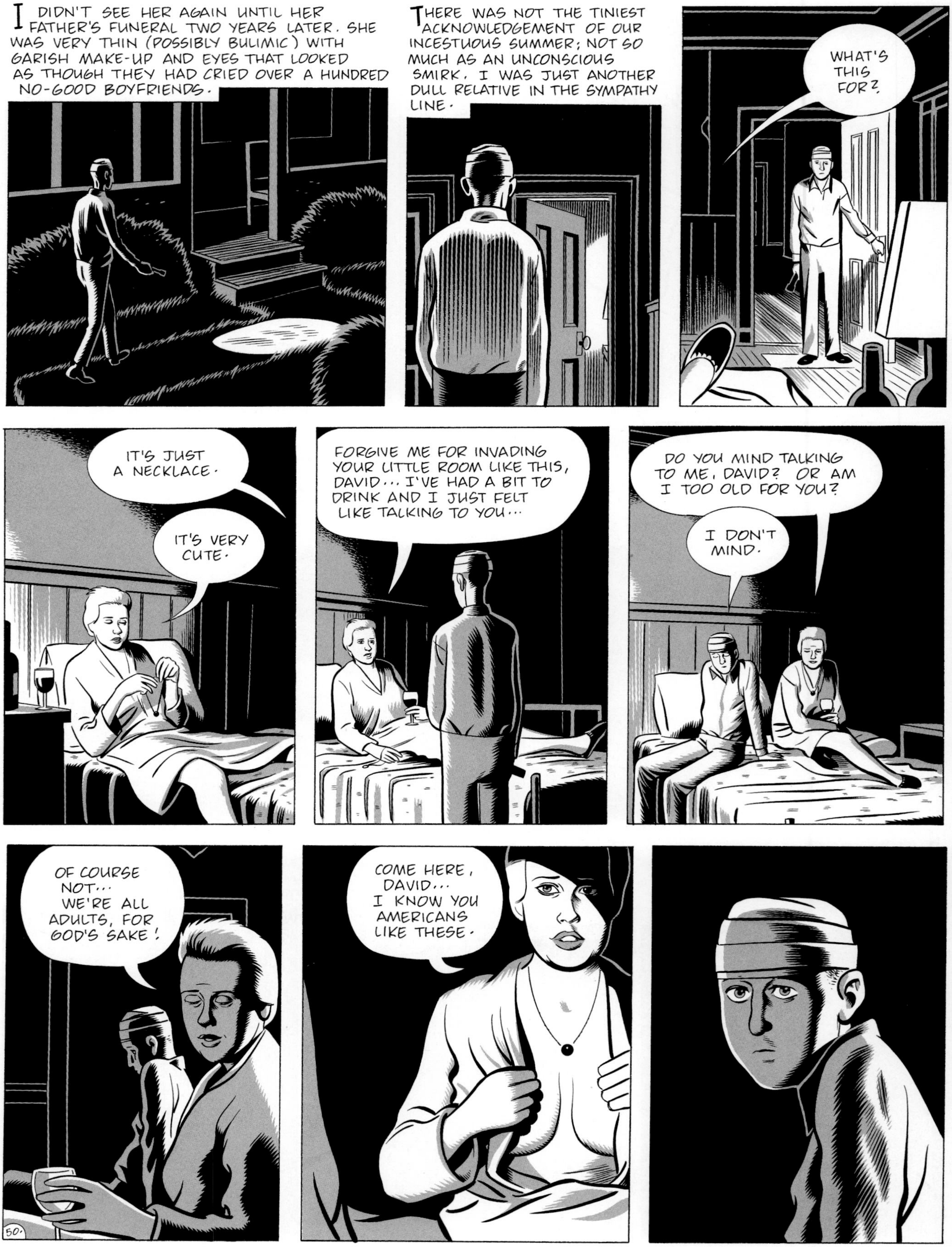
I DIDN'T SEE HER AGAIN UNTIL HER FATHER'S FUNERAL TWO YEARS LATER. SHE WAS VERY THIN (POSSIBLY BULIMIC) WITH GARISH MAKE-UP AND EYES THAT LOOKED AS THOUGH THEY HAD CRIED OVER A HUNDRED NO-GOOD BOYFRIENDS.
THERE WAS NOT THE TINIEST ACKNOWLEDGEMENT OF OUR INCESTUOUS SUMMER; NOT SO MUCH AS AN UNCONSCIOUS SMIRK. I WAS JUST ANOTHER DULL RELATIVE IN THE SYMPATHY LINE.
WHAT'S THIS FOR?
IT'S JUST A NECKLACE.
IT'S VERY CUTE.
FORGIVE ME FOR INVADING YOUR LITTLE ROOM LIKE THIS, DAVID... I'VE HAD A BIT TO DRINK AND I JUST FELT LIKE TALKING TO YOU...
DO YOU MIND TALKING TO ME, DAVID? OR AM I TOO OLD FOR YOU?
I DON'T MIND.
OF COURSE NOT... WE'RE ALL ADULTS, FOR GOD'S SAKE!
COME HERE, DAVID... I KNOW YOU AMERICANS LIKE THESE.

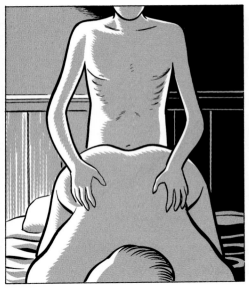

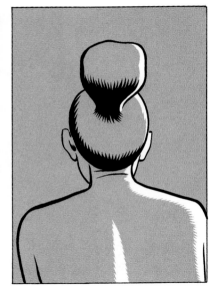

WHAT'S THIS ONE ABOUT?

IT'S KIND OF HARD TO EXPLAIN...

I REALLY NEED TO GET MY PROJECTOR FIXED...

I WAS IN A MOVIE ONCE.

I BET YOU'D GET A KICK OUT OF IT.

WHY DOES YOUR FAMILY HATE ME SO MUCH?

FACE IT, YOU'RE AN ASSHOLE!

I ONLY CAME ALONG ON THIS FUCKING TRIP BECAUSE I THOUGHT WE COULD WORK THINGS OUT BETWEEN YOUR MOTHER AND ME...

YEAH, WELL, THAT WAS PRETTY STUPID!

51

CAN'T SHE AT LEAST HAVE SOME FUCKING HUMAN DECENCY? I GREW UP WITHOUT A MOTHER IN THE HOUSE; I DON'T NEED THIS SHIT FROM HER!

=SIGH= LOOK, SHE JUST HATES YOU.. DEAL WITH IT.

FUCK HER!

IT'S NOTHING PERSONAL, IT'S JUST THE WAY YOU ACT-- SHE ALWAYS HATES PEOPLE LIKE THAT...

AND BASICALLY SHE'LL JUST NEVER FORGIVE YOU FOR RUINING MY LIFE.... OKAY?

SOMETIMES I THINK THAT'S THE ONLY REASON YOU MARRIED ME: TO PISS HER OFF...

WHAT'S THAT NOISE?

SCREEK SCREEK SCR

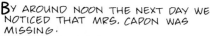

BY AROUND NOON THE NEXT DAY WE NOTICED THAT MRS. CAPON WAS MISSING.

SHE TOOK ONE OF THE BOATS.

DO YOU SEE ANYTHING?

OH NO...

AUGUST AND HULLIGAN WENT OUT TO LOOK AROUND BUT THERE WAS NO SIGN OF A BODY. HAD I FALLEN ASLEEP BEFORE SHE LEFT THE ROOM? I CAN'T REMEMBER. HAD I DRIVEN HER TO SUICIDE? AM I THE MONSTER IN MY OWN HORROR STORY?

WE CAN'T JUST SIT AROUND-- WE'VE GOT TO FIND HER!

52.

THERE'S NOWHERE LEFT TO LOOK.

WHAT ABOUT YOU, DAVID.... DID YOU TALK TO HER LAST NIGHT?

WHO KNOWS, MAYBE THE POISON GOT TO HER... MAYBE IT DOES SOMETHING TO YOUR MIND...

YEAH, MAYBE SO... MAYBE THAT'S EXACTLY WHAT HAPPENED...

POOR LITTLE IRIS... THANK GOD SHE STILL HAS MANFRED.

SO DAVID, AUGUST TELLS ME YOU'RE A MOVIE DIRECTOR?

OH... NO, NOT REALLY...

WELL THANK GOD FOR THAT!

YOU POOR THING... WE REALLY NEED TO GET YOU AWAY FROM ALL THIS TUMULT!

THERE IT WAS! THE LONG-AWAITED OPENING SALVO IN HER CAMPAIGN TO GET ME BACK INTO THE FAMILY HOME (SURELY MERRYVALE HAD BEEN SPARED BY THE TERRORISTS!). LUCKILY, A SPONTANEOUS HEADACHE ALLOWED ME TO WITHDRAW BEFORE THE FOLLOW-THROUGH.

TUMULT! I HAD FORGOTTEN THE EERIE CALLOUSNESS THAT CAME TO HER IN TIMES OF DISTRESS. ALL SUFFERERS WERE BELITTLED WITH QUAINT DIM-INUTIVES AS THOUGH, BY CONTRAST, HER SOLITARY, SEXLESS ADULTHOOD WAS THE ONLY VALID TRAGEDY.

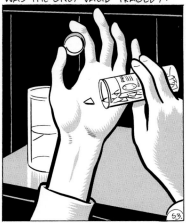

53.

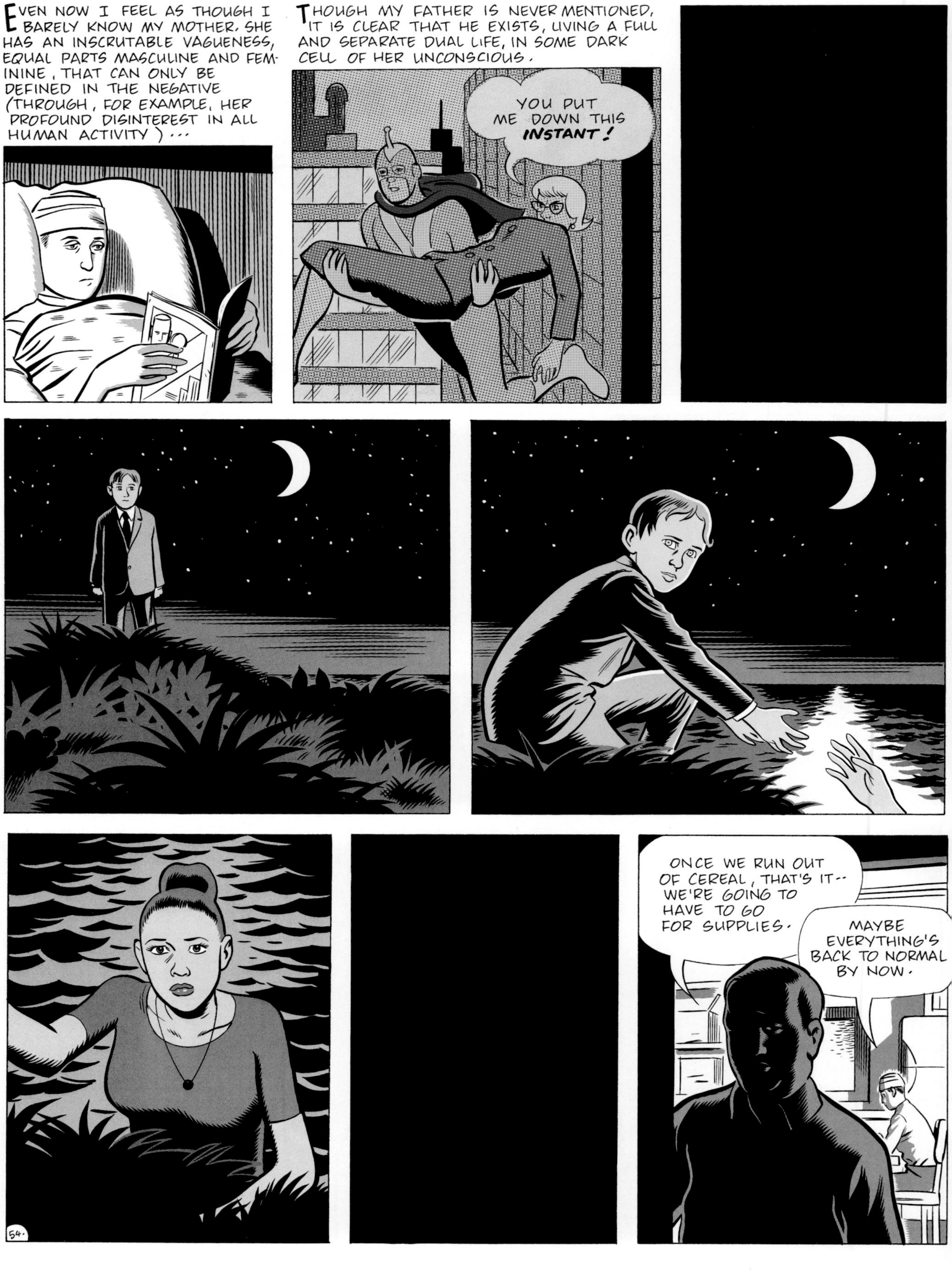
EVEN NOW I FEEL AS THOUGH I BARELY KNOW MY MOTHER. SHE HAS AN INSCRUTABLE VAGUENESS, EQUAL PARTS MASCULINE AND FEMININE, THAT CAN ONLY BE DEFINED IN THE NEGATIVE (THROUGH, FOR EXAMPLE, HER PROFOUND DISINTEREST IN ALL HUMAN ACTIVITY)...
THOUGH MY FATHER IS NEVER MENTIONED, IT IS CLEAR THAT HE EXISTS, LIVING A FULL AND SEPARATE DUAL LIFE, IN SOME DARK CELL OF HER UNCONSCIOUS.
YOU PUT ME DOWN THIS INSTANT!
ONCE WE RUN OUT OF CEREAL, THAT'S IT-- WE'RE GOING TO HAVE TO GO FOR SUPPLIES.
MAYBE EVERYTHING'S BACK TO NORMAL BY NOW.
54.

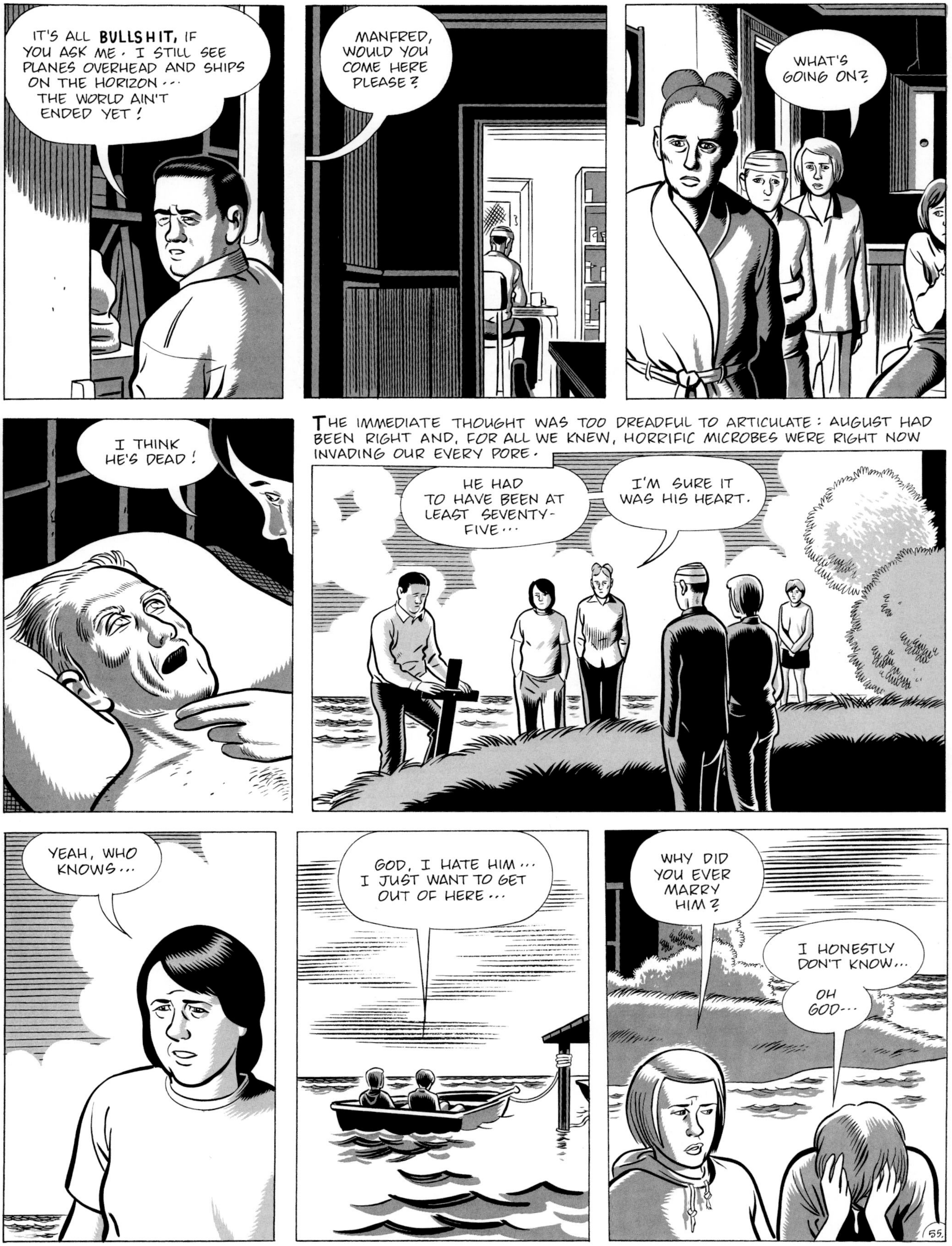
IT'S ALL BULLSHIT, IF YOU ASK ME. I STILL SEE PLANES OVERHEAD AND SHIPS ON THE HORIZON... THE WORLD AIN'T ENDED YET!
MANFRED, WOULD YOU COME HERE PLEASE?
WHAT'S GOING ON?
I THINK HE'S DEAD!
THE IMMEDIATE THOUGHT WAS TOO DREADFUL TO ARTICULATE: AUGUST HAD BEEN RIGHT AND, FOR ALL WE KNEW, HORRIFIC MICROBES WERE RIGHT NOW INVADING OUR EVERY PORE.
HE HAD TO HAVE BEEN AT LEAST SEVENTY-FIVE...
I'M SURE IT WAS HIS HEART.
YEAH, WHO KNOWS...
GOD, I HATE HIM... I JUST WANT TO GET OUT OF HERE...
WHY DID YOU EVER MARRY HIM?
I HONESTLY DON'T KNOW...
OH GOD...

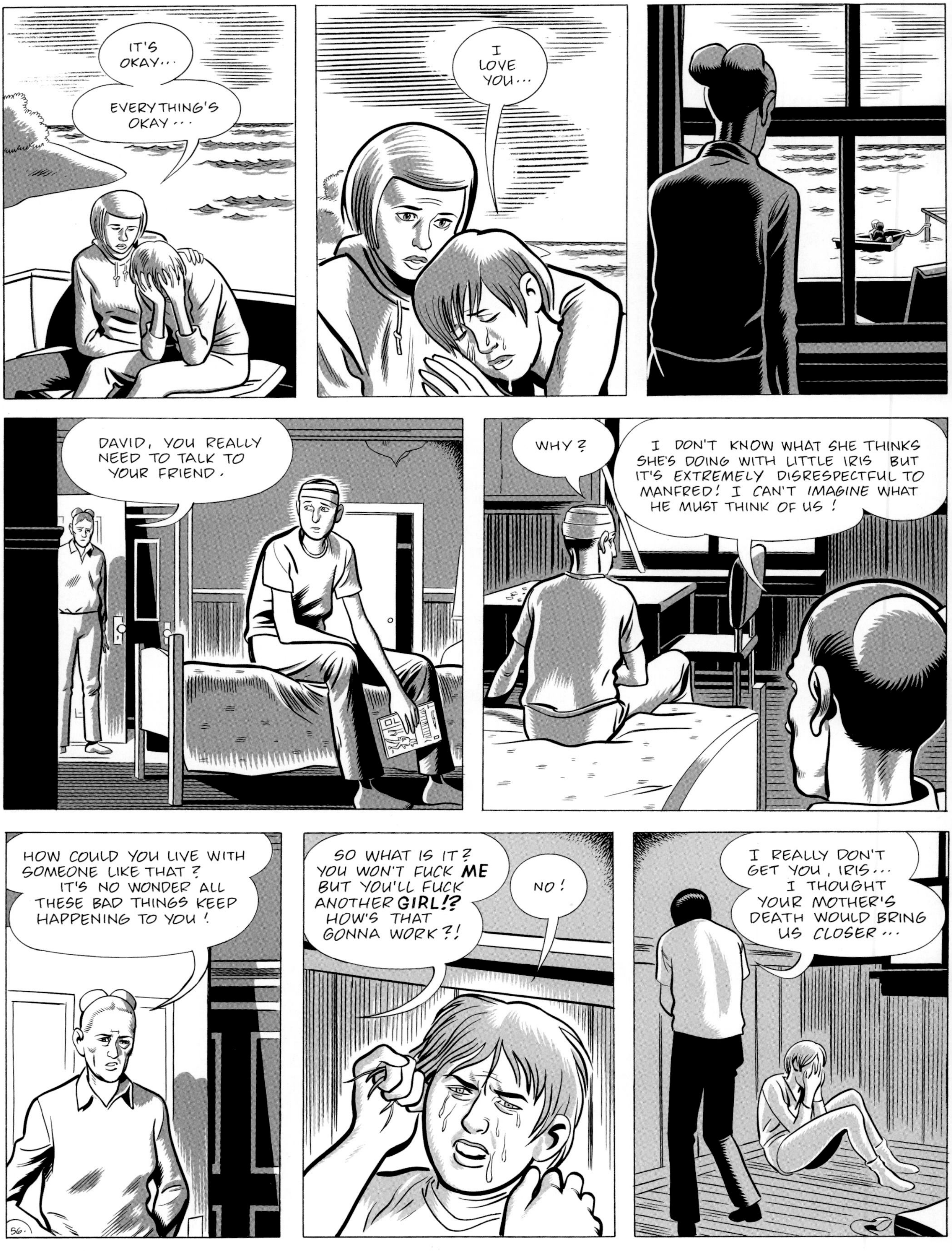
IT'S OKAY...
EVERYTHING'S OKAY...
I LOVE YOU...
DAVID, YOU REALLY NEED TO TALK TO YOUR FRIEND.
WHY?
I DON'T KNOW WHAT SHE THINKS SHE'S DOING WITH LITTLE IRIS BUT IT'S EXTREMELY DISRESPECTFUL TO MANFRED! I CAN'T IMAGINE WHAT HE MUST THINK OF US!
HOW COULD YOU LIVE WITH SOMEONE LIKE THAT? IT'S NO WONDER ALL THESE BAD THINGS KEEP HAPPENING TO YOU!
SO WHAT IS IT? YOU WON'T FUCK ME BUT YOU'LL FUCK ANOTHER GIRL!? HOW'S THAT GONNA WORK?!
NO!
I REALLY DON'T GET YOU, IRIS... I THOUGHT YOUR MOTHER'S DEATH WOULD BRING US CLOSER...

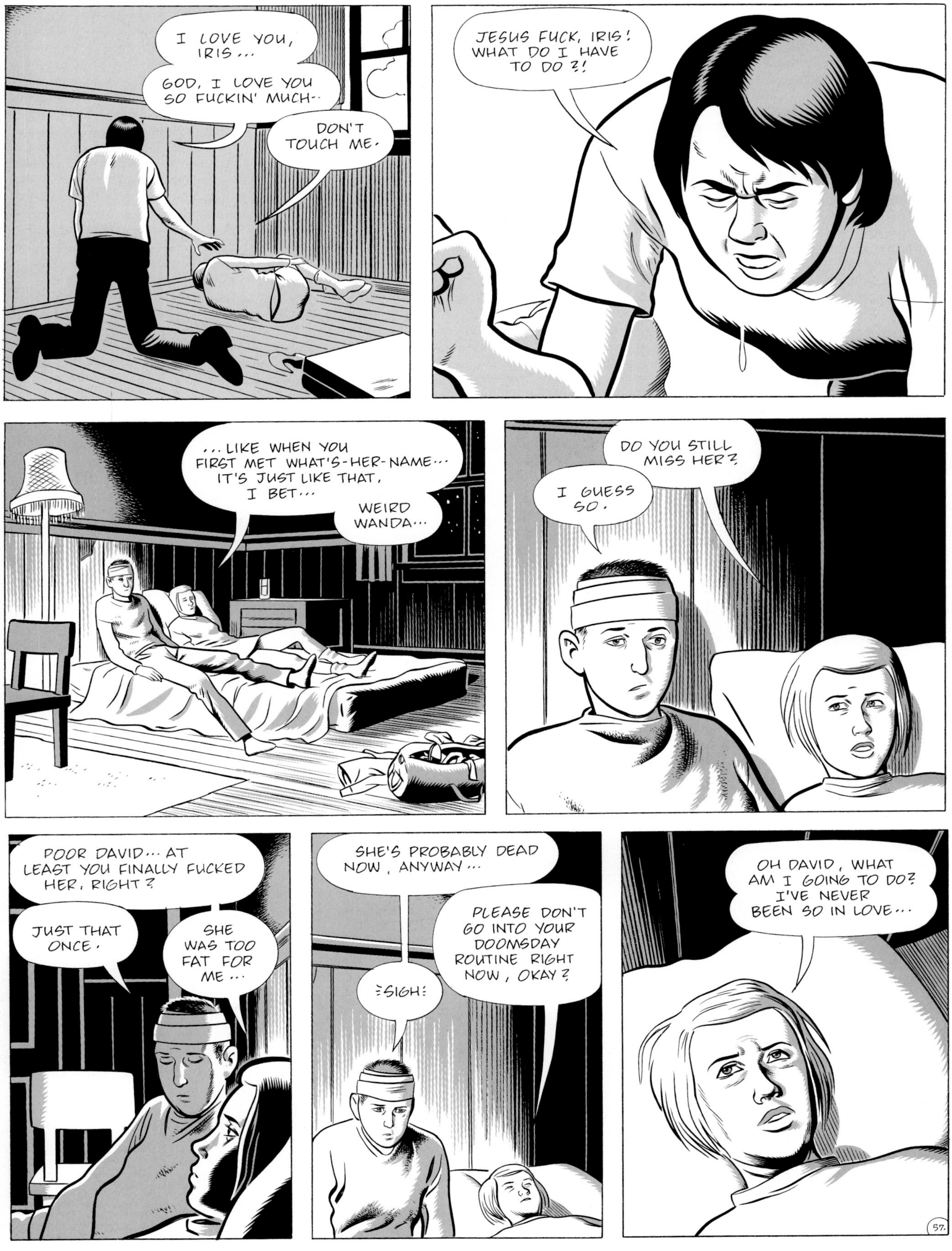

I LOVE YOU, IRIS...
GOD, I LOVE YOU SO FUCKIN' MUCH--
DON'T TOUCH ME.
JESUS FUCK, IRIS! WHAT DO I HAVE TO DO?!
...LIKE WHEN YOU FIRST MET WHAT'S-HER-NAME... IT'S JUST LIKE THAT, I BET...
WEIRD WANDA...
DO YOU STILL MISS HER?
I GUESS SO.
POOR DAVID... AT LEAST YOU FINALLY FUCKED HER, RIGHT?
JUST THAT ONCE.
SHE WAS TOO FAT FOR ME...
SHE'S PROBABLY DEAD NOW, ANYWAY...
PLEASE DON'T GO INTO YOUR DOOMSDAY ROUTINE RIGHT NOW, OKAY?
SIGH
OH DAVID, WHAT AM I GOING TO DO? I'VE NEVER BEEN SO IN LOVE...

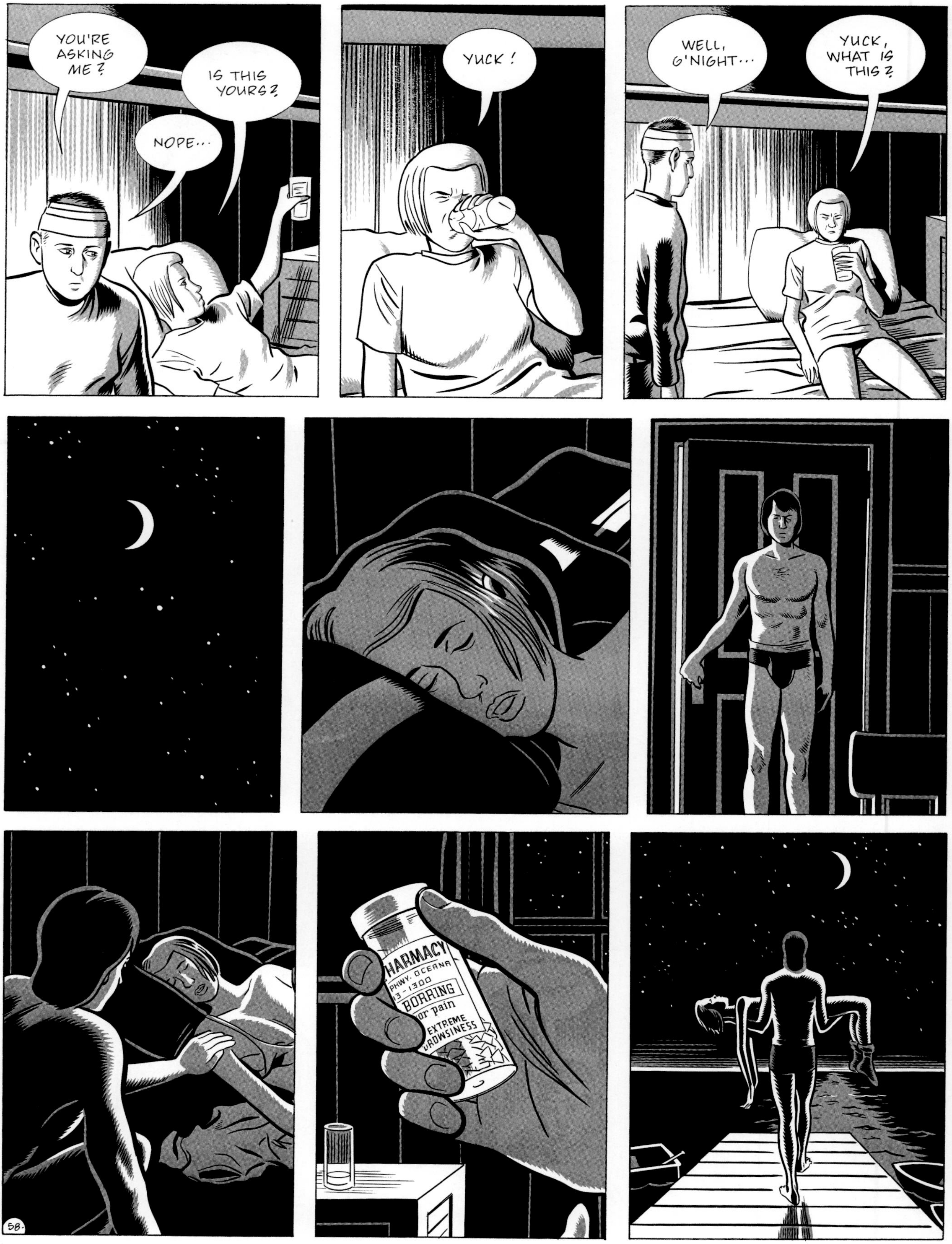

YOU'RE ASKING ME?
IS THIS YOURS?
NOPE...
YUCK!
WELL, G'NIGHT...
YUCK, WHAT IS THIS?
HARMACY
PKWY. OCEANA
3-1300
BORRING
for Pain
EXTREME

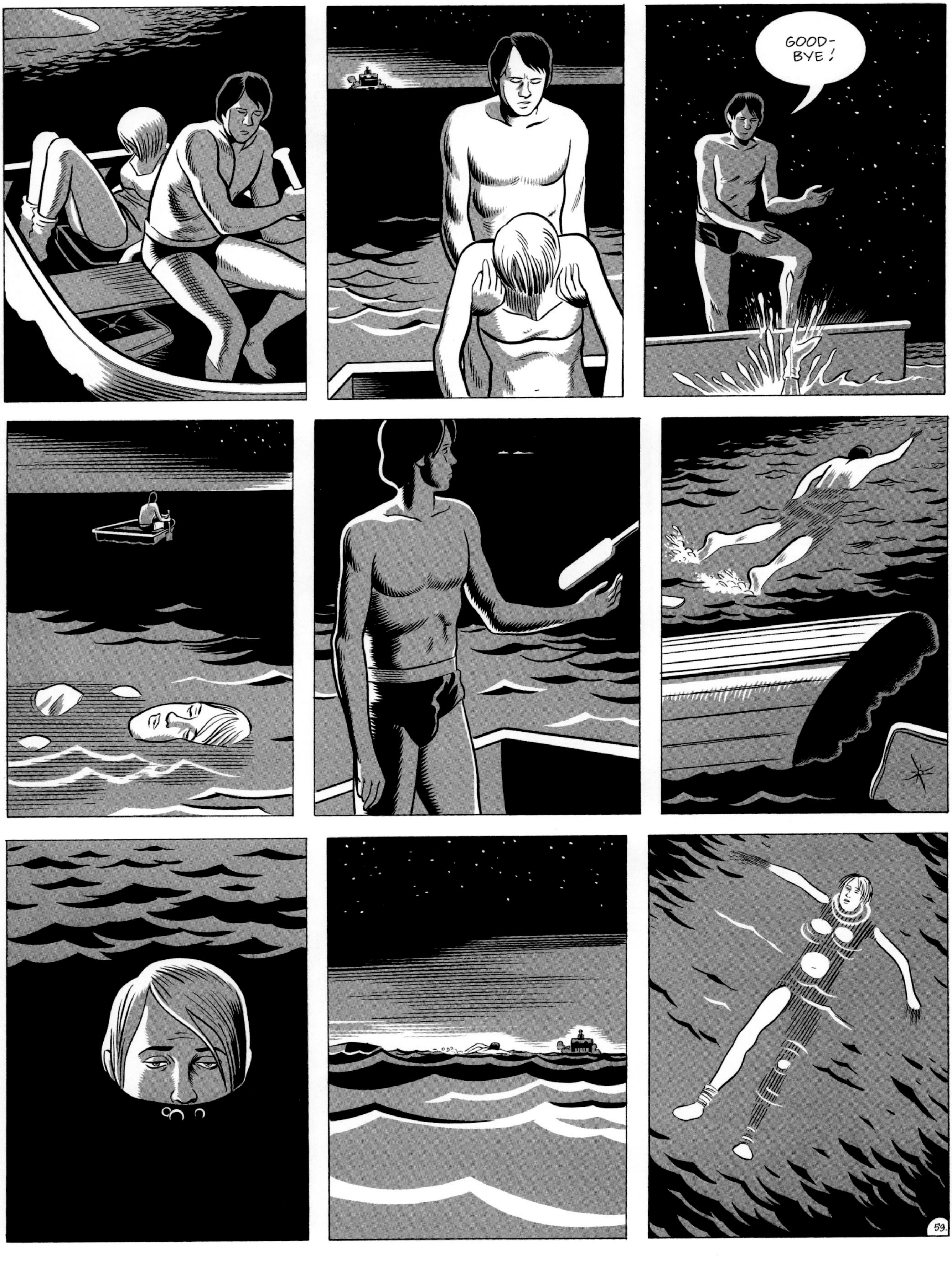
GOOD-BYE!

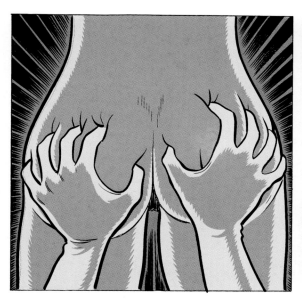

CLICK

WHAT HAPPENED?

WERE YOU SWIMMING?

DO YOU THINK YOU'D BE OKAY WITHOUT ME?

60.

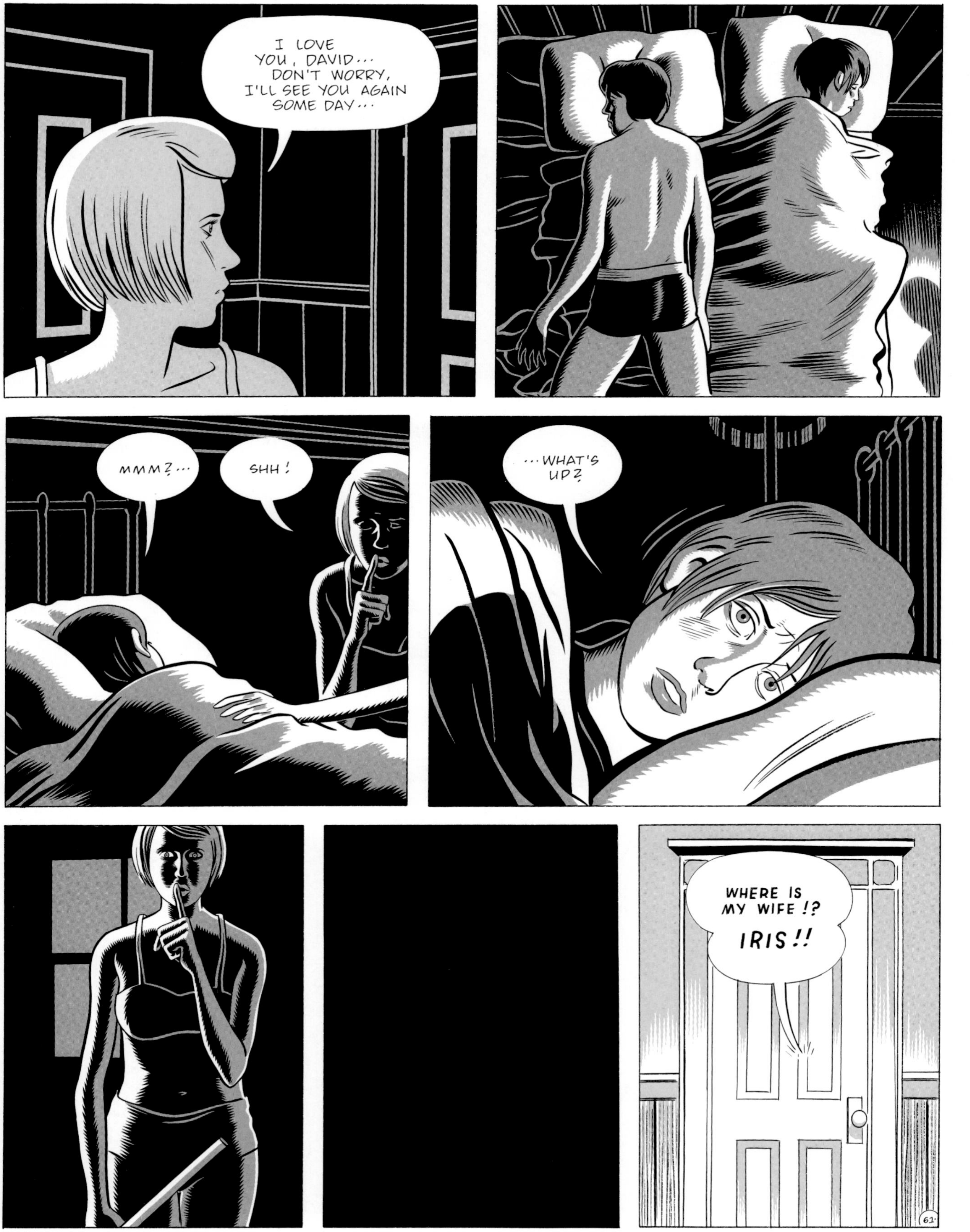
I LOVE YOU, DAVID... DON'T WORRY, I'LL SEE YOU AGAIN SOME DAY...
MMM?...
SHH!
...WHAT'S UP?
WHERE IS MY WIFE!?
IRIS!!

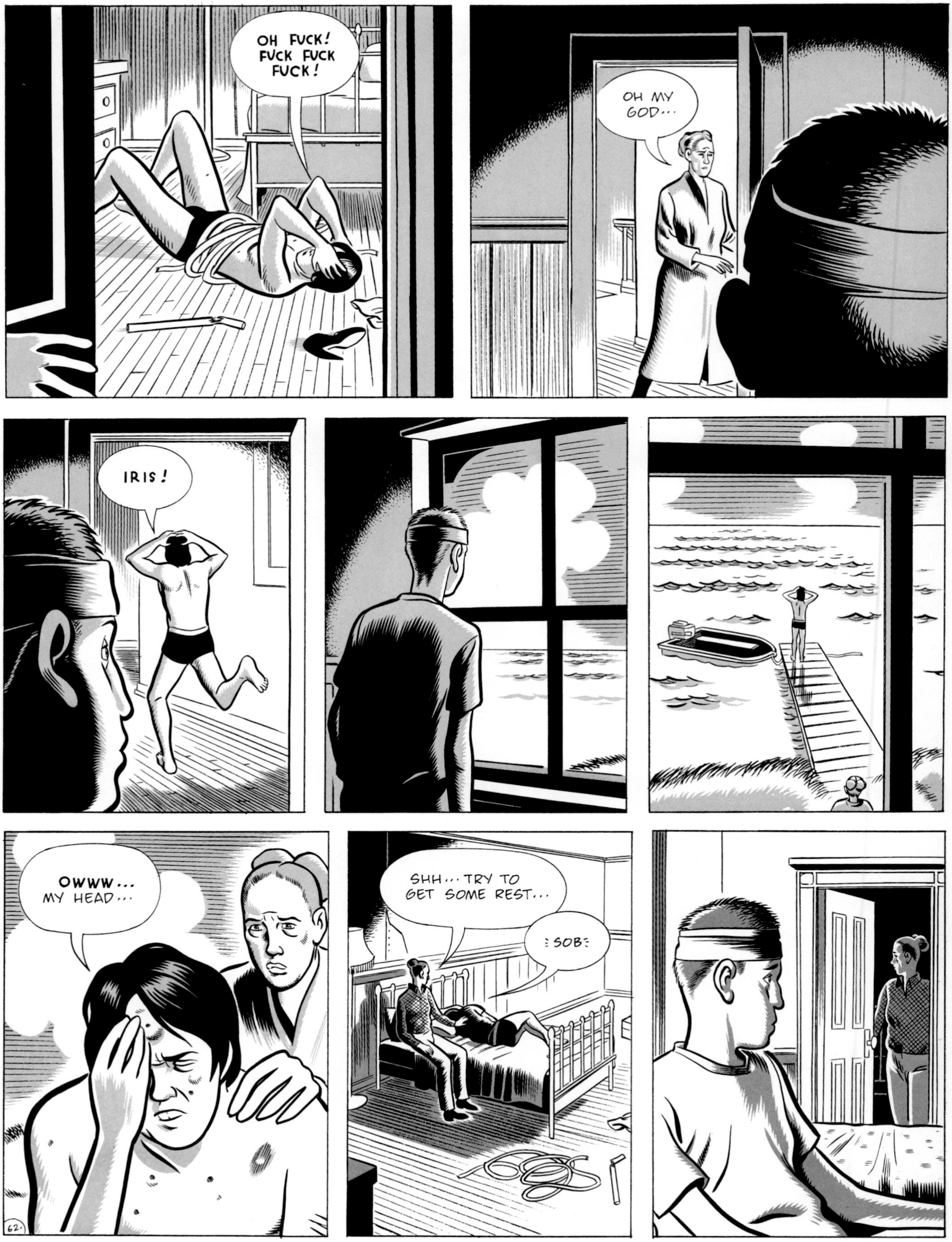

OH FUCK! FUCK FUCK FUCK!
OH MY GOD...
IRIS!
OWWW... MY HEAD...
SHH... TRY TO GET SOME REST...
SOB
62.

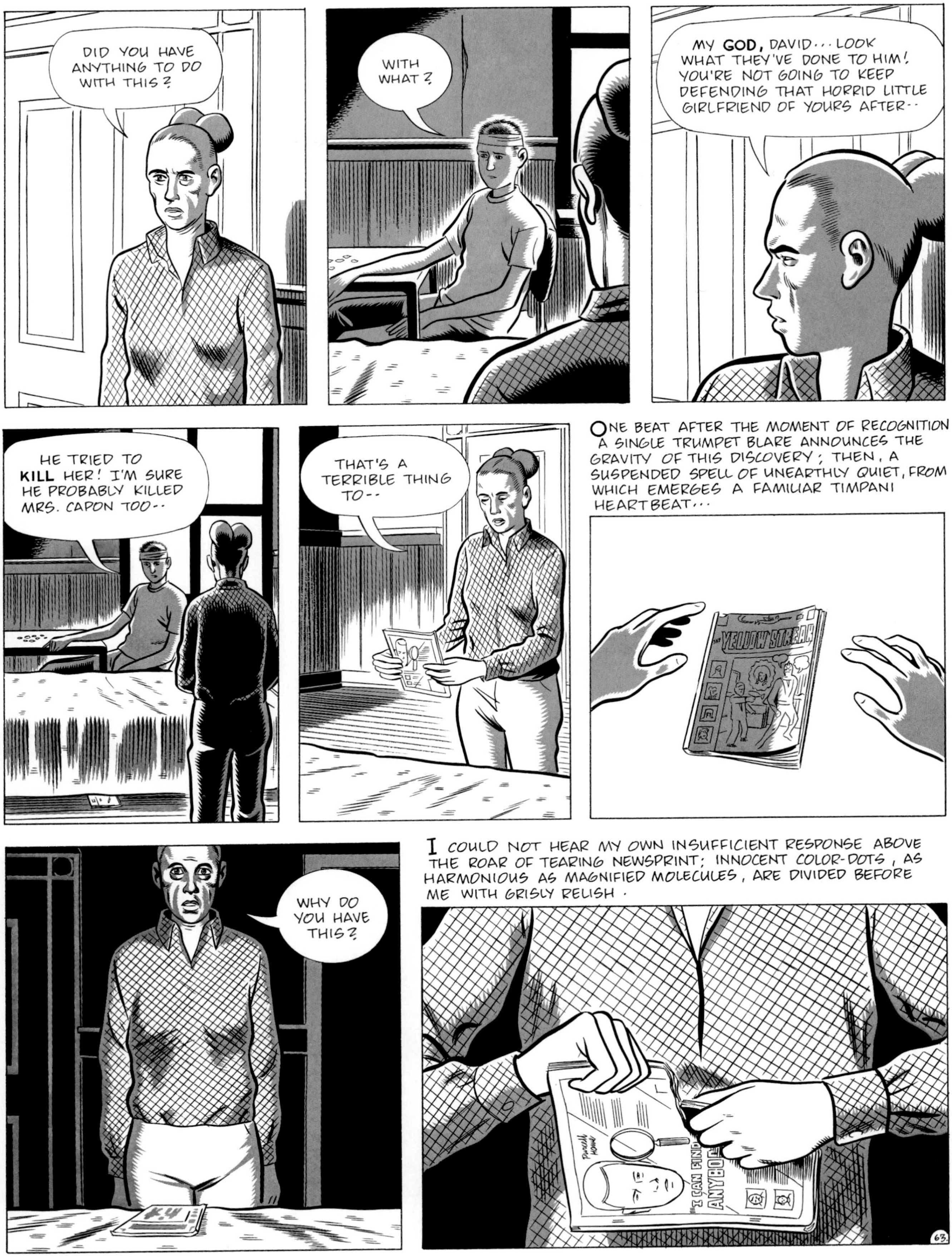
DID YOU HAVE ANYTHING TO DO WITH THIS?
WITH WHAT?
MY **GOD,** DAVID... LOOK WHAT THEY'VE DONE TO HIM! YOU'RE NOT GOING TO KEEP DEFENDING THAT HORRID LITTLE GIRLFRIEND OF YOURS AFTER--
HE TRIED TO **KILL** HER! I'M SURE HE PROBABLY KILLED MRS. CAPON TOO--
THAT'S A TERRIBLE THING TO--
ONE BEAT AFTER THE MOMENT OF RECOGNITION A SINGLE TRUMPET BLARE ANNOUNCES THE GRAVITY OF THIS DISCOVERY; THEN, A SUSPENDED SPELL OF UNEARTHLY QUIET, FROM WHICH EMERGES A FAMILIAR TIMPANI HEARTBEAT...
WHY DO YOU HAVE THIS?
I COULD NOT HEAR MY OWN INSUFFICIENT RESPONSE ABOVE THE ROAR OF TEARING NEWSPRINT; INNOCENT COLOR-DOTS, AS HARMONIOUS AS MAGNIFIED MOLECULES, ARE DIVIDED BEFORE ME WITH GRISLY RELISH.

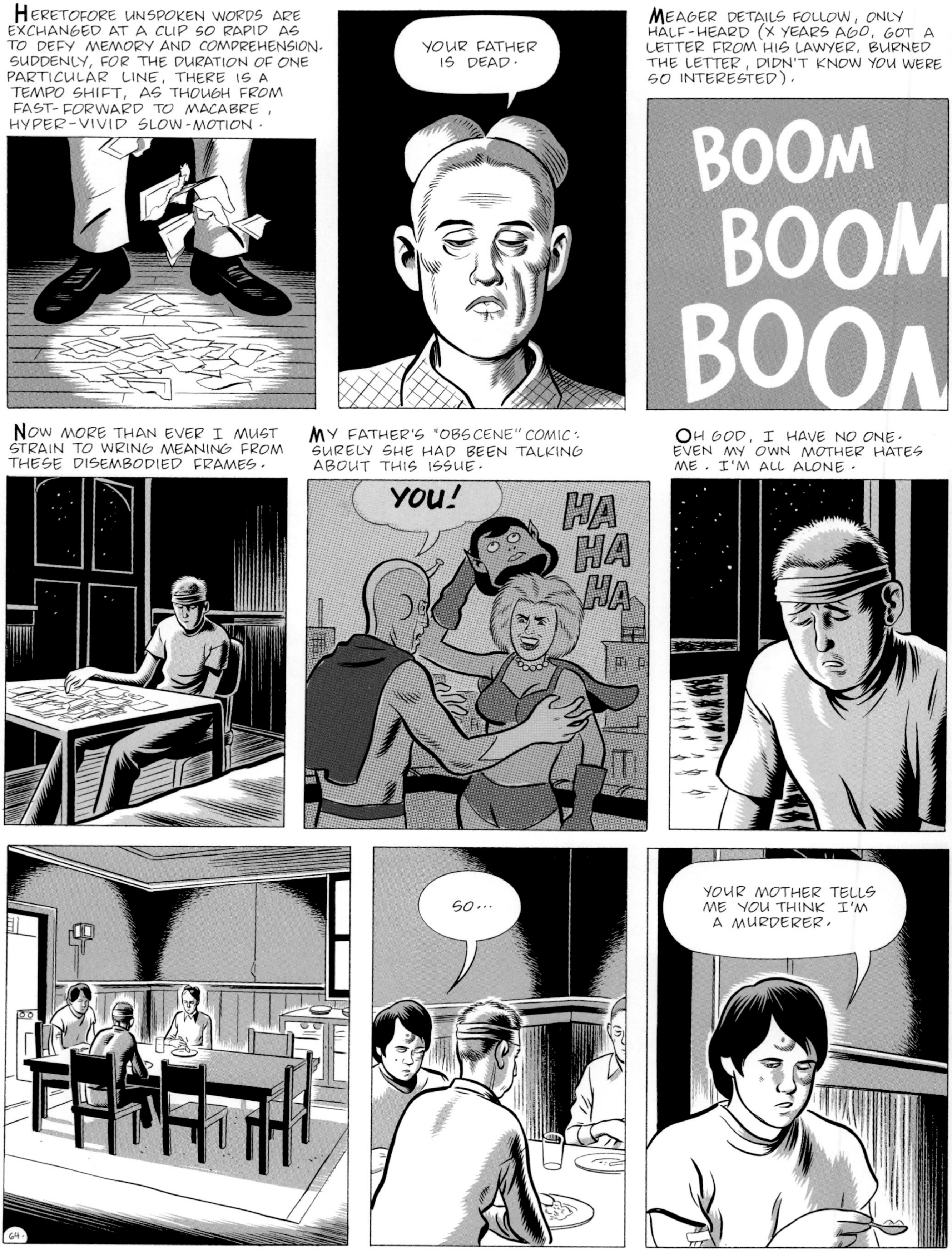
HERETOFORE UNSPOKEN WORDS ARE EXCHANGED AT A CLIP SO RAPID AS TO DEFY MEMORY AND COMPREHENSION. SUDDENLY, FOR THE DURATION OF ONE PARTICULAR LINE, THERE IS A TEMPO SHIFT, AS THOUGH FROM FAST-FORWARD TO MACABRE, HYPER-VIVID SLOW-MOTION.
YOUR FATHER IS DEAD.
MEAGER DETAILS FOLLOW, ONLY HALF-HEARD (X YEARS AGO, GOT A LETTER FROM HIS LAWYER, BURNED THE LETTER, DIDN'T KNOW YOU WERE SO INTERESTED).
BOOM
BOOM
BOOM
NOW MORE THAN EVER I MUST STRAIN TO WRING MEANING FROM THESE DISEMBODIED FRAMES.
MY FATHER'S "OBSCENE" COMIC: SURELY SHE HAD BEEN TALKING ABOUT THIS ISSUE.
YOU!
HA HA HA HA
OH GOD, I HAVE NO ONE. EVEN MY OWN MOTHER HATES ME. I'M ALL ALONE.
SO...
YOUR MOTHER TELLS ME YOU THINK I'M A MURDERER.

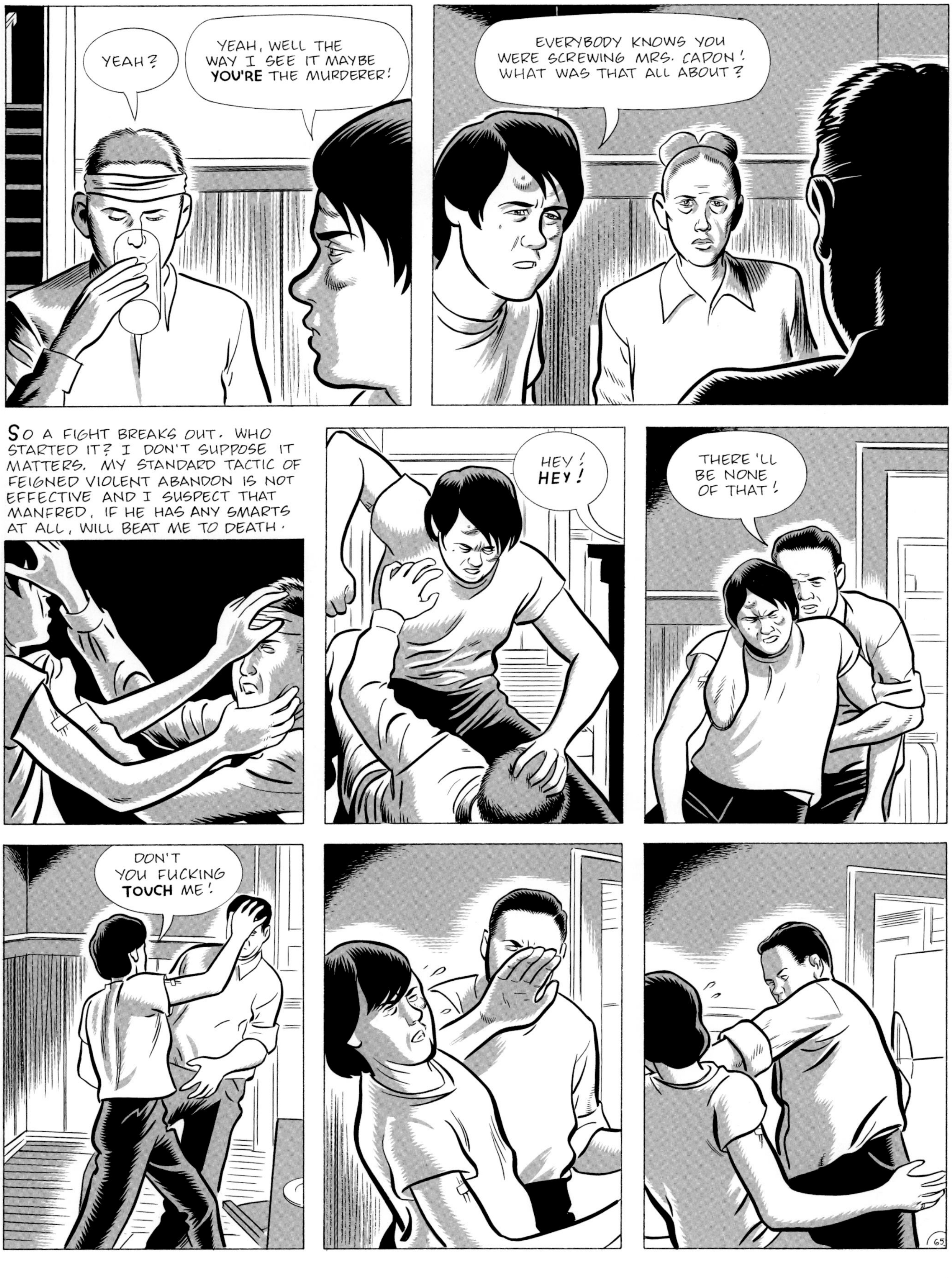
YEAH?
YEAH, WELL THE WAY I SEE IT MAYBE **YOU'RE** THE MURDERER!
EVERYBODY KNOWS YOU WERE SCREWING MRS. CAPON! WHAT WAS THAT ALL ABOUT?
SO A FIGHT BREAKS OUT. WHO STARTED IT? I DON'T SUPPOSE IT MATTERS. MY STANDARD TACTIC OF FEIGNED VIOLENT ABANDON IS NOT EFFECTIVE AND I SUSPECT THAT MANFRED, IF HE HAS ANY SMARTS AT ALL, WILL BEAT ME TO DEATH.
HEY! **HEY!**
THERE'LL BE NONE OF THAT!
DON'T YOU FUCKING **TOUCH** ME!

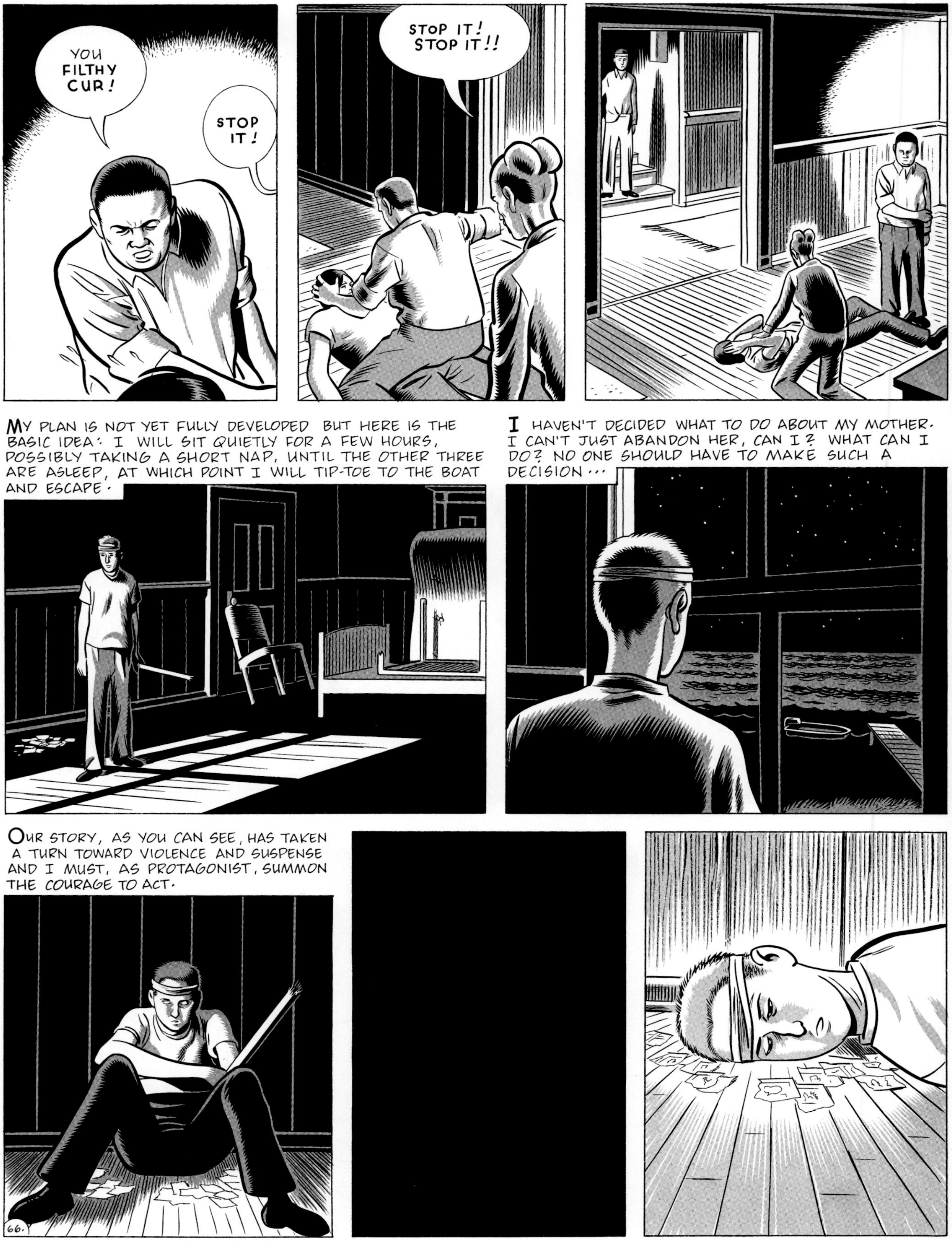
YOU FILTHY CUR!
STOP IT!
STOP IT! STOP IT!!
MY PLAN IS NOT YET FULLY DEVELOPED BUT HERE IS THE BASIC IDEA: I WILL SIT QUIETLY FOR A FEW HOURS, POSSIBLY TAKING A SHORT NAP, UNTIL THE OTHER THREE ARE ASLEEP, AT WHICH POINT I WILL TIP-TOE TO THE BOAT AND ESCAPE.
I HAVEN'T DECIDED WHAT TO DO ABOUT MY MOTHER. I CAN'T JUST ABANDON HER, CAN I? WHAT CAN I DO? NO ONE SHOULD HAVE TO MAKE SUCH A DECISION...
OUR STORY, AS YOU CAN SEE, HAS TAKEN A TURN TOWARD VIOLENCE AND SUSPENSE AND I MUST, AS PROTAGONIST, SUMMON THE COURAGE TO ACT.
66.

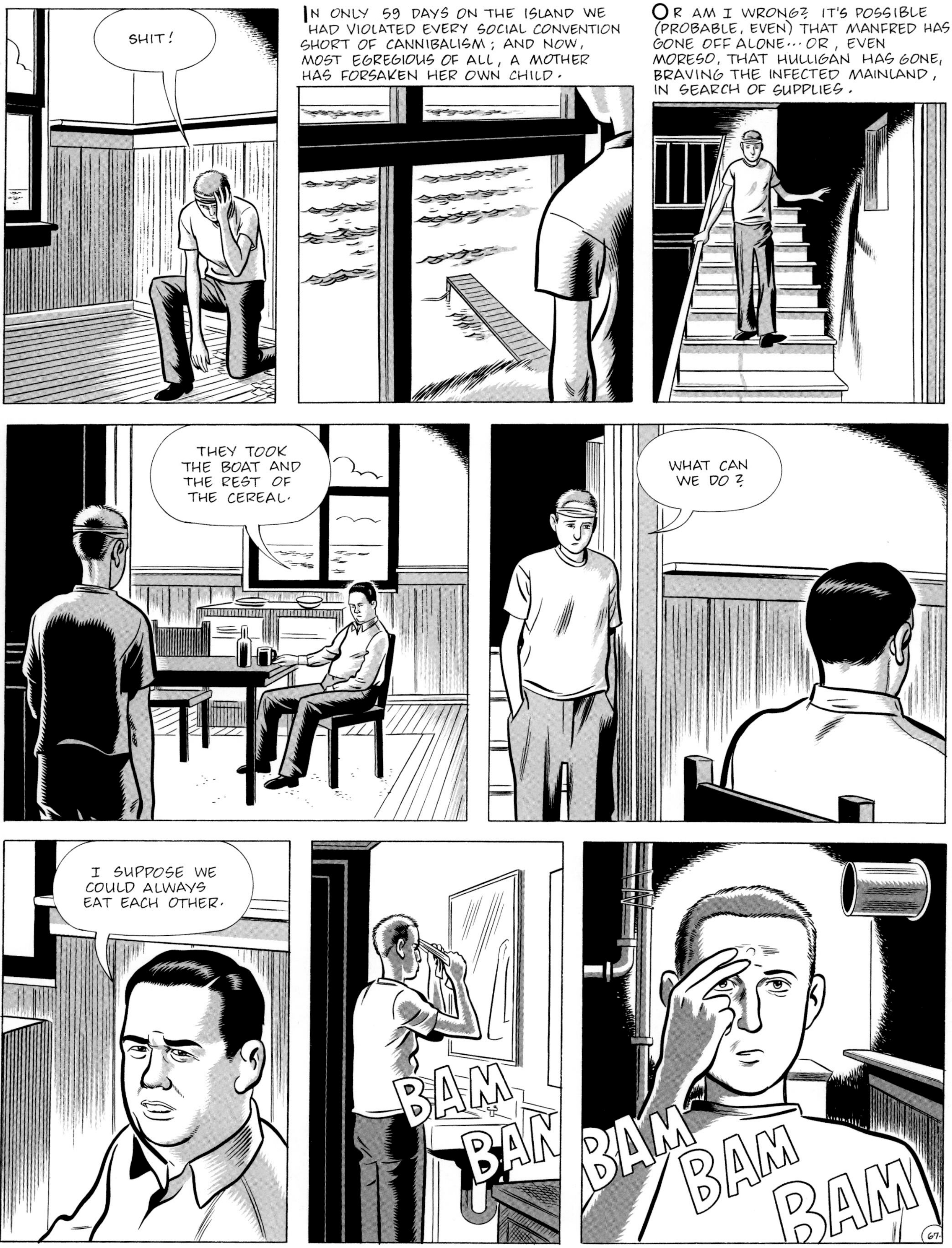
SHIT!
IN ONLY 59 DAYS ON THE ISLAND WE HAD VIOLATED EVERY SOCIAL CONVENTION SHORT OF CANNIBALISM; AND NOW, MOST EGREGIOUS OF ALL, A MOTHER HAS FORSAKEN HER OWN CHILD.
OR AM I WRONG? IT'S POSSIBLE (PROBABLE, EVEN) THAT MANFRED HAS GONE OFF ALONE... OR, EVEN MORESO, THAT HULLIGAN HAS GONE, BRAVING THE INFECTED MAINLAND, IN SEARCH OF SUPPLIES.
THEY TOOK THE BOAT AND THE REST OF THE CEREAL.
WHAT CAN WE DO?
I SUPPOSE WE COULD ALWAYS EAT EACH OTHER.
BAM
BAM
BAM
BAM
BAM
67.

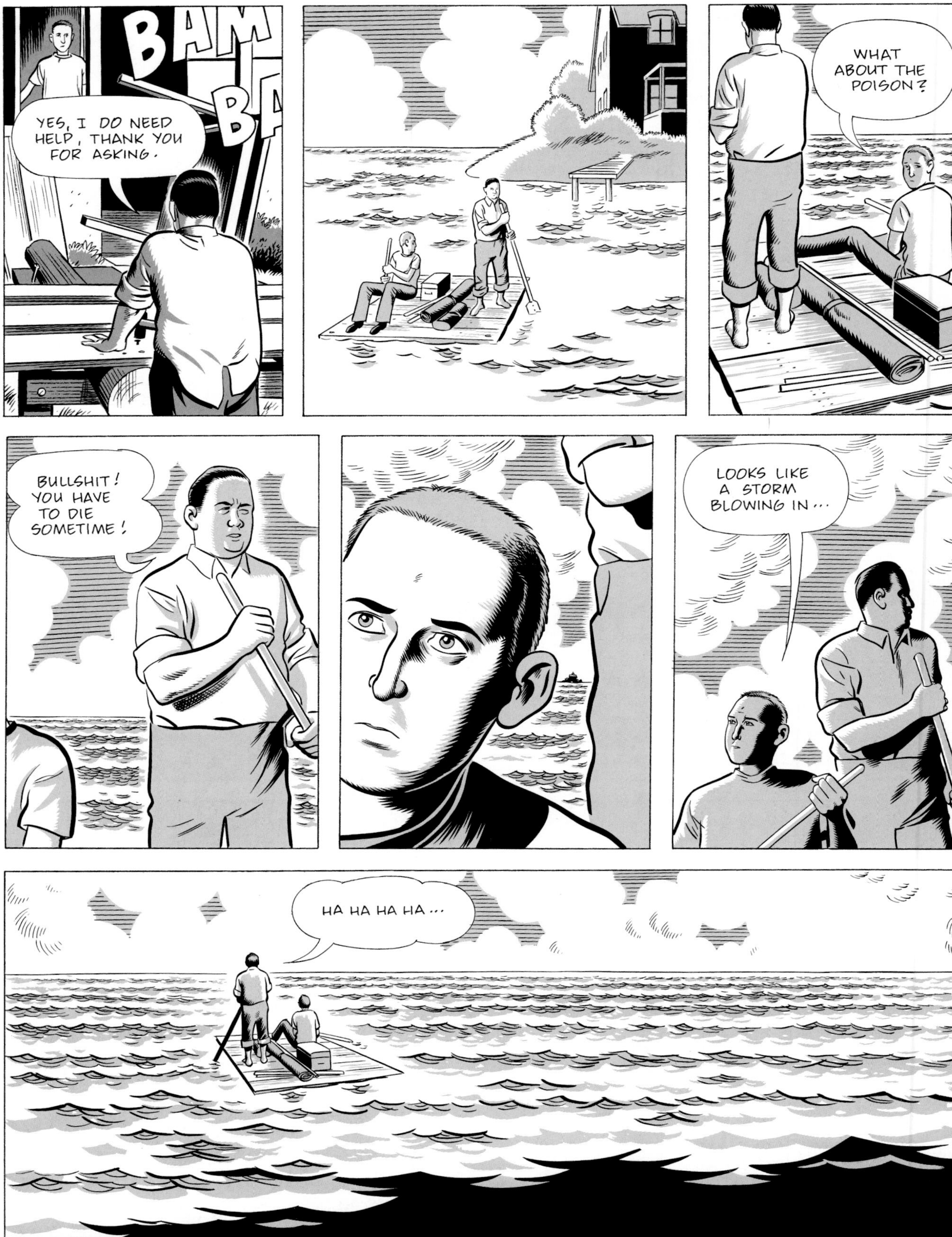
BAM
BA
YES, I DO NEED HELP, THANK YOU FOR ASKING.
WHAT ABOUT THE POISON?
BULLSHIT! YOU HAVE TO DIE SOMETIME!
LOOKS LIKE A STORM BLOWING IN...
HA HA HA HA...
END OF ACT TWO...

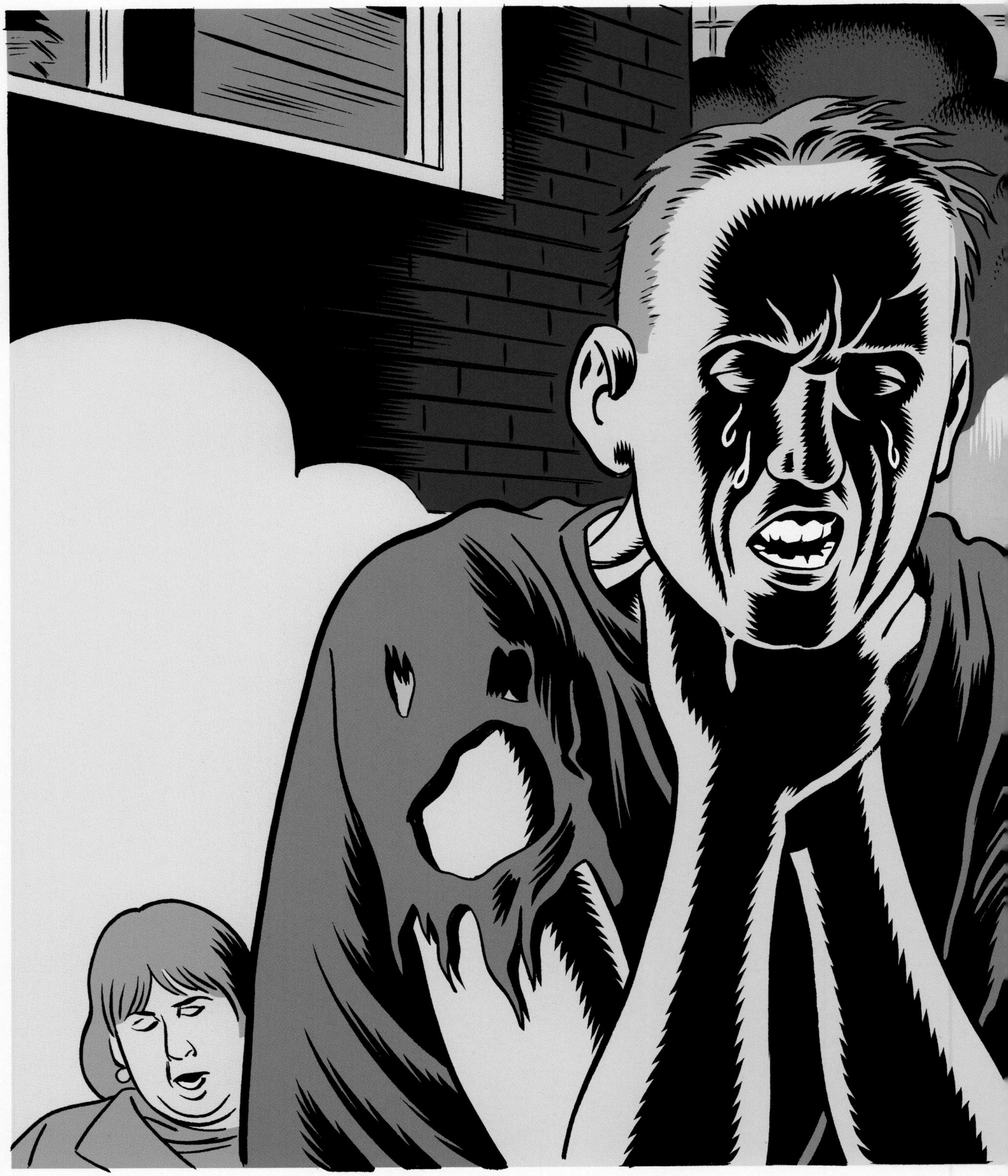

DAVID BORING · DOT PAA

COUNTRY OF ORIGIN USA

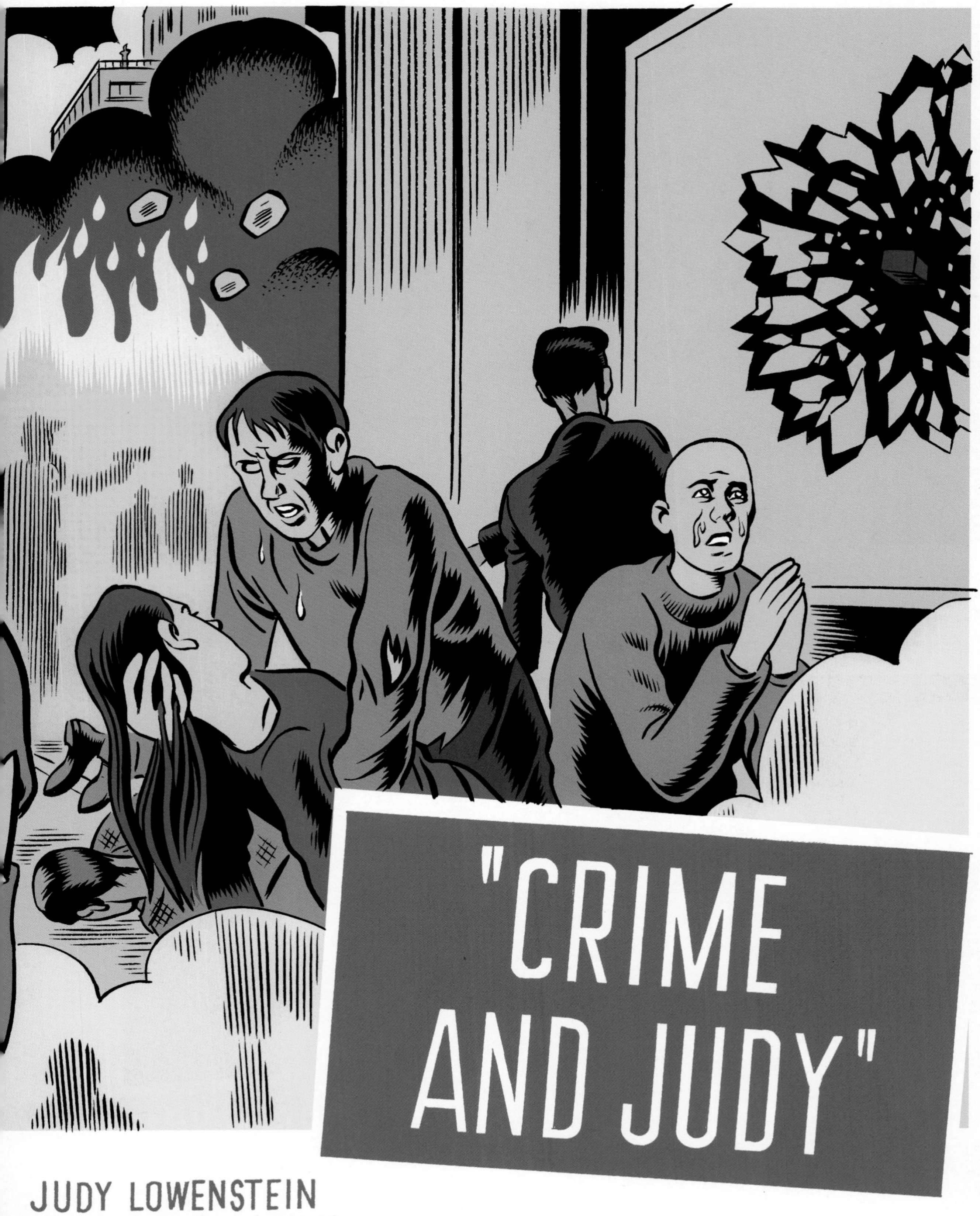
"CRIME
AND JUDY"

JUDY LOWENSTEIN
FERDINAND KARKES

 00/333

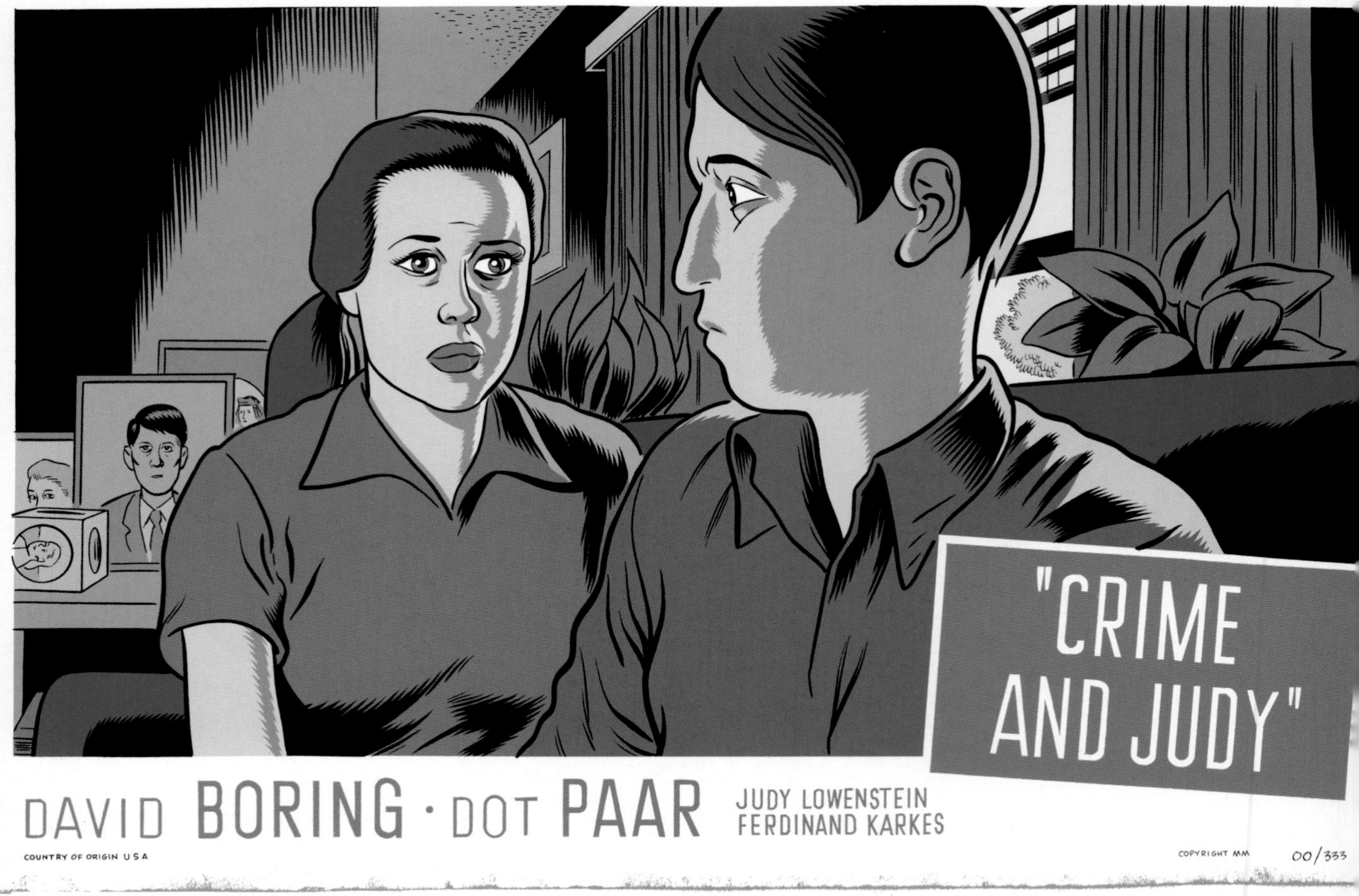
"CRIME AND JUDY"
DAVID BORING · DOT PAAR
JUDY LOWENSTEIN
FERDINAND KARKES
COUNTRY OF ORIGIN U S A
COPYRIGHT MM
00/333

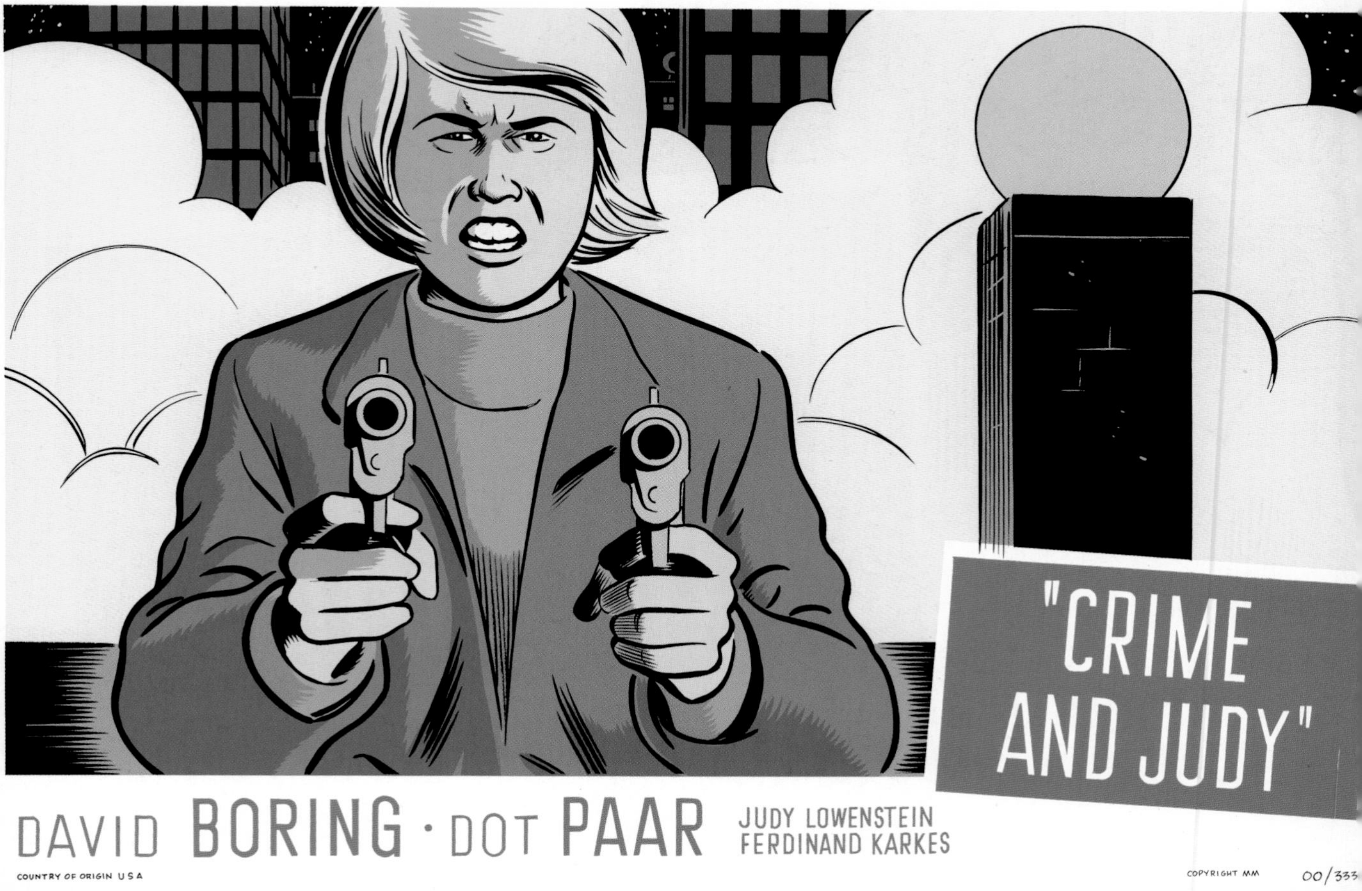
"CRIME AND JUDY"
DAVID BORING · DOT PAAR
JUDY LOWENSTEIN
FERDINAND KARKES
COUNTRY OF ORIGIN U S A
COPYRIGHT MM
00/333

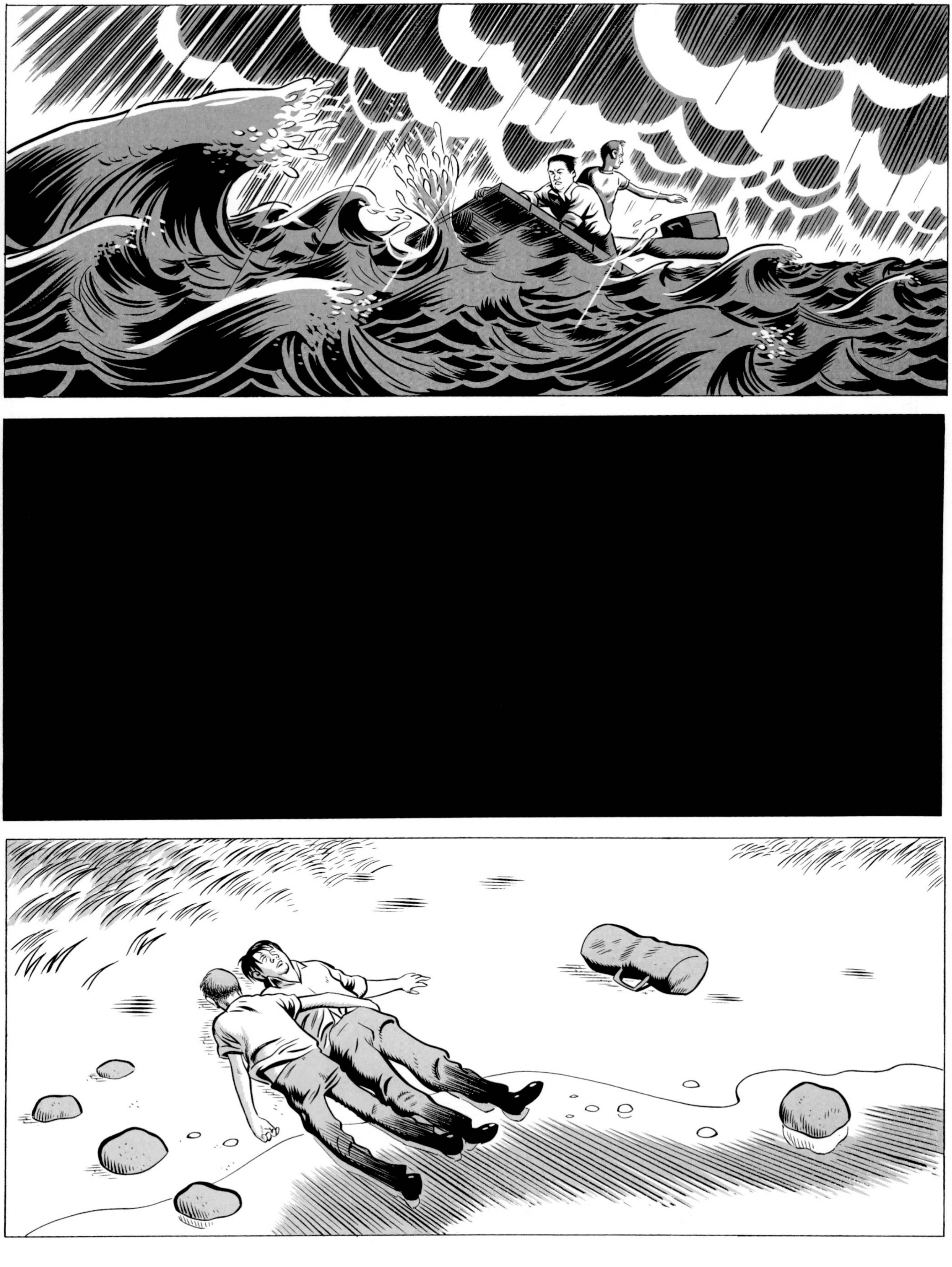

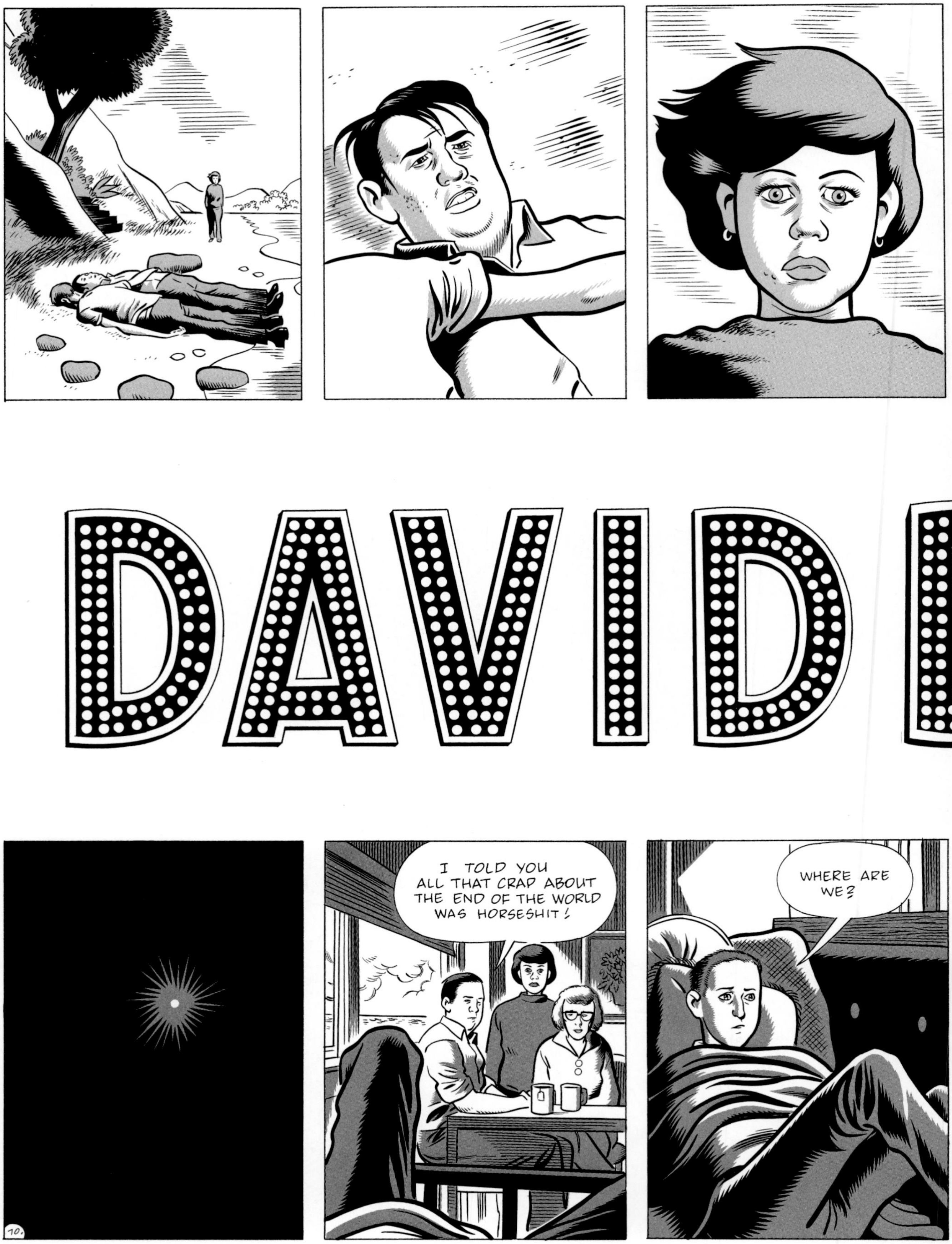
DAVID
I TOLD YOU ALL THAT CRAP ABOUT THE END OF THE WORLD WAS HORSESHIT!
WHERE ARE WE?

IN THE HOME OF OUR RESCUERS, IN SOUTHERN NEW LAPLAND COUNTY.

HELLO, DAVID.

IT WAS ALL OVER IN A DAY, SHE SAYS. OUR BOYS TOOK CARE OF THEM BEFORE THEY HAD A CHANCE TO DO MUCH DAMAGE... YOUR UNCLE GOT US ALL WORKED UP OVER NOTHING!

IT WASN'T NOTHING! I'VE NEVER BEEN SO SCARED!

IT'S JUST THE BEGINNING. THEY'LL KILL US ALL BEFORE THEY'RE DONE.

  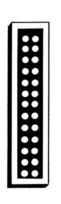  

BORING

NO, NO... THANKS FOR YOUR OFFER, DAVID, BUT I'M STAYING ON...

I FEEL AS THOUGH THE HAND OF PROVIDENCE HAS PLACED ME EXACTLY WHERE I BELONG!

71

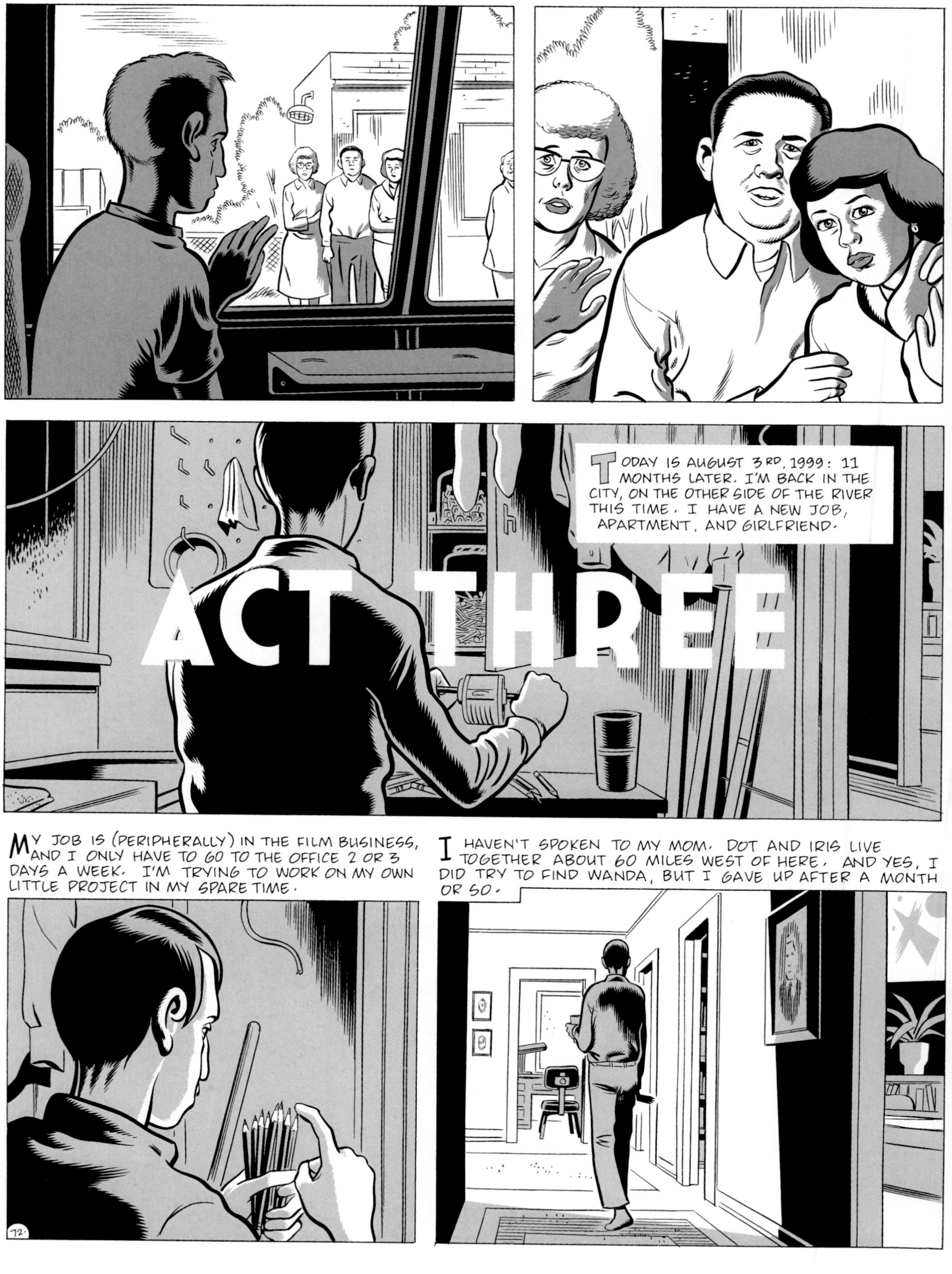
TODAY IS AUGUST 3RD, 1999: 11 MONTHS LATER. I'M BACK IN THE CITY, ON THE OTHER SIDE OF THE RIVER THIS TIME. I HAVE A NEW JOB, APARTMENT, AND GIRLFRIEND.
ACT THREE
MY JOB IS (PERIPHERALLY) IN THE FILM BUSINESS, AND I ONLY HAVE TO GO TO THE OFFICE 2 OR 3 DAYS A WEEK. I'M TRYING TO WORK ON MY OWN LITTLE PROJECT IN MY SPARE TIME.
I HAVEN'T SPOKEN TO MY MOM. DOT AND IRIS LIVE TOGETHER ABOUT 60 MILES WEST OF HERE. AND YES, I DID TRY TO FIND WANDA, BUT I GAVE UP AFTER A MONTH OR SO.
72.

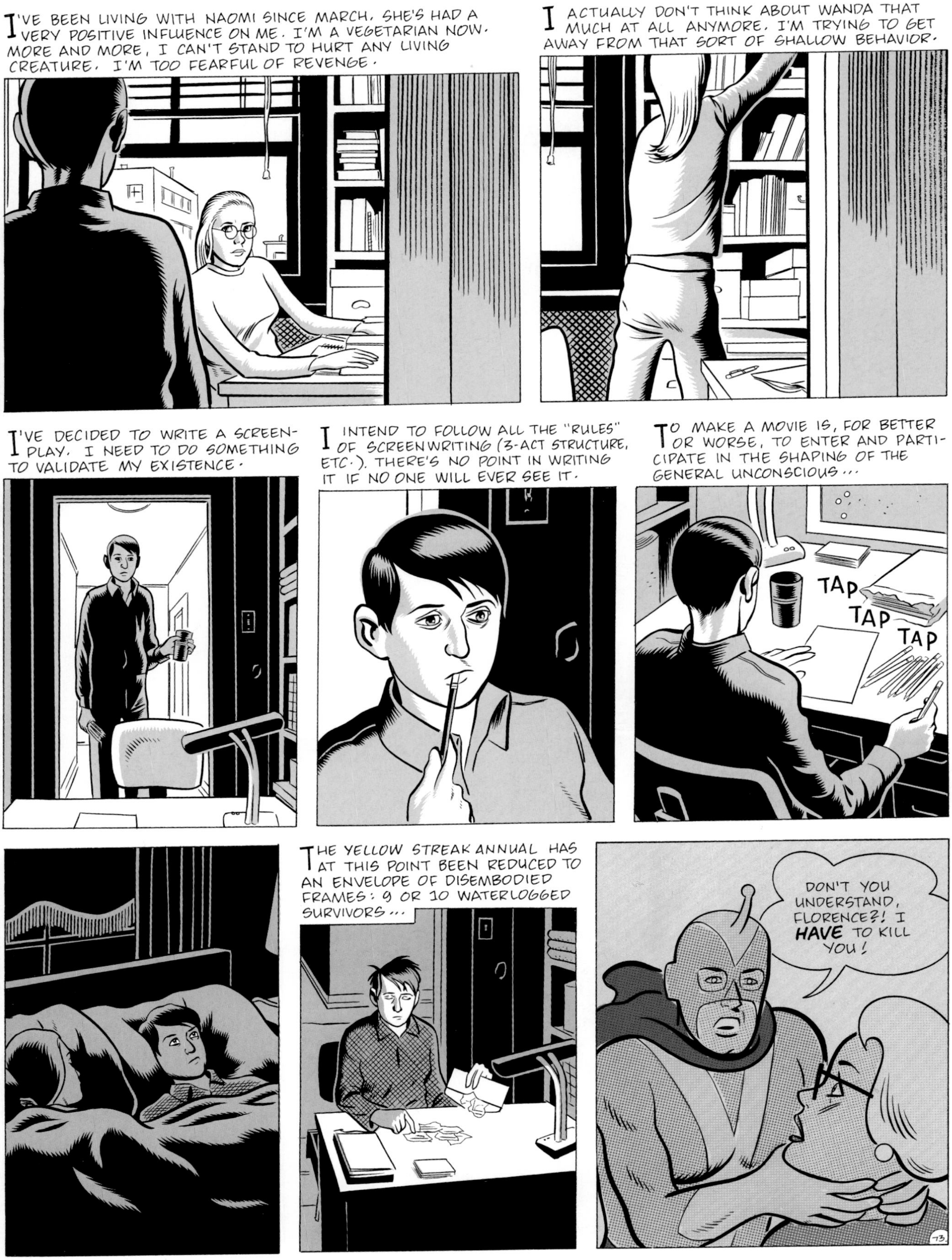
I'VE BEEN LIVING WITH NAOMI SINCE MARCH. SHE'S HAD A VERY POSITIVE INFLUENCE ON ME. I'M A VEGETARIAN NOW. MORE AND MORE, I CAN'T STAND TO HURT ANY LIVING CREATURE. I'M TOO FEARFUL OF REVENGE.
I ACTUALLY DON'T THINK ABOUT WANDA THAT MUCH AT ALL ANYMORE. I'M TRYING TO GET AWAY FROM THAT SORT OF SHALLOW BEHAVIOR.
I'VE DECIDED TO WRITE A SCREENPLAY. I NEED TO DO SOMETHING TO VALIDATE MY EXISTENCE.
I INTEND TO FOLLOW ALL THE "RULES" OF SCREENWRITING (3-ACT STRUCTURE, ETC.). THERE'S NO POINT IN WRITING IT IF NO ONE WILL EVER SEE IT.
TO MAKE A MOVIE IS, FOR BETTER OR WORSE, TO ENTER AND PARTICIPATE IN THE SHAPING OF THE GENERAL UNCONSCIOUS...
TAP
TAP
TAP
THE YELLOW STREAK ANNUAL HAS AT THIS POINT BEEN REDUCED TO AN ENVELOPE OF DISEMBODIED FRAMES: 9 OR 10 WATERLOGGED SURVIVORS...
DON'T YOU UNDERSTAND, FLORENCE?! I **HAVE** TO KILL YOU!
73

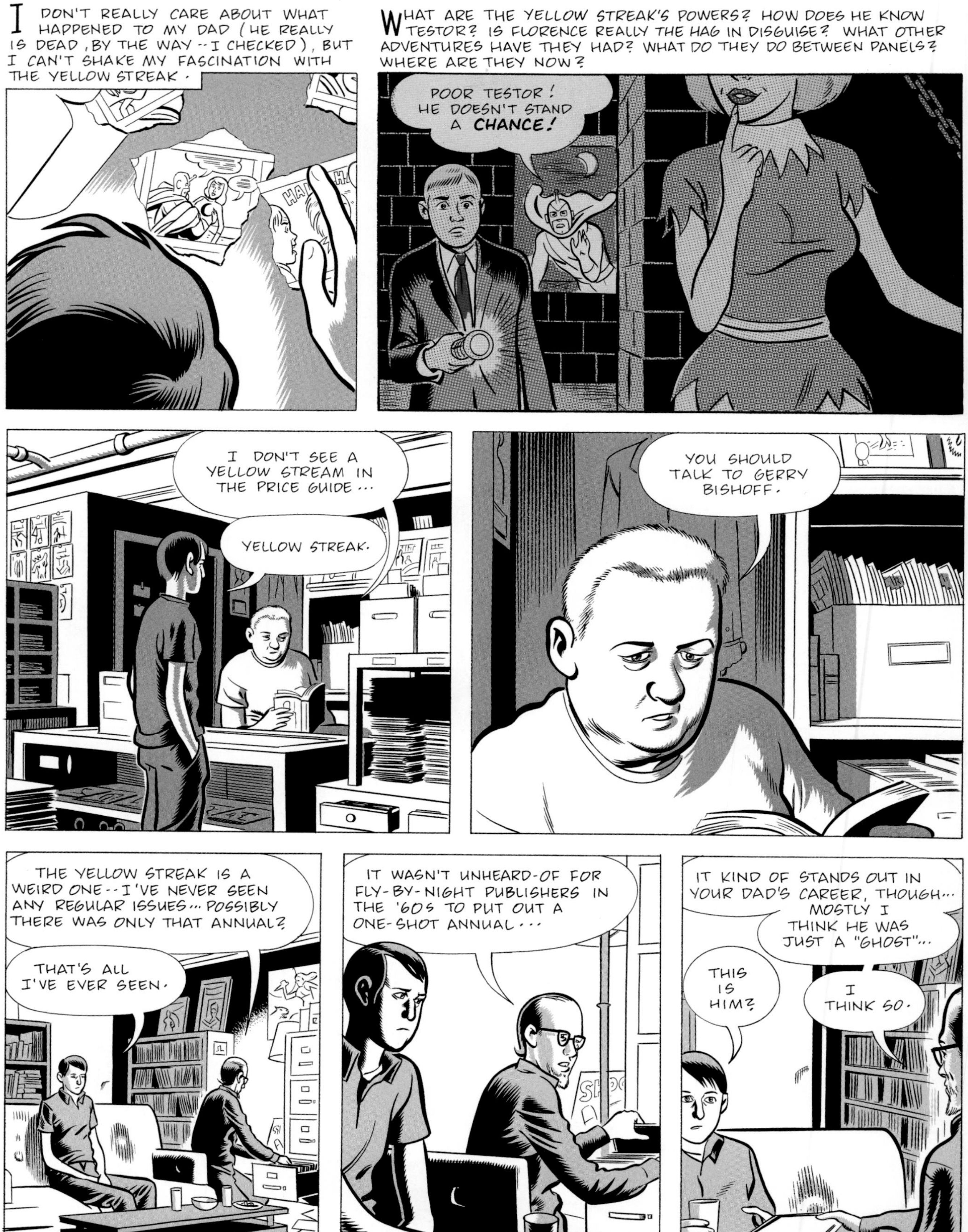
I DON'T REALLY CARE ABOUT WHAT HAPPENED TO MY DAD (HE REALLY IS DEAD, BY THE WAY -- I CHECKED), BUT I CAN'T SHAKE MY FASCINATION WITH THE YELLOW STREAK.
WHAT ARE THE YELLOW STREAK'S POWERS? HOW DOES HE KNOW TESTOR? IS FLORENCE REALLY THE HAG IN DISGUISE? WHAT OTHER ADVENTURES HAVE THEY HAD? WHAT DO THEY DO BETWEEN PANELS? WHERE ARE THEY NOW?
POOR TESTOR! HE DOESN'T STAND A **CHANCE!**
I DON'T SEE A YELLOW STREAM IN THE PRICE GUIDE...
YELLOW STREAK.
YOU SHOULD TALK TO GERRY BISHOFF.
THE YELLOW STREAK IS A WEIRD ONE -- I'VE NEVER SEEN ANY REGULAR ISSUES... POSSIBLY THERE WAS ONLY THAT ANNUAL?
THAT'S ALL I'VE EVER SEEN.
IT WASN'T UNHEARD-OF FOR FLY-BY-NIGHT PUBLISHERS IN THE '60S TO PUT OUT A ONE-SHOT ANNUAL...
IT KIND OF STANDS OUT IN YOUR DAD'S CAREER, THOUGH...
MOSTLY I THINK HE WAS JUST A "GHOST"...
THIS IS HIM?
I THINK SO.

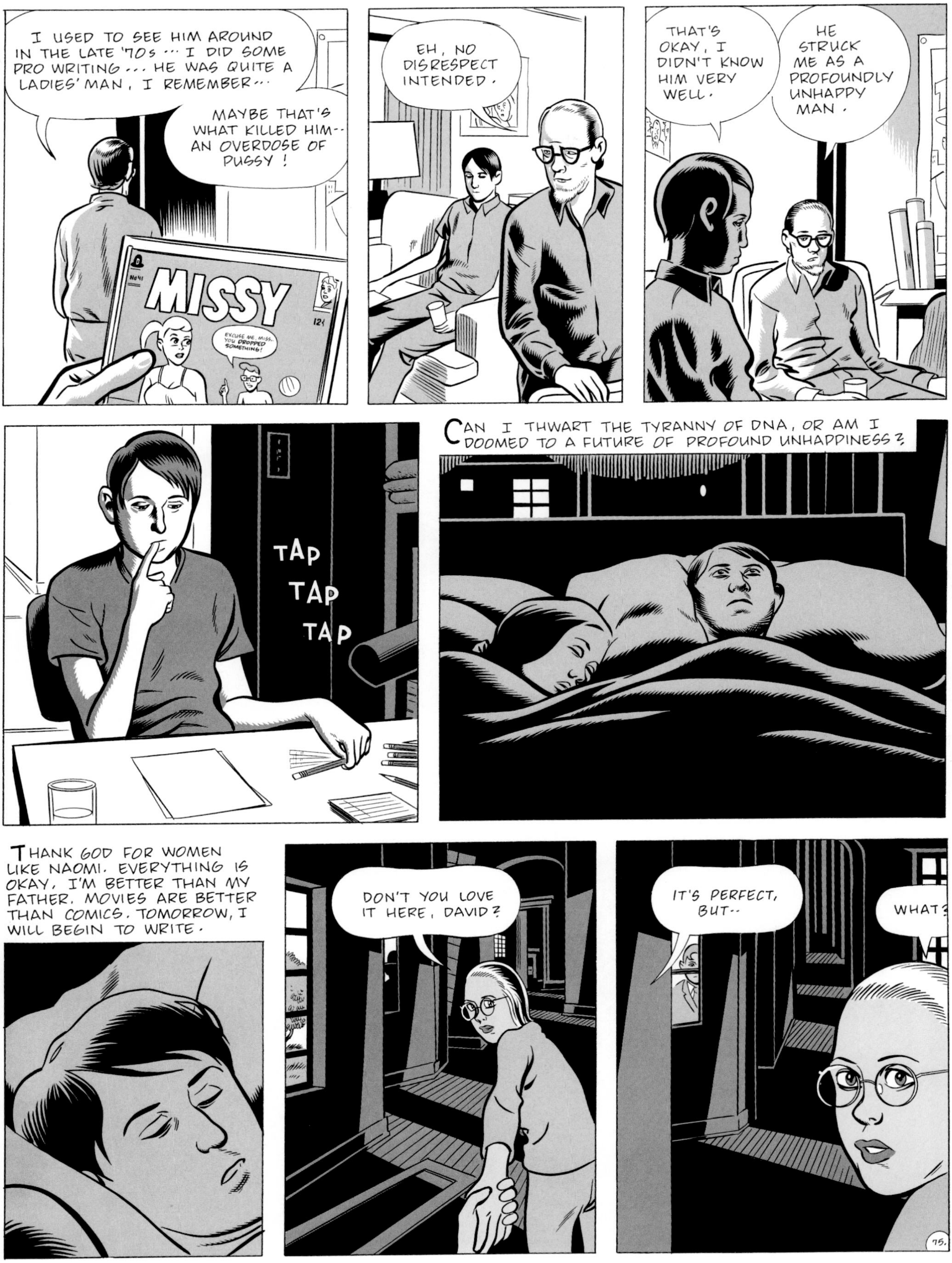

I USED TO SEE HIM AROUND IN THE LATE '70s ··· I DID SOME PRO WRITING ··· HE WAS QUITE A LADIES' MAN, I REMEMBER ···
MAYBE THAT'S WHAT KILLED HIM -- AN OVERDOSE OF PUSSY!
MISSY
No 41
12¢
EXCUSE ME, MISS. YOU DROPPED SOMETHING!
EH, NO DISRESPECT INTENDED.
THAT'S OKAY, I DIDN'T KNOW HIM VERY WELL.
HE STRUCK ME AS A PROFOUNDLY UNHAPPY MAN.
TAP
TAP
TAP
CAN I THWART THE TYRANNY OF DNA, OR AM I DOOMED TO A FUTURE OF PROFOUND UNHAPPINESS?
THANK GOD FOR WOMEN LIKE NAOMI. EVERYTHING IS OKAY. I'M BETTER THAN MY FATHER. MOVIES ARE BETTER THAN COMICS. TOMORROW, I WILL BEGIN TO WRITE.
DON'T YOU LOVE IT HERE, DAVID?
IT'S PERFECT, BUT --
WHAT?

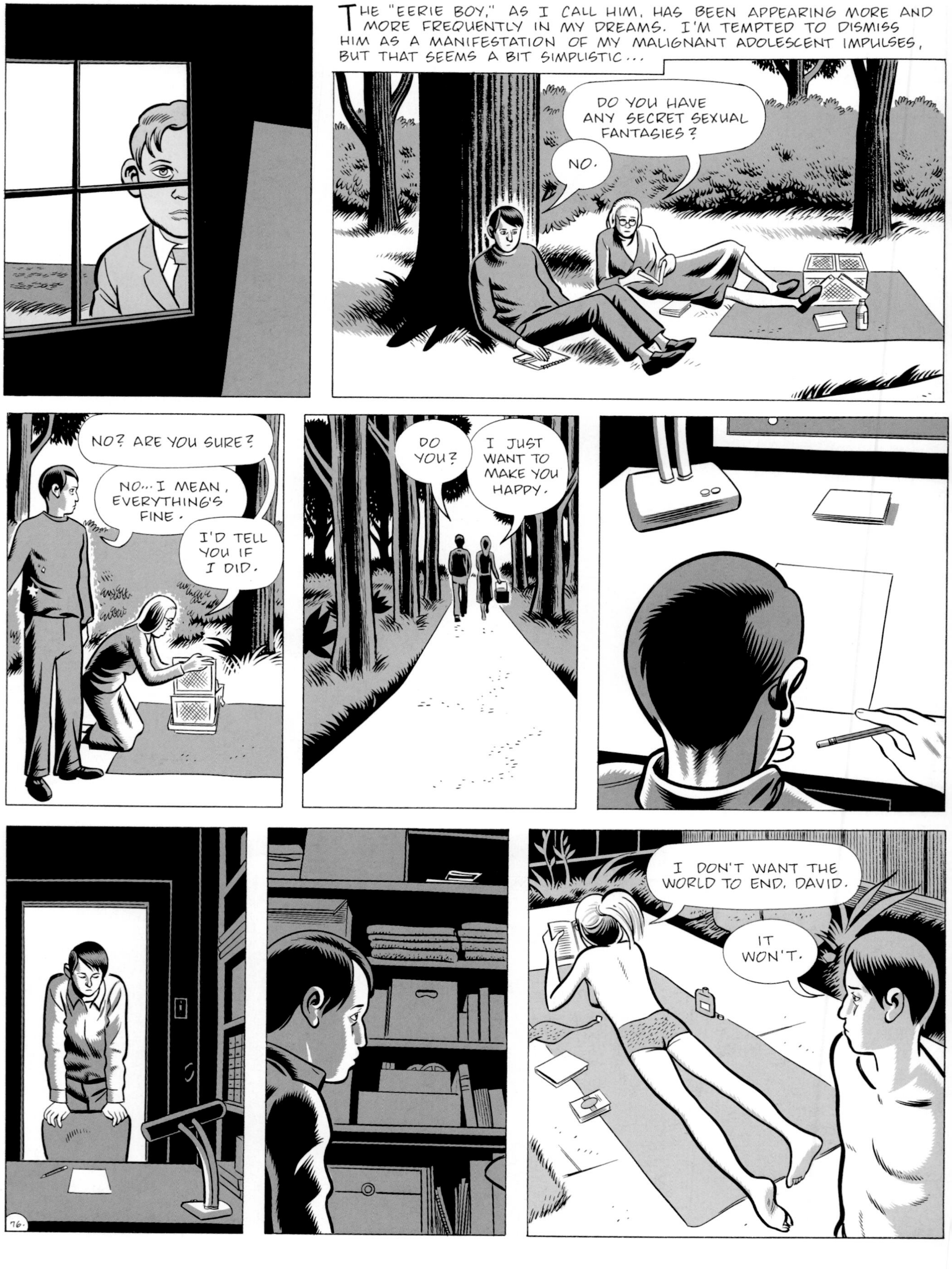
THE "EERIE BOY," AS I CALL HIM, HAS BEEN APPEARING MORE AND MORE FREQUENTLY IN MY DREAMS. I'M TEMPTED TO DISMISS HIM AS A MANIFESTATION OF MY MALIGNANT ADOLESCENT IMPULSES, BUT THAT SEEMS A BIT SIMPLISTIC...
DO YOU HAVE ANY SECRET SEXUAL FANTASIES?
NO.
NO? ARE YOU SURE?
NO... I MEAN, EVERYTHING'S FINE.
I'D TELL YOU IF I DID.
DO YOU?
I JUST WANT TO MAKE YOU HAPPY.
I DON'T WANT THE WORLD TO END, DAVID.
IT WON'T.
76.

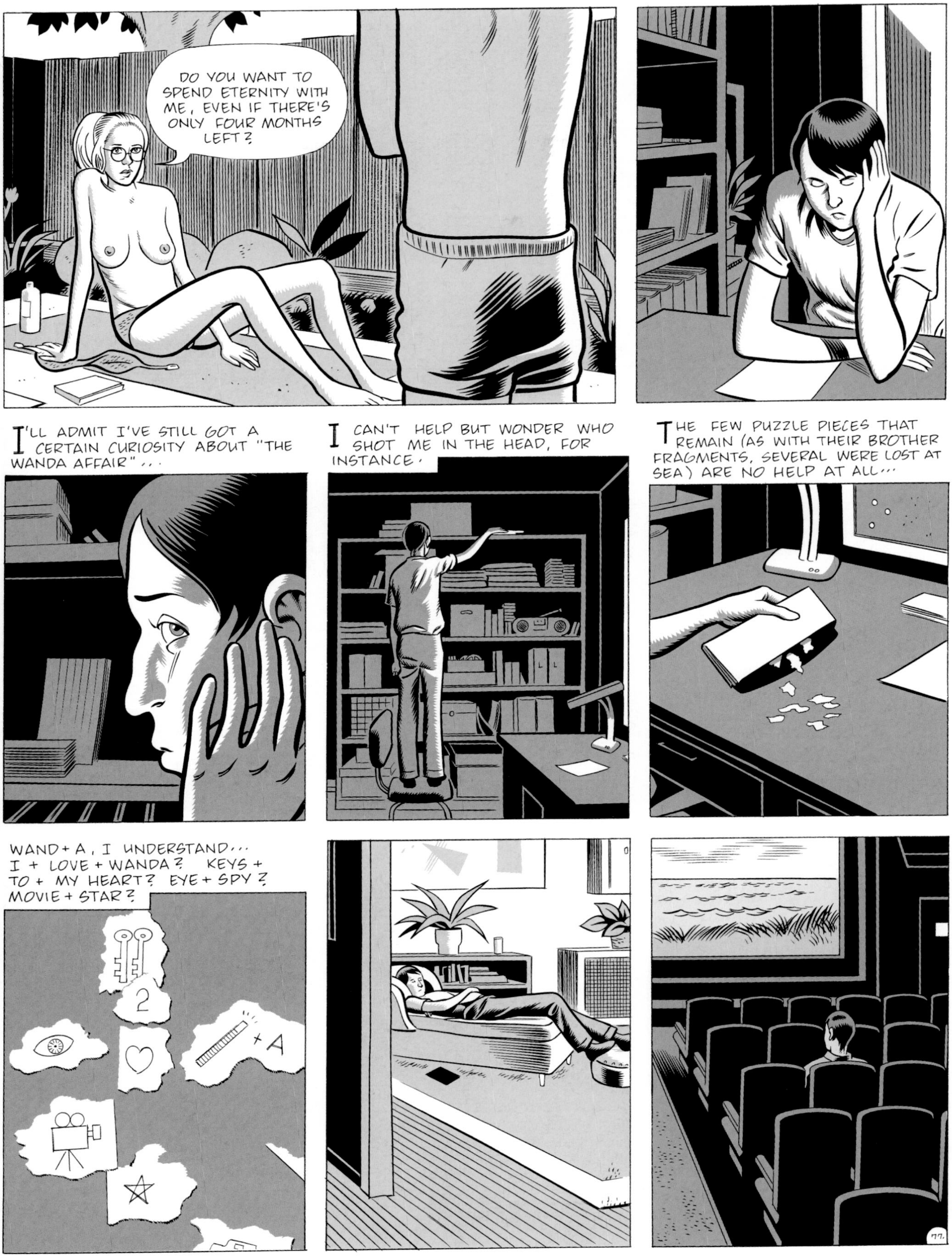

DO YOU WANT TO SPEND ETERNITY WITH ME, EVEN IF THERE'S ONLY FOUR MONTHS LEFT?
I'LL ADMIT I'VE STILL GOT A CERTAIN CURIOSITY ABOUT "THE WANDA AFFAIR"...
I CAN'T HELP BUT WONDER WHO SHOT ME IN THE HEAD, FOR INSTANCE.
THE FEW PUZZLE PIECES THAT REMAIN (AS WITH THEIR BROTHER FRAGMENTS, SEVERAL WERE LOST AT SEA) ARE NO HELP AT ALL...
WAND + A, I UNDERSTAND... I + LOVE + WANDA? KEYS + TO + MY HEART? EYE + SPY? MOVIE + STAR?
2
+A

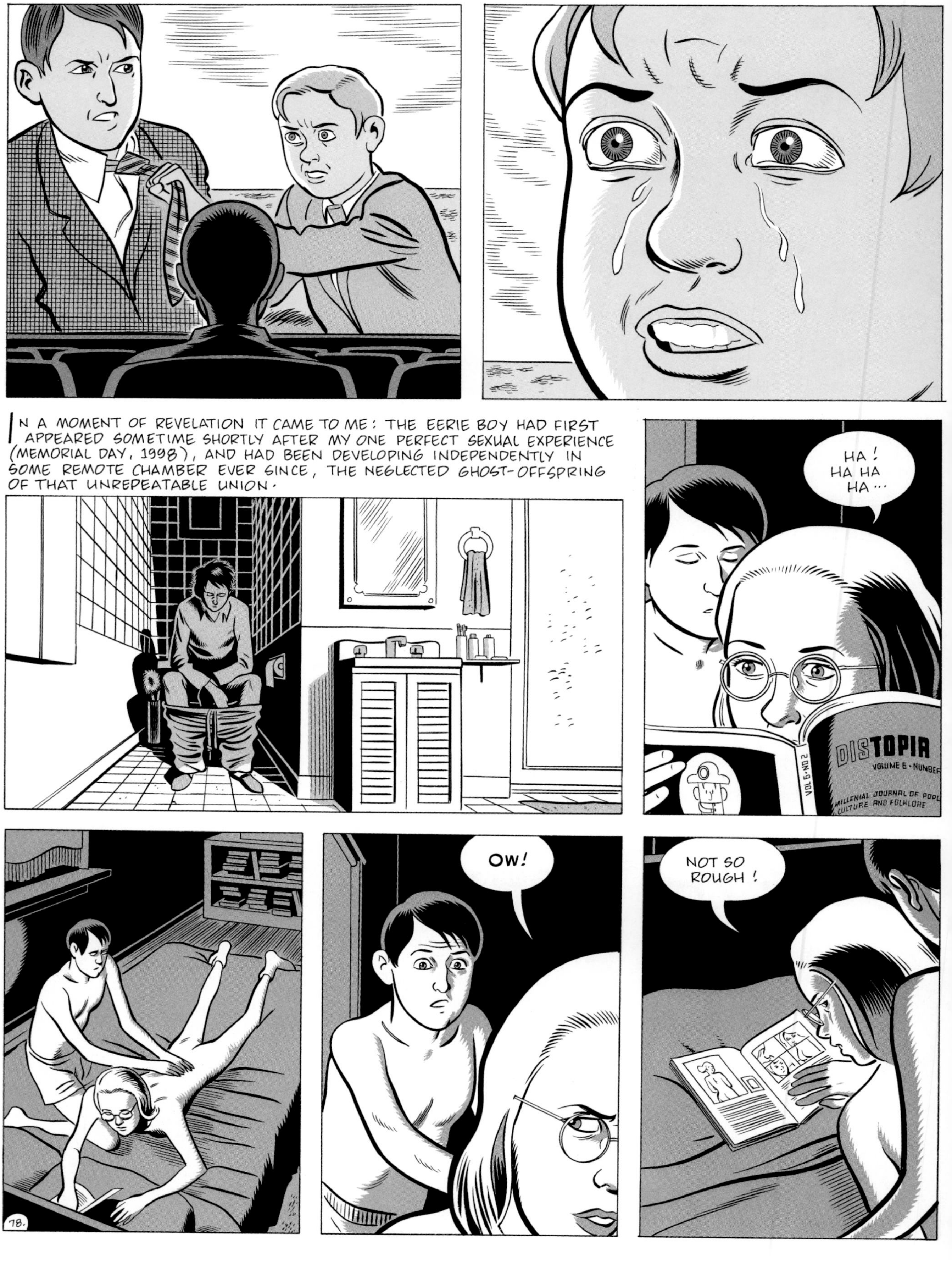

IN A MOMENT OF REVELATION IT CAME TO ME: THE EERIE BOY HAD FIRST APPEARED SOMETIME SHORTLY AFTER MY ONE PERFECT SEXUAL EXPERIENCE (MEMORIAL DAY, 1998), AND HAD BEEN DEVELOPING INDEPENDENTLY IN SOME REMOTE CHAMBER EVER SINCE, THE NEGLECTED GHOST-OFFSPRING OF THAT UNREPEATABLE UNION.
HA! HA HA HA...
DISTOPIA
VOL 6 • NO 2
CULTURE AND FOLKLORE
OW!
NOT SO ROUGH!

...WHAT *IS* THAT?

WHAT ARE YOU READING?

THAN 'REALIT ... EGULTS IN THE COLLECTOR' ... DISFUNCTION, AT TIMES ...

I TOLD YOU--IT'S AN ARTICLE ABOUT-- THE AUTHOR HAS THESE OLD PHOTO ALBUMS AND SCRAPBOOKS MADE BY SEXUAL DEVIANTS...

HIS ANALYSIS IS REALLY HILARIOUS-- IT'S SO MEAN-SPIRITED AND OVER-THE-TOP! THESE POOR, LONELY OLD MEN WITH THEIR SAD LITTLE ALBUMS...

WHO IS IT? WHO'S THE AUTHOR?

THE INDULGENT READER WILL RECALL THAT THE SCRAPBOOK FROM WHICH SEVERAL OF THESE EXAMPLES APPEAR TO HAVE BEEN TAKEN WAS GIVEN, UNDER DURESS, BY YOUR NARRATOR TO WANDA KRAML ON THE EVENING OF MAY 15, 1998.

JESUS, DAVID...

PERVE... COLLEC... THE VISU...

FERDINAND B HARKES...

... ERATED ...

YOU DON'T HAVE TO PRETEND TO BE INTERESTED!

NO, I--

CLAP

JUST SHUT UP AND KISS ME!

...DAVID?

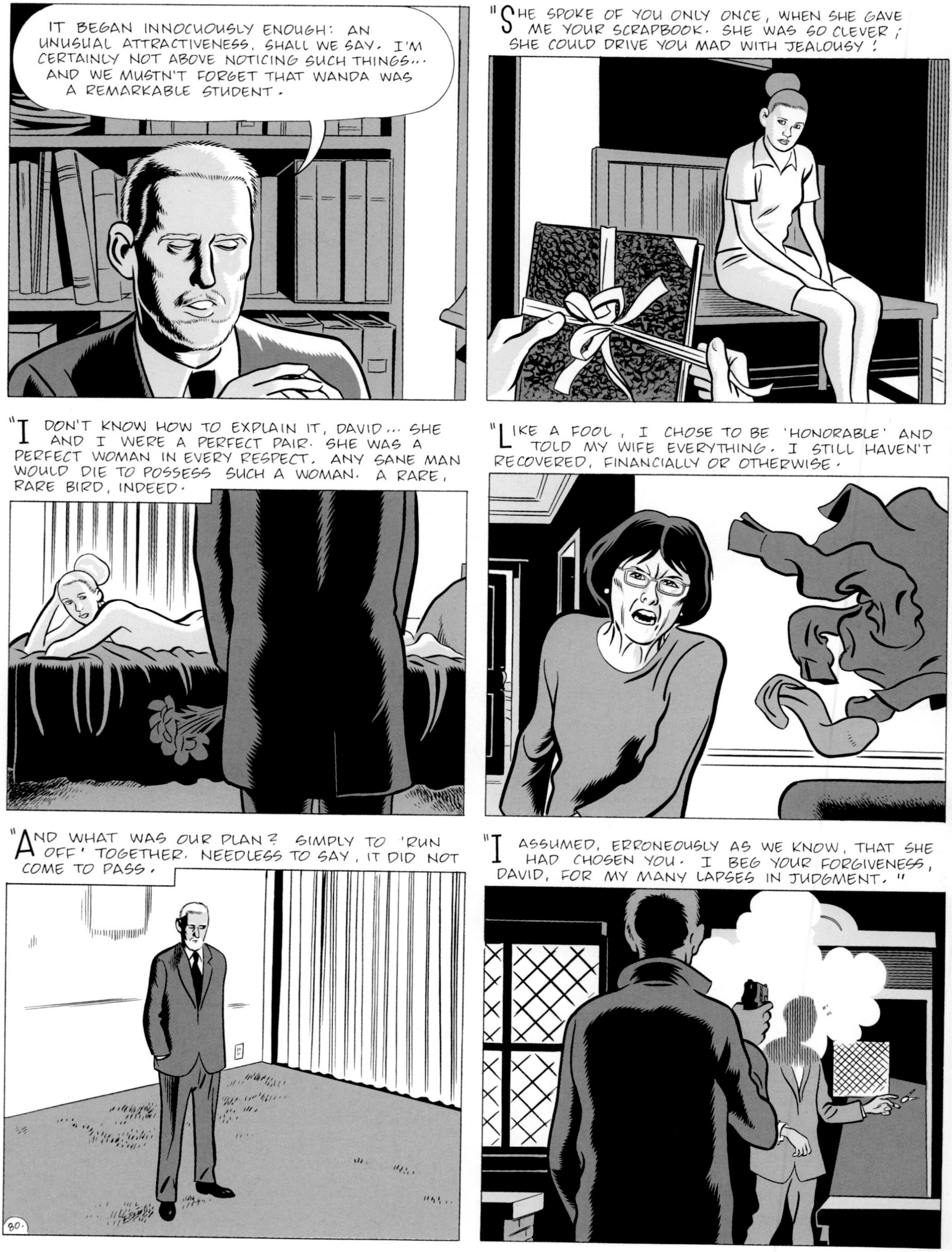
IT BEGAN INNOCUOUSLY ENOUGH: AN UNUSUAL ATTRACTIVENESS, SHALL WE SAY. I'M CERTAINLY NOT ABOVE NOTICING SUCH THINGS... AND WE MUSTN'T FORGET THAT WANDA WAS A REMARKABLE STUDENT.
"SHE SPOKE OF YOU ONLY ONCE, WHEN SHE GAVE ME YOUR SCRAPBOOK. SHE WAS SO CLEVER; SHE COULD DRIVE YOU MAD WITH JEALOUSY!
"I DON'T KNOW HOW TO EXPLAIN IT, DAVID... SHE AND I WERE A PERFECT PAIR. SHE WAS A PERFECT WOMAN IN EVERY RESPECT. ANY SANE MAN WOULD DIE TO POSSESS SUCH A WOMAN. A RARE, RARE BIRD, INDEED.
"LIKE A FOOL, I CHOSE TO BE 'HONORABLE' AND TOLD MY WIFE EVERYTHING. I STILL HAVEN'T RECOVERED, FINANCIALLY OR OTHERWISE.
"AND WHAT WAS OUR PLAN? SIMPLY TO 'RUN OFF' TOGETHER. NEEDLESS TO SAY, IT DID NOT COME TO PASS.
"I ASSUMED, ERRONEOUSLY AS WE KNOW, THAT SHE HAD CHOSEN YOU. I BEG YOUR FORGIVENESS, DAVID, FOR MY MANY LAPSES IN JUDGMENT."

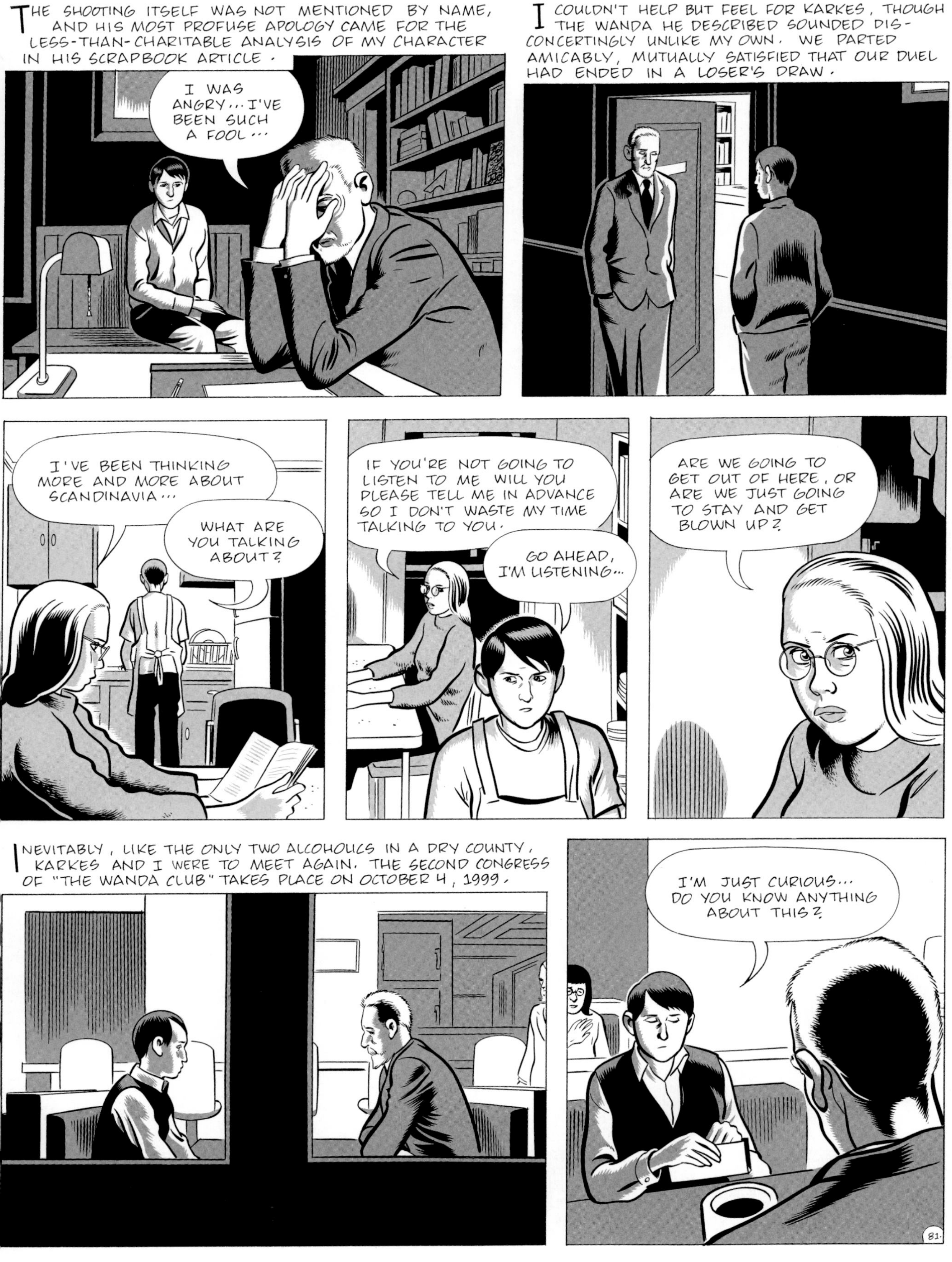
THE SHOOTING ITSELF WAS NOT MENTIONED BY NAME, AND HIS MOST PROFUSE APOLOGY CAME FOR THE LESS-THAN-CHARITABLE ANALYSIS OF MY CHARACTER IN HIS SCRAPBOOK ARTICLE.
I WAS ANGRY... I'VE BEEN SUCH A FOOL...
I COULDN'T HELP BUT FEEL FOR KARKES, THOUGH THE WANDA HE DESCRIBED SOUNDED DISCONCERTINGLY UNLIKE MY OWN. WE PARTED AMICABLY, MUTUALLY SATISFIED THAT OUR DUEL HAD ENDED IN A LOSER'S DRAW.
I'VE BEEN THINKING MORE AND MORE ABOUT SCANDINAVIA...
WHAT ARE YOU TALKING ABOUT?
IF YOU'RE NOT GOING TO LISTEN TO ME WILL YOU PLEASE TELL ME IN ADVANCE SO I DON'T WASTE MY TIME TALKING TO YOU.
GO AHEAD, I'M LISTENING...
ARE WE GOING TO GET OUT OF HERE, OR ARE WE JUST GOING TO STAY AND GET BLOWN UP?
INEVITABLY, LIKE THE ONLY TWO ALCOHOLICS IN A DRY COUNTY, KARKES AND I WERE TO MEET AGAIN. THE SECOND CONGRESS OF "THE WANDA CLUB" TAKES PLACE ON OCTOBER 4, 1999.
I'M JUST CURIOUS... DO YOU KNOW ANYTHING ABOUT THIS?

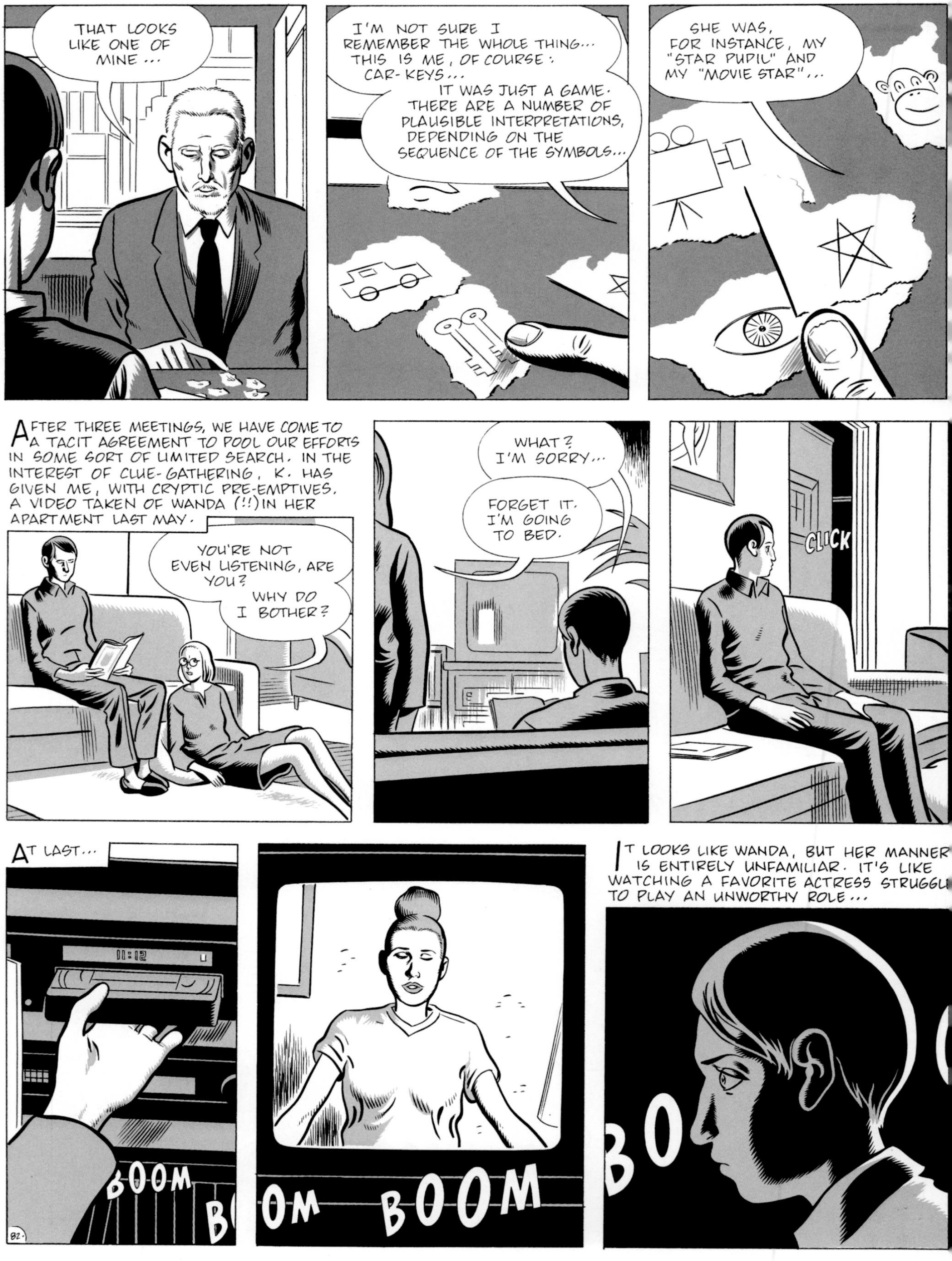
THAT LOOKS LIKE ONE OF MINE...
I'M NOT SURE I REMEMBER THE WHOLE THING... THIS IS ME, OF COURSE: CAR-KEYS...
IT WAS JUST A GAME. THERE ARE A NUMBER OF PLAUSIBLE INTERPRETATIONS, DEPENDING ON THE SEQUENCE OF THE SYMBOLS...
SHE WAS, FOR INSTANCE, MY "STAR PUPIL" AND MY "MOVIE STAR",..
AFTER THREE MEETINGS, WE HAVE COME TO A TACIT AGREEMENT TO POOL OUR EFFORTS IN SOME SORT OF LIMITED SEARCH. IN THE INTEREST OF CLUE-GATHERING, K. HAS GIVEN ME, WITH CRYPTIC PRE-EMPTIVES, A VIDEO TAKEN OF WANDA (!!) IN HER APARTMENT LAST MAY.
YOU'RE NOT EVEN LISTENING, ARE YOU?
WHY DO I BOTHER?
WHAT? I'M SORRY...
FORGET IT. I'M GOING TO BED.
CLICK
AT LAST...
11:12
BOOM
B
OM
BOOM
IT LOOKS LIKE WANDA, BUT HER MANNER IS ENTIRELY UNFAMILIAR. IT'S LIKE WATCHING A FAVORITE ACTRESS STRUGGL TO PLAY AN UNWORTHY ROLE...
BO
82.

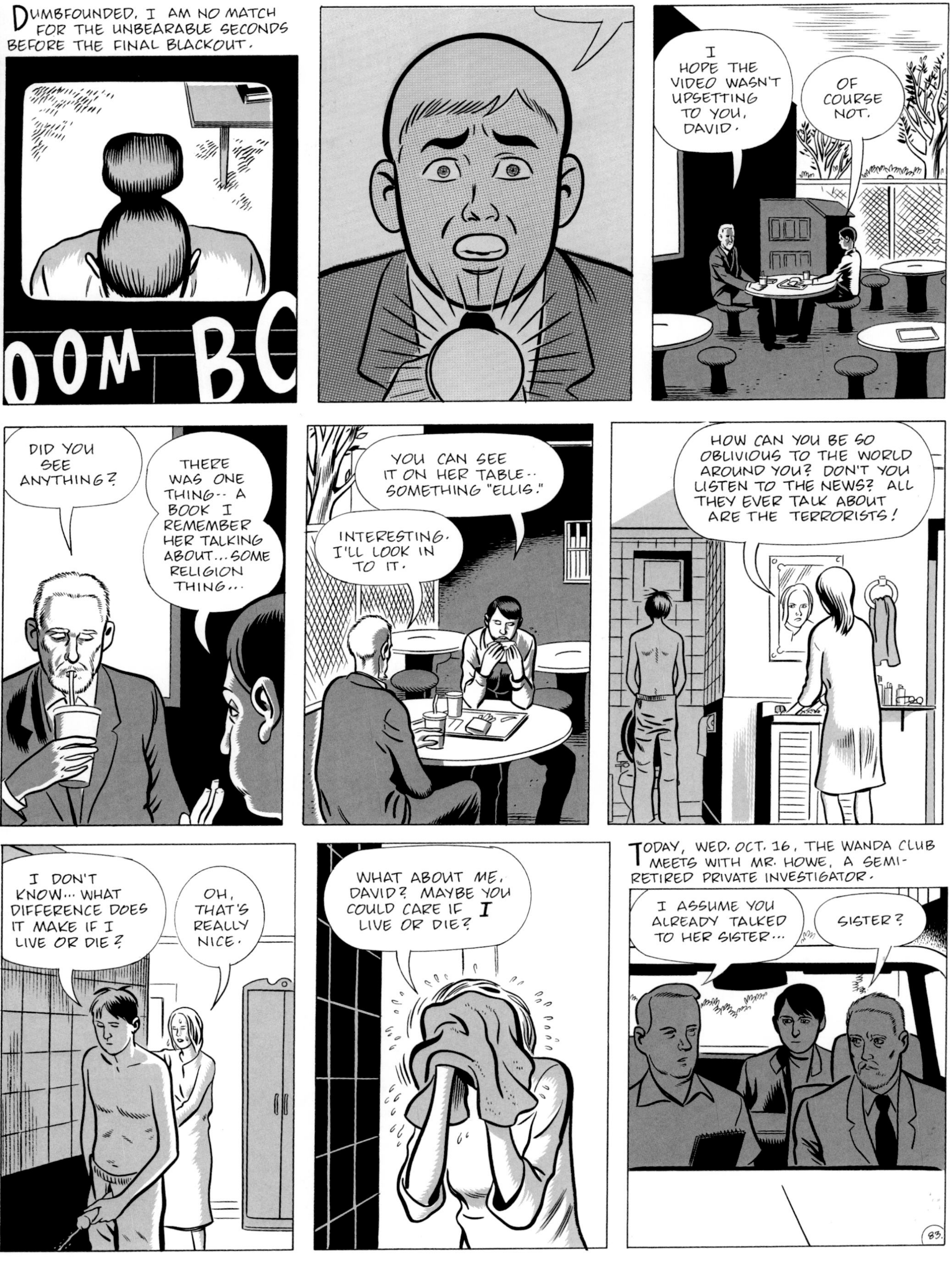
DUMBFOUNDED, I AM NO MATCH FOR THE UNBEARABLE SECONDS BEFORE THE FINAL BLACKOUT.
OOM BO
I HOPE THE VIDEO WASN'T UPSETTING TO YOU, DAVID.
OF COURSE NOT.
DID YOU SEE ANYTHING?
THERE WAS ONE THING-- A BOOK I REMEMBER HER TALKING ABOUT... SOME RELIGION THING...
YOU CAN SEE IT ON HER TABLE.. SOMETHING "ELLIS."
INTERESTING. I'LL LOOK IN TO IT.
HOW CAN YOU BE SO OBLIVIOUS TO THE WORLD AROUND YOU? DON'T YOU LISTEN TO THE NEWS? ALL THEY EVER TALK ABOUT ARE THE TERRORISTS!
I DON'T KNOW... WHAT DIFFERENCE DOES IT MAKE IF I LIVE OR DIE?
OH, THAT'S REALLY NICE.
WHAT ABOUT ME, DAVID? MAYBE YOU COULD CARE IF I LIVE OR DIE?
TODAY, WED. OCT. 16, THE WANDA CLUB MEETS WITH MR. HOWE, A SEMI-RETIRED PRIVATE INVESTIGATOR.
I ASSUME YOU ALREADY TALKED TO HER SISTER...
SISTER?

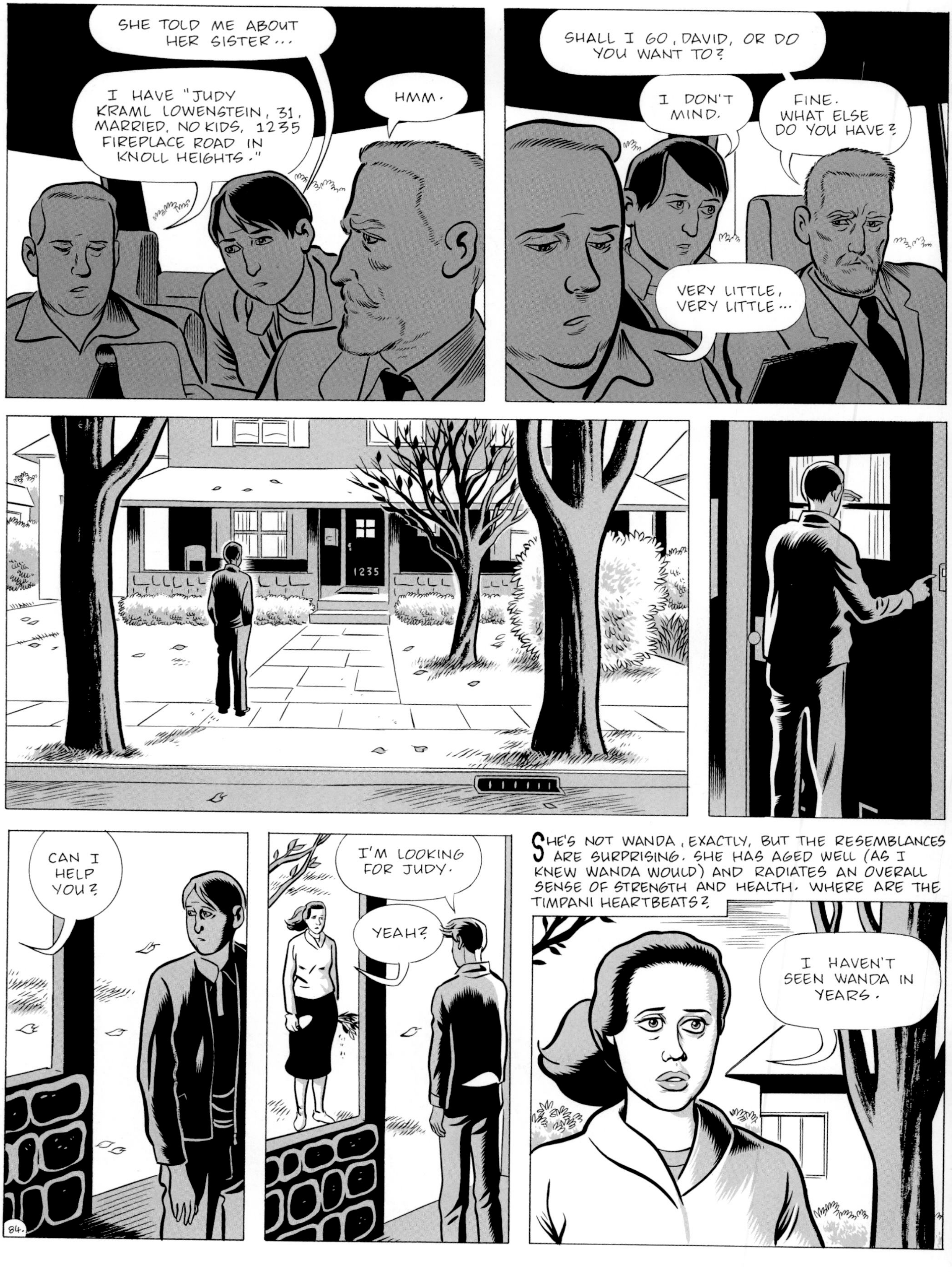
SHE TOLD ME ABOUT HER SISTER...
I HAVE "JUDY KRAML LOWENSTEIN, 31, MARRIED, NO KIDS, 1235 FIREPLACE ROAD IN KNOLL HEIGHTS."
HMM.
SHALL I GO, DAVID, OR DO YOU WANT TO?
I DON'T MIND.
FINE. WHAT ELSE DO YOU HAVE?
VERY LITTLE, VERY LITTLE...
1235
CAN I HELP YOU?
I'M LOOKING FOR JUDY.
YEAH?
SHE'S NOT WANDA, EXACTLY, BUT THE RESEMBLANCES ARE SURPRISING. SHE HAS AGED WELL (AS I KNEW WANDA WOULD) AND RADIATES AN OVERALL SENSE OF STRENGTH AND HEALTH. WHERE ARE THE TIMPANI HEARTBEATS?
I HAVEN'T SEEN WANDA IN YEARS.

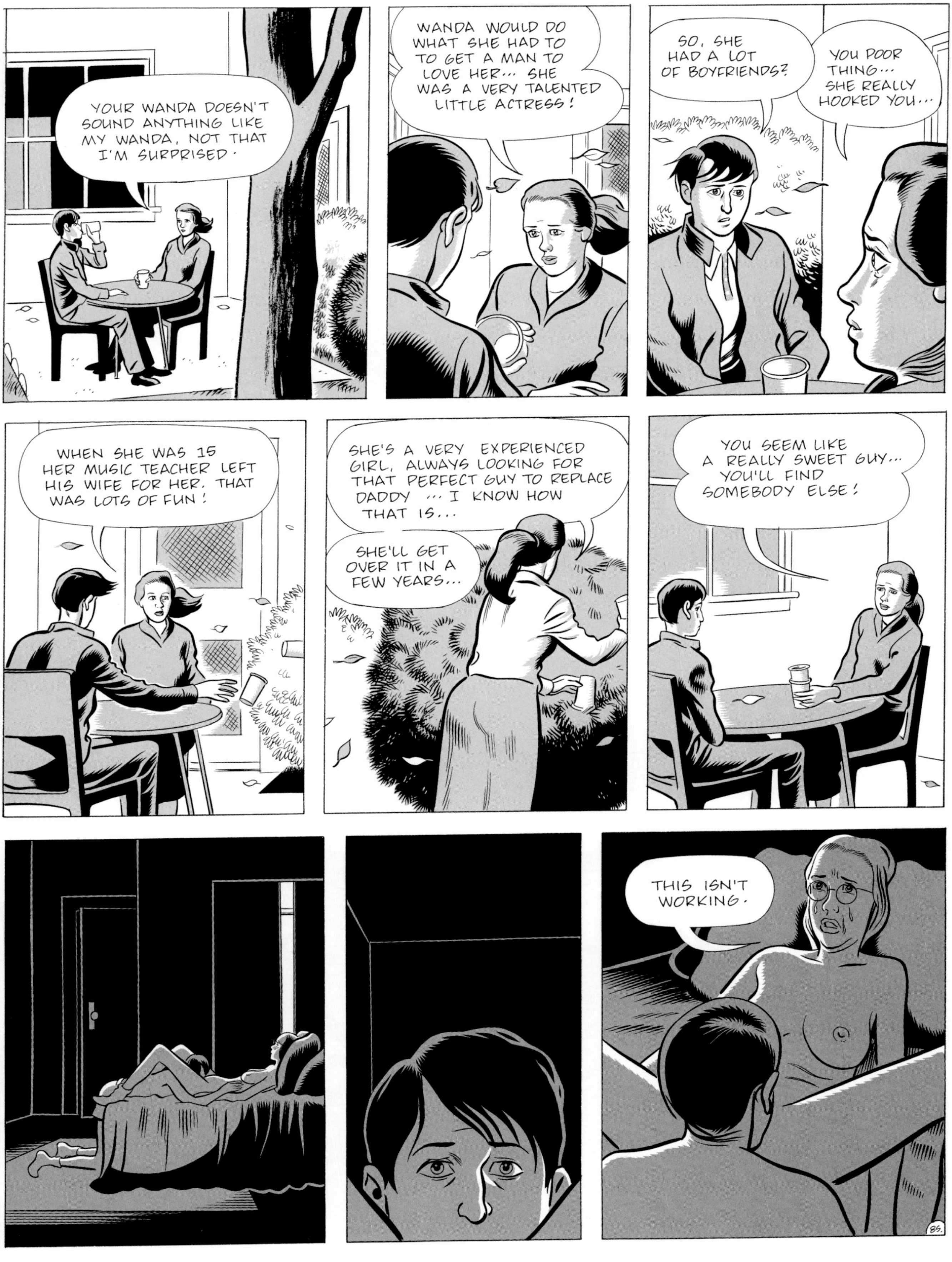
YOUR WANDA DOESN'T SOUND ANYTHING LIKE MY WANDA, NOT THAT I'M SURPRISED.
WANDA WOULD DO WHAT SHE HAD TO TO GET A MAN TO LOVE HER... SHE WAS A VERY TALENTED LITTLE ACTRESS!
SO, SHE HAD A LOT OF BOYFRIENDS?
YOU POOR THING... SHE REALLY HOOKED YOU...
WHEN SHE WAS 15 HER MUSIC TEACHER LEFT HIS WIFE FOR HER. THAT WAS LOTS OF FUN!
SHE'S A VERY EXPERIENCED GIRL, ALWAYS LOOKING FOR THAT PERFECT GUY TO REPLACE DADDY ... I KNOW HOW THAT IS...
SHE'LL GET OVER IT IN A FEW YEARS...
YOU SEEM LIKE A REALLY SWEET GUY... YOU'LL FIND SOMEBODY ELSE!
THIS ISN'T WORKING.

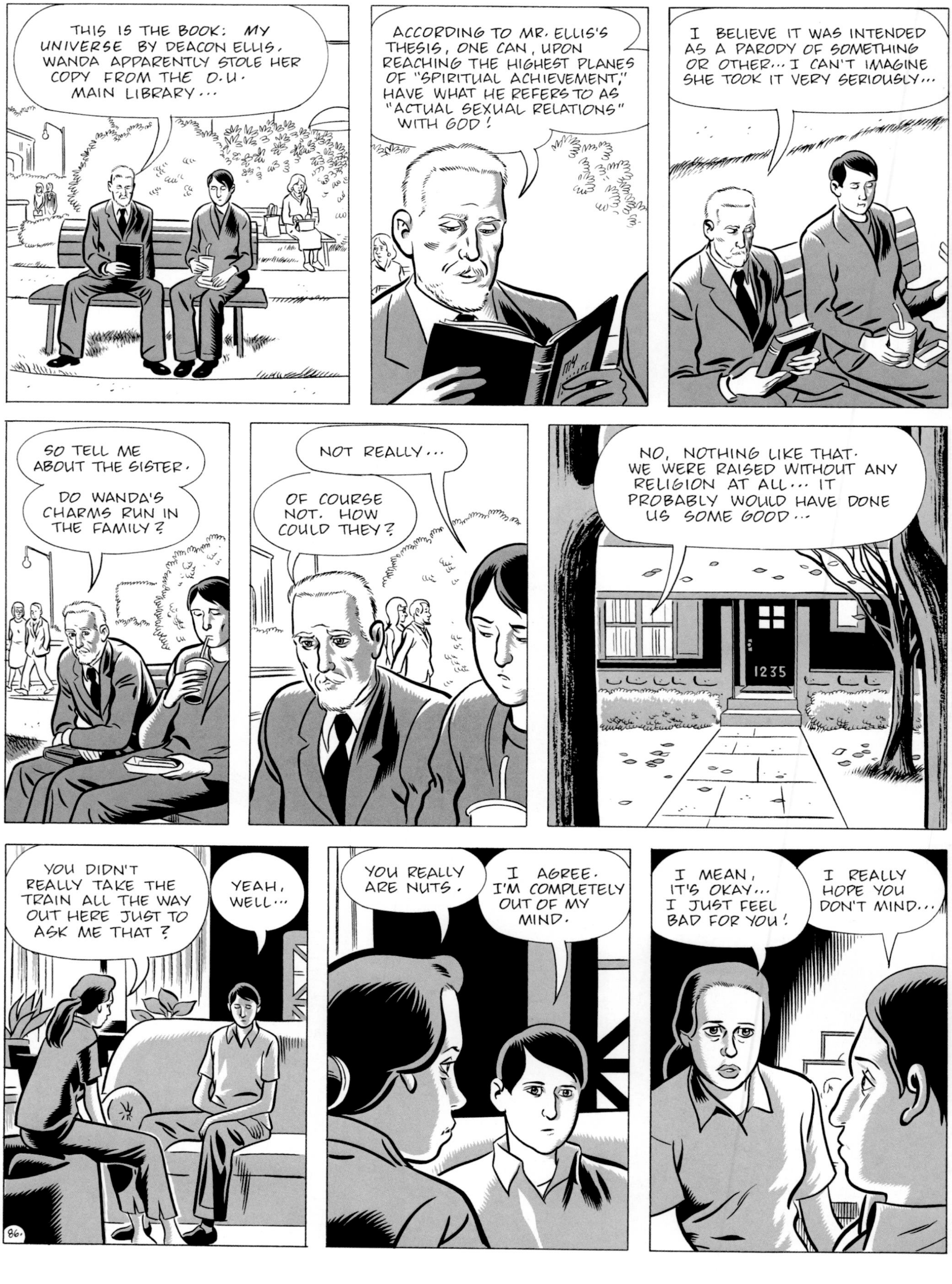
THIS IS THE BOOK: MY UNIVERSE BY DEACON ELLIS. WANDA APPARENTLY STOLE HER COPY FROM THE O.U. MAIN LIBRARY...
ACCORDING TO MR. ELLIS'S THESIS, ONE CAN, UPON REACHING THE HIGHEST PLANES OF "SPIRITUAL ACHIEVEMENT," HAVE WHAT HE REFERS TO AS "ACTUAL SEXUAL RELATIONS" WITH GOD!
I BELIEVE IT WAS INTENDED AS A PARODY OF SOMETHING OR OTHER... I CAN'T IMAGINE SHE TOOK IT VERY SERIOUSLY...
SO TELL ME ABOUT THE SISTER.
DO WANDA'S CHARMS RUN IN THE FAMILY?
NOT REALLY...
OF COURSE NOT. HOW COULD THEY?
NO, NOTHING LIKE THAT. WE WERE RAISED WITHOUT ANY RELIGION AT ALL... IT PROBABLY WOULD HAVE DONE US SOME GOOD...
1235
YOU DIDN'T REALLY TAKE THE TRAIN ALL THE WAY OUT HERE JUST TO ASK ME THAT?
YEAH, WELL...
YOU REALLY ARE NUTS.
I AGREE. I'M COMPLETELY OUT OF MY MIND.
I MEAN, IT'S OKAY... I JUST FEEL BAD FOR YOU!
I REALLY HOPE YOU DON'T MIND...

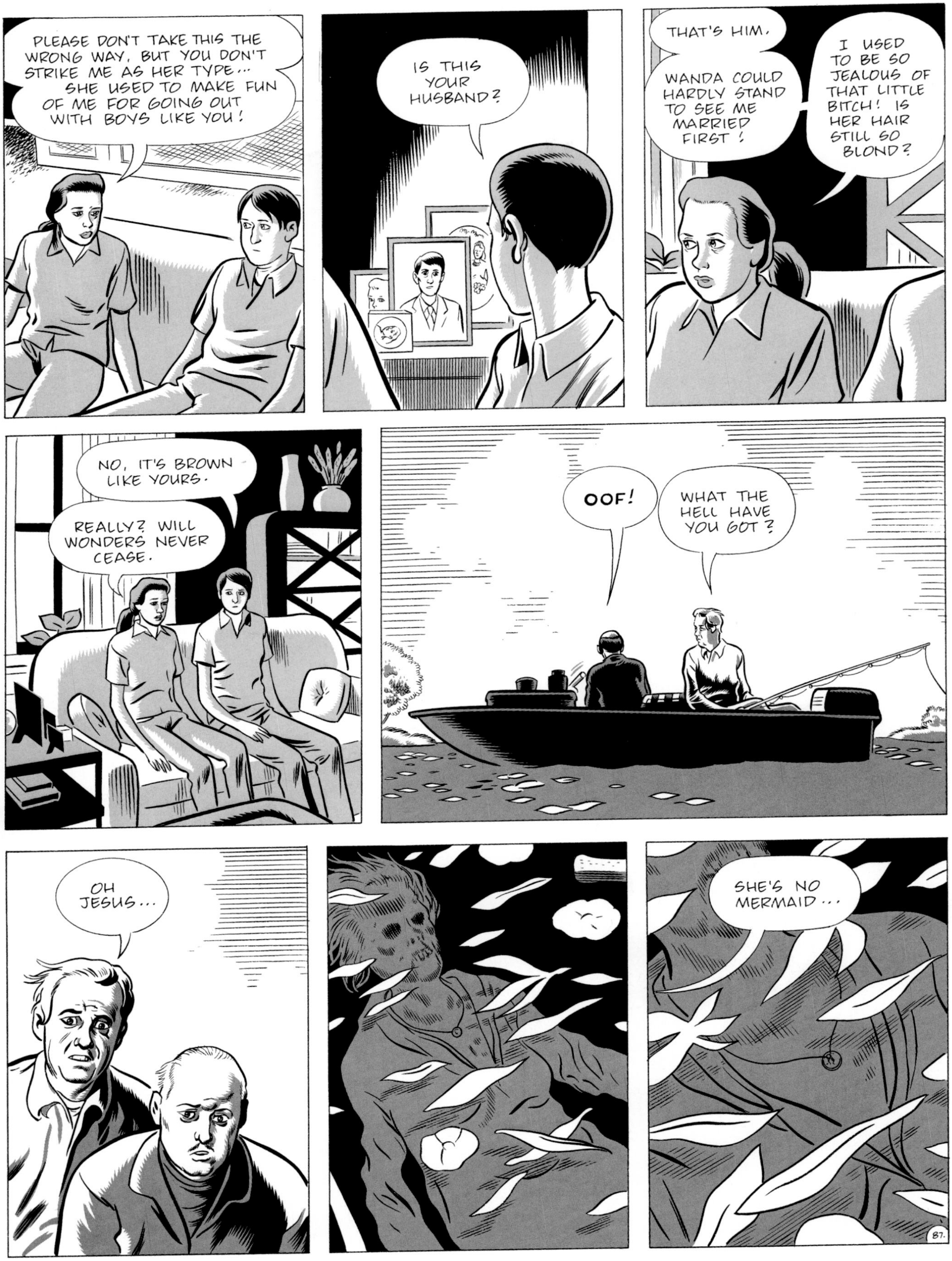
PLEASE DON'T TAKE THIS THE WRONG WAY, BUT YOU DON'T STRIKE ME AS HER TYPE... SHE USED TO MAKE FUN OF ME FOR GOING OUT WITH BOYS LIKE YOU!
IS THIS YOUR HUSBAND?
THAT'S HIM.
WANDA COULD HARDLY STAND TO SEE ME MARRIED FIRST!
I USED TO BE SO JEALOUS OF THAT LITTLE BITCH! IS HER HAIR STILL SO BLOND?
NO, IT'S BROWN LIKE YOURS.
REALLY? WILL WONDERS NEVER CEASE.
OOF!
WHAT THE HELL HAVE YOU GOT?
OH JESUS...
SHE'S NO MERMAID...

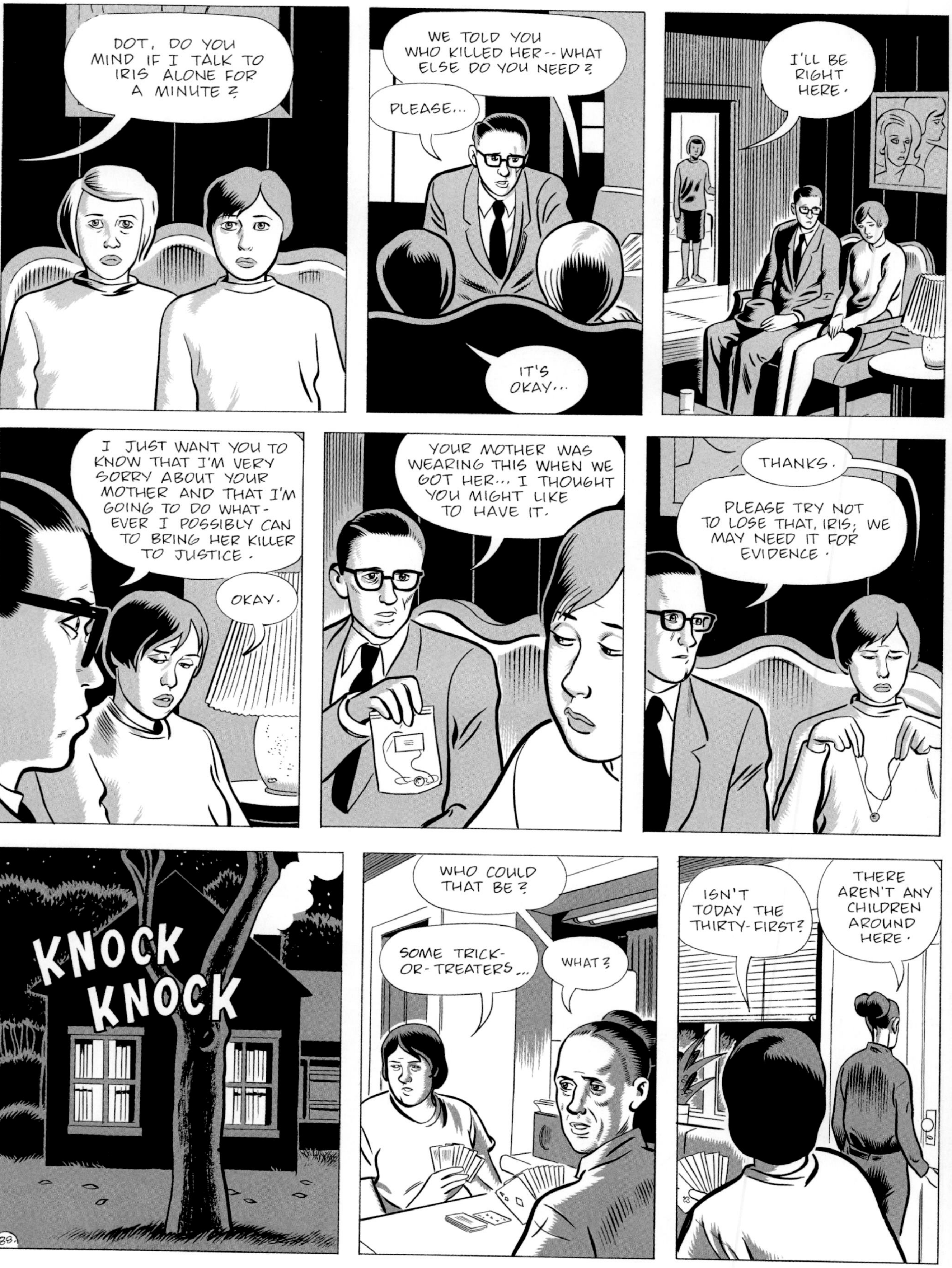
DOT, DO YOU MIND IF I TALK TO IRIS ALONE FOR A MINUTE?
WE TOLD YOU WHO KILLED HER--WHAT ELSE DO YOU NEED?
PLEASE...
IT'S OKAY...
I'LL BE RIGHT HERE.
I JUST WANT YOU TO KNOW THAT I'M VERY SORRY ABOUT YOUR MOTHER AND THAT I'M GOING TO DO WHATEVER I POSSIBLY CAN TO BRING HER KILLER TO JUSTICE.
OKAY.
YOUR MOTHER WAS WEARING THIS WHEN WE GOT HER... I THOUGHT YOU MIGHT LIKE TO HAVE IT.
THANKS.
PLEASE TRY NOT TO LOSE THAT, IRIS; WE MAY NEED IT FOR EVIDENCE.
KNOCK KNOCK
WHO COULD THAT BE?
SOME TRICK-OR-TREATERS...
WHAT?
ISN'T TODAY THE THIRTY-FIRST?
THERE AREN'T ANY CHILDREN AROUND HERE.

HELLO?

GOOD EVENING MA'AM, AGENT ROY SMITH. I'M LOOKING FOR MR. MANFRED ROLAND, JR.

I'M NOT LEAVING FOREVER, DAVID... I'LL BE BACK IN FEBRUARY IF THE CITY ISN'T BLOWN UP BY THEN.

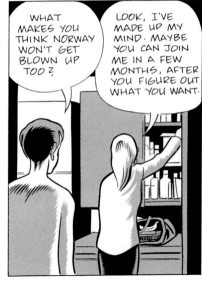

WHAT MAKES YOU THINK NORWAY WON'T GET BLOWN UP TOO?

LOOK, I'VE MADE UP MY MIND. MAYBE YOU CAN JOIN ME IN A FEW MONTHS, AFTER YOU FIGURE OUT WHAT YOU WANT.

I KNOW WHAT I WANT.

YOU THINK YOU KNOW EVERYTHING, DAVID, THAT'S YOUR PROBLEM.

JUST BECAUSE YOU'RE COLD AND DISTANT DOESN'T MEAN YOU'RE SMART.

I NEVER SAID I WAS SMART -- YOU'RE PROJECTING...

LOOK, I JUST CAN'T STAND IT ANY MORE. FORGIVE ME, DAVID, BUT IT'S BORING!

ANYTHING ELSE?

GOODBYE, DAVID.

89.

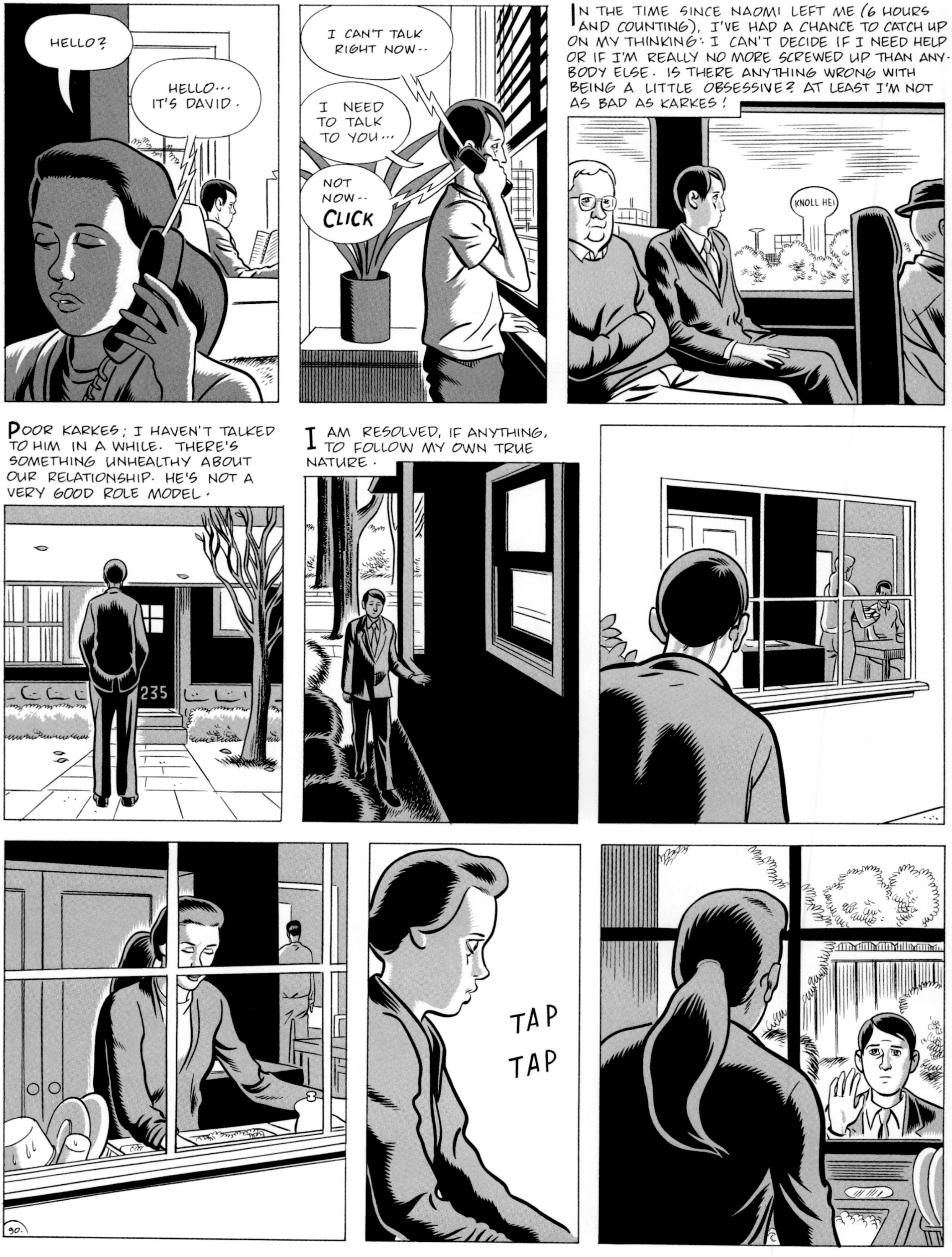
HELLO?
HELLO... IT'S DAVID.
I CAN'T TALK RIGHT NOW--
I NEED TO TALK TO YOU...
NOT NOW-- CLICK
IN THE TIME SINCE NAOMI LEFT ME (6 HOURS AND COUNTING), I'VE HAD A CHANCE TO CATCH UP ON MY THINKING: I CAN'T DECIDE IF I NEED HELP OR IF I'M REALLY NO MORE SCREWED UP THAN ANYBODY ELSE. IS THERE ANYTHING WRONG WITH BEING A LITTLE OBSESSIVE? AT LEAST I'M NOT AS BAD AS KARKES!
KNOLL HEI
POOR KARKES; I HAVEN'T TALKED TO HIM IN A WHILE. THERE'S SOMETHING UNHEALTHY ABOUT OUR RELATIONSHIP. HE'S NOT A VERY GOOD ROLE MODEL.
235
I AM RESOLVED, IF ANYTHING, TO FOLLOW MY OWN TRUE NATURE.
TAP TAP

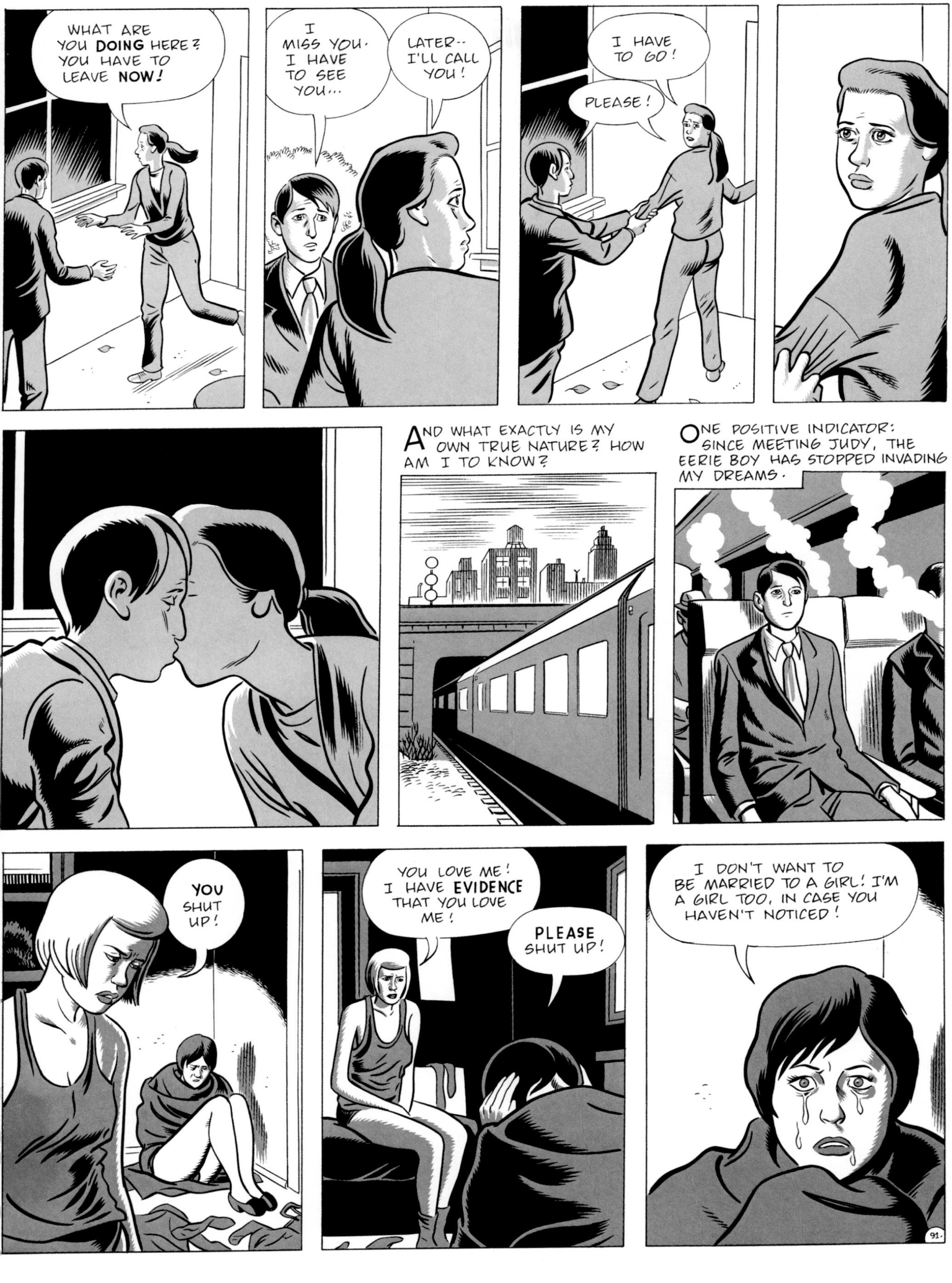
WHAT ARE YOU **DOING** HERE? YOU HAVE TO LEAVE **NOW!**
I MISS YOU. I HAVE TO SEE YOU...
LATER-- I'LL CALL YOU!
I HAVE TO GO!
PLEASE!
AND WHAT EXACTLY IS MY OWN TRUE NATURE? HOW AM I TO KNOW?
ONE POSITIVE INDICATOR: SINCE MEETING JUDY, THE EERIE BOY HAS STOPPED INVADING MY DREAMS.
YOU SHUT UP!
YOU LOVE ME! I HAVE **EVIDENCE** THAT YOU LOVE ME!
PLEASE SHUT UP!
I DON'T WANT TO BE MARRIED TO A GIRL! I'M A GIRL TOO, IN CASE YOU HAVEN'T NOTICED!

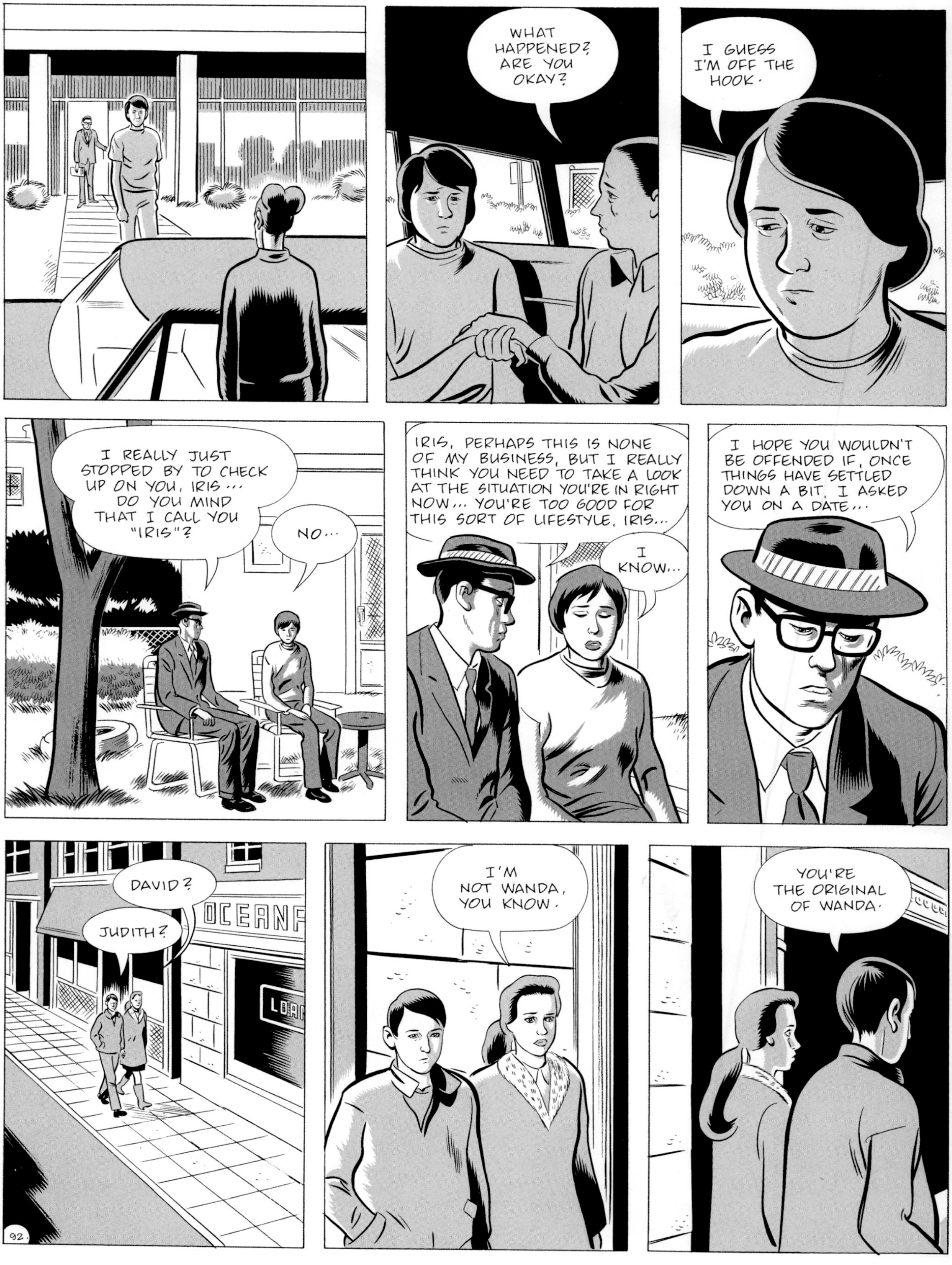
WHAT HAPPENED? ARE YOU OKAY?
I GUESS I'M OFF THE HOOK.
I REALLY JUST STOPPED BY TO CHECK UP ON YOU, IRIS... DO YOU MIND THAT I CALL YOU "IRIS"?
NO...
IRIS, PERHAPS THIS IS NONE OF MY BUSINESS, BUT I REALLY THINK YOU NEED TO TAKE A LOOK AT THE SITUATION YOU'RE IN RIGHT NOW... YOU'RE TOO GOOD FOR THIS SORT OF LIFESTYLE, IRIS...
I KNOW...
I HOPE YOU WOULDN'T BE OFFENDED IF, ONCE THINGS HAVE SETTLED DOWN A BIT, I ASKED YOU ON A DATE...
DAVID?
JUDITH?
OCEANA
I'M NOT WANDA, YOU KNOW.
YOU'RE THE ORIGINAL OF WANDA.

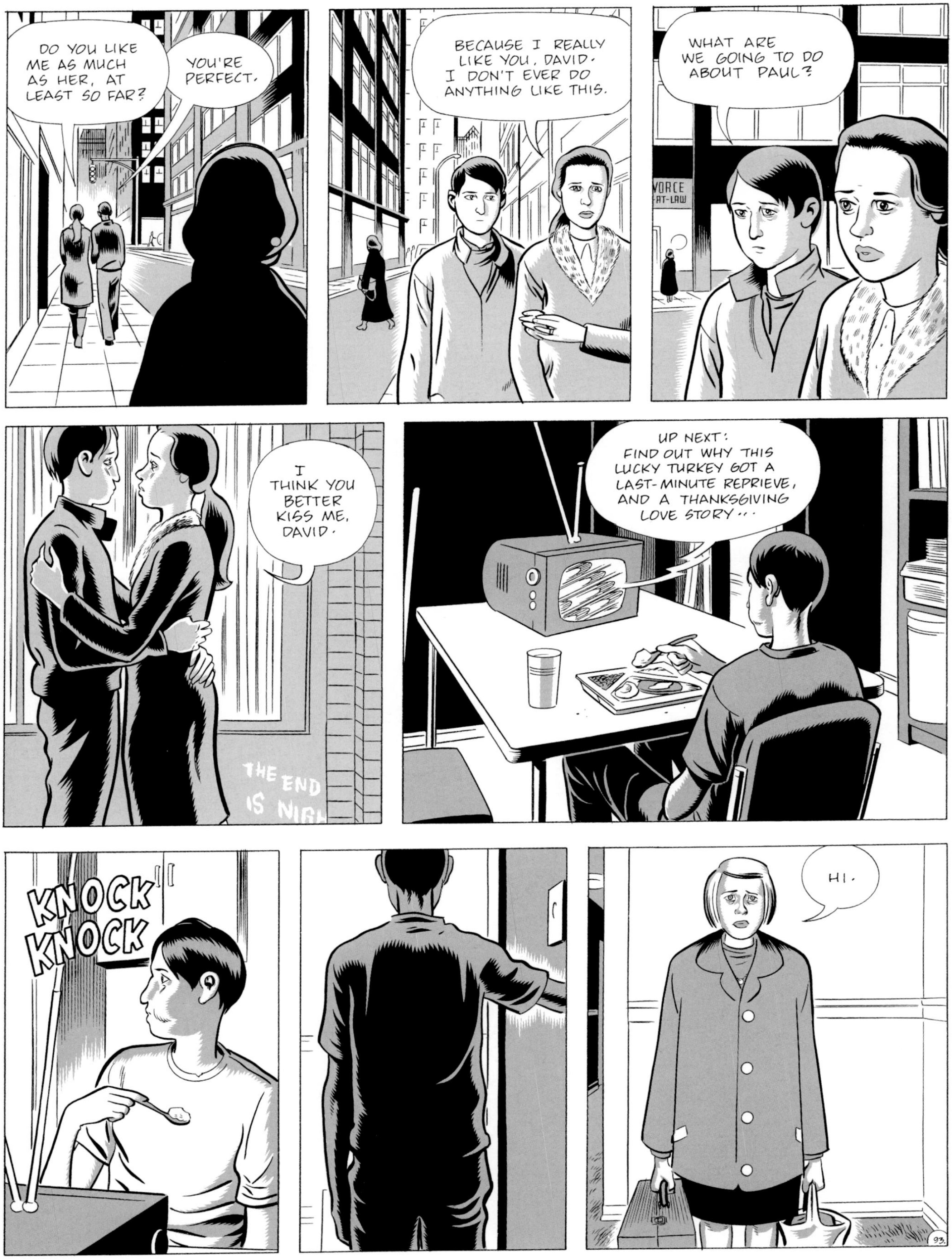
DO YOU LIKE ME AS MUCH AS HER, AT LEAST SO FAR?
YOU'RE PERFECT.
BECAUSE I REALLY LIKE YOU, DAVID. I DON'T EVER DO ANYTHING LIKE THIS.
WHAT ARE WE GOING TO DO ABOUT PAUL?
VORCE
AT-LAW
I THINK YOU BETTER KISS ME, DAVID.
THE END
IS NIG
UP NEXT: FIND OUT WHY THIS LUCKY TURKEY GOT A LAST-MINUTE REPRIEVE, AND A THANKSGIVING LOVE STORY...
KNOCK KNOCK
HI.

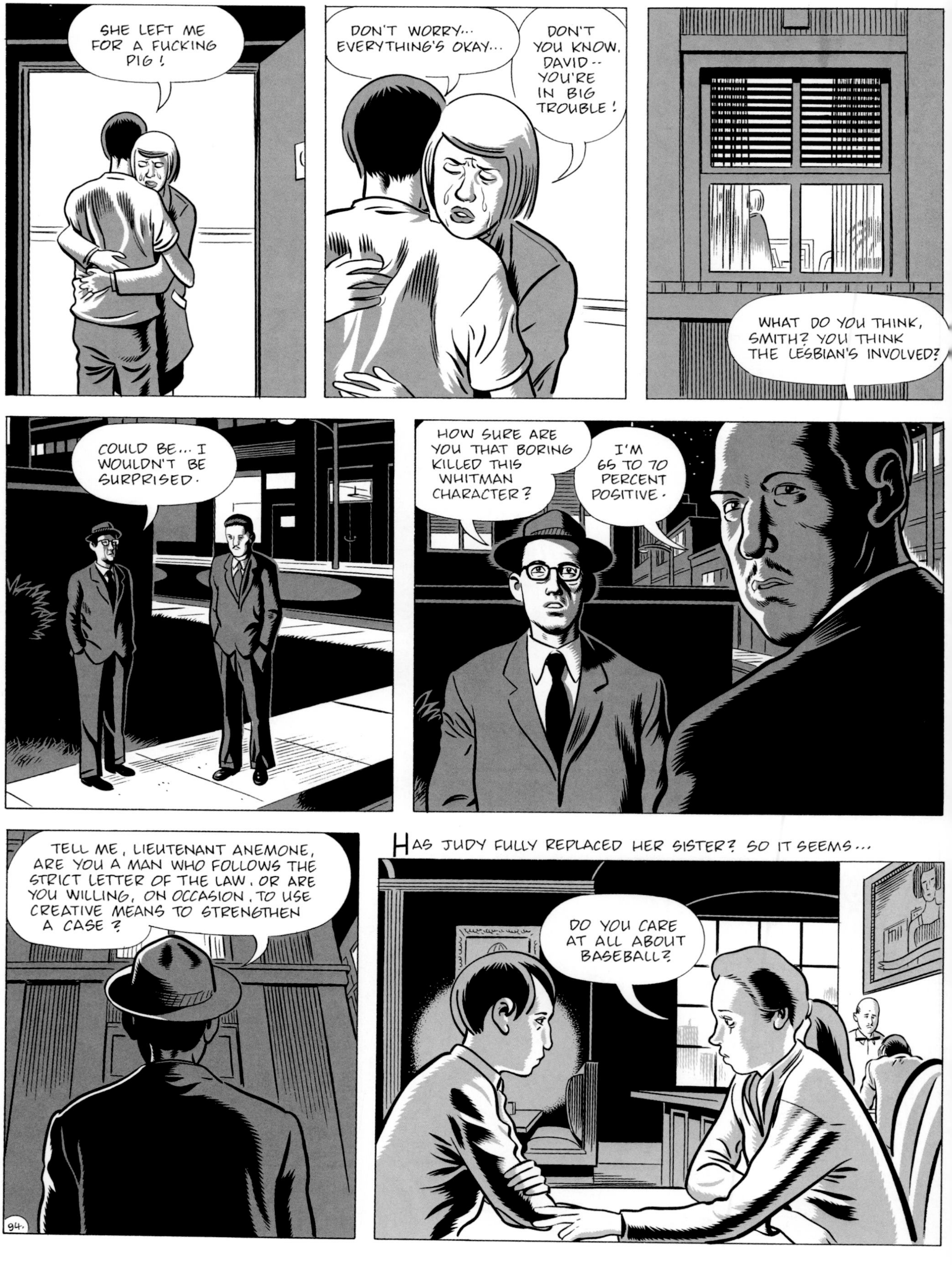
SHE LEFT ME FOR A FUCKING PIG!
DON'T WORRY... EVERYTHING'S OKAY...
DON'T YOU KNOW, DAVID-- YOU'RE IN BIG TROUBLE!
WHAT DO YOU THINK, SMITH? YOU THINK THE LESBIAN'S INVOLVED?
COULD BE... I WOULDN'T BE SURPRISED.
HOW SURE ARE YOU THAT BORING KILLED THIS WHITMAN CHARACTER?
I'M 65 TO 70 PERCENT POSITIVE.
TELL ME, LIEUTENANT ANEMONE, ARE YOU A MAN WHO FOLLOWS THE STRICT LETTER OF THE LAW, OR ARE YOU WILLING, ON OCCASION, TO USE CREATIVE MEANS TO STRENGTHEN A CASE?
HAS JUDY FULLY REPLACED HER SISTER? SO IT SEEMS...
DO YOU CARE AT ALL ABOUT BASEBALL?
94.

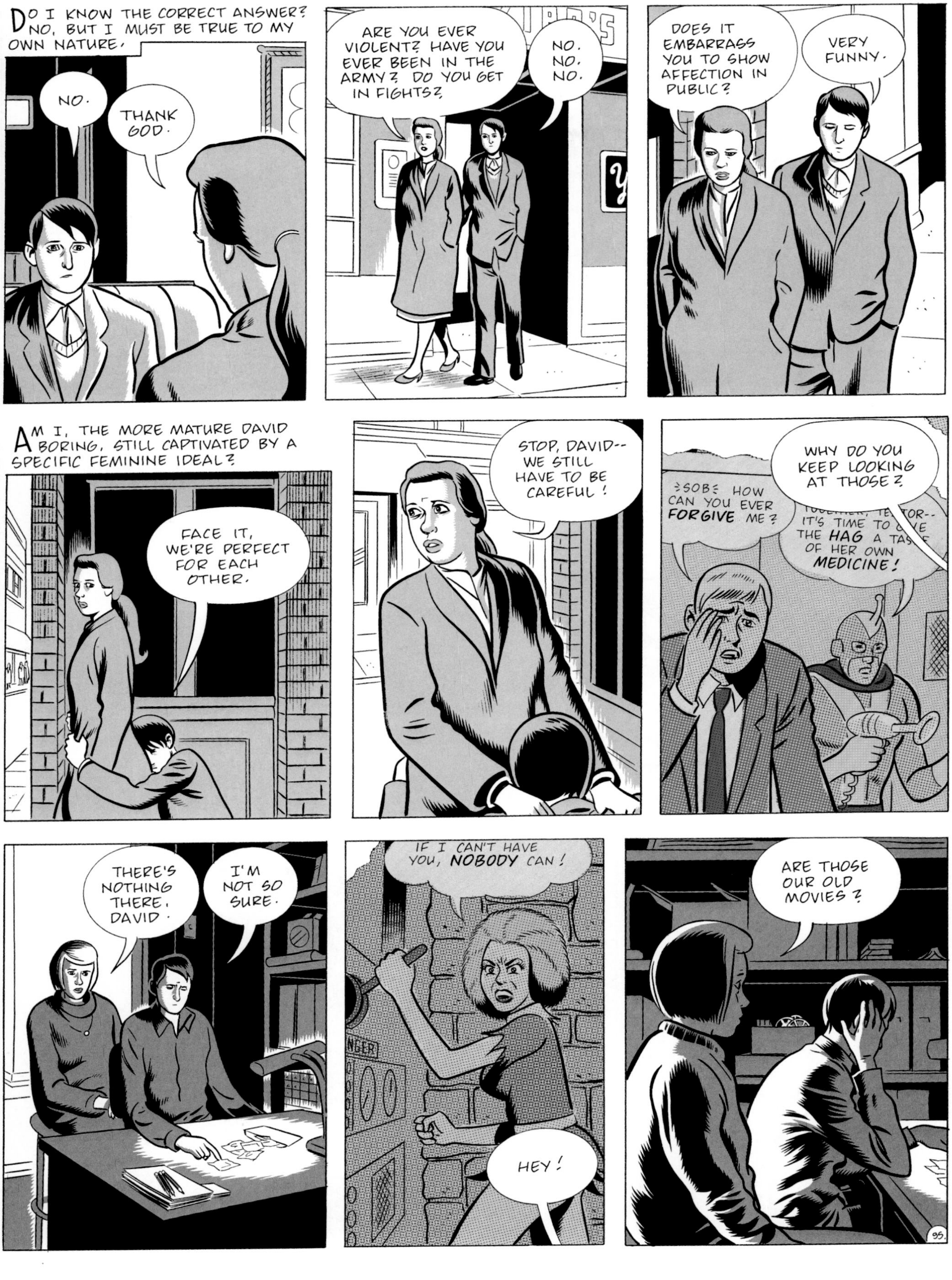
DO I KNOW THE CORRECT ANSWER? NO, BUT I MUST BE TRUE TO MY OWN NATURE.
NO.
THANK GOD.
ARE YOU EVER VIOLENT? HAVE YOU EVER BEEN IN THE ARMY? DO YOU GET IN FIGHTS?
NO. NO. NO.
DOES IT EMBARRASS YOU TO SHOW AFFECTION IN PUBLIC?
VERY FUNNY.
AM I, THE MORE MATURE DAVID BORING, STILL CAPTIVATED BY A SPECIFIC FEMININE IDEAL?
FACE IT, WE'RE PERFECT FOR EACH OTHER.
STOP, DAVID-- WE STILL HAVE TO BE CAREFUL!
SOB HOW CAN YOU EVER **FORGIVE** ME?
WHY DO YOU KEEP LOOKING AT THOSE?
IT'S TIME TO
THE **HAG** A TA
OF HER OWN **MEDICINE!**
THERE'S NOTHING THERE, DAVID.
I'M NOT SO SURE.
IF I CAN'T HAVE YOU, **NOBODY** CAN!
HEY!
ARE THOSE OUR OLD MOVIES?

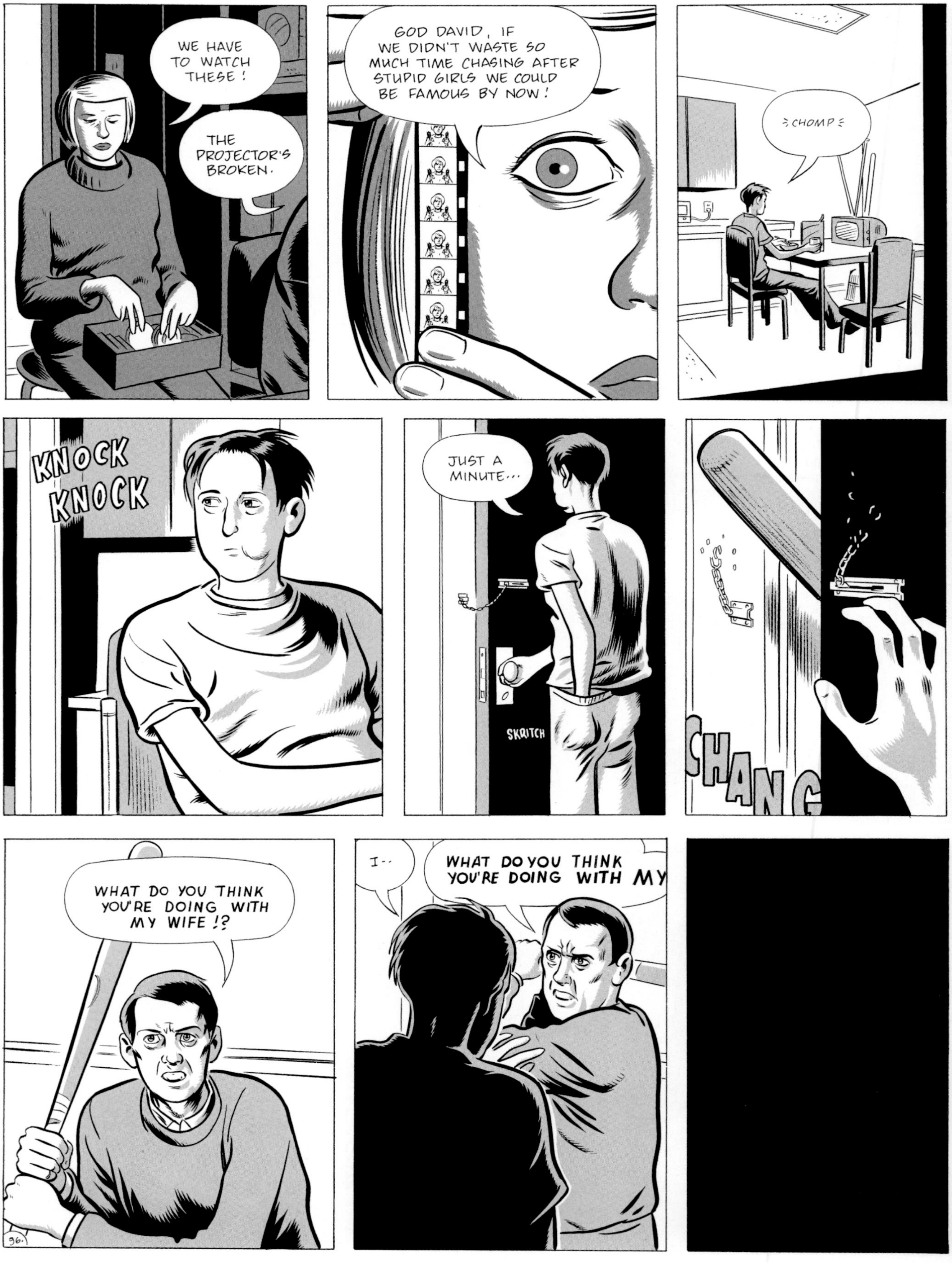
WE HAVE TO WATCH THESE!
THE PROJECTOR'S BROKEN.
GOD DAVID, IF WE DIDN'T WASTE SO MUCH TIME CHASING AFTER STUPID GIRLS WE COULD BE FAMOUS BY NOW!
CHOMP
KNOCK KNOCK
JUST A MINUTE...
SKRITCH
CHANG
WHAT DO YOU THINK YOU'RE DOING WITH MY WIFE!?
I--
WHAT DO YOU THINK YOU'RE DOING WITH MY

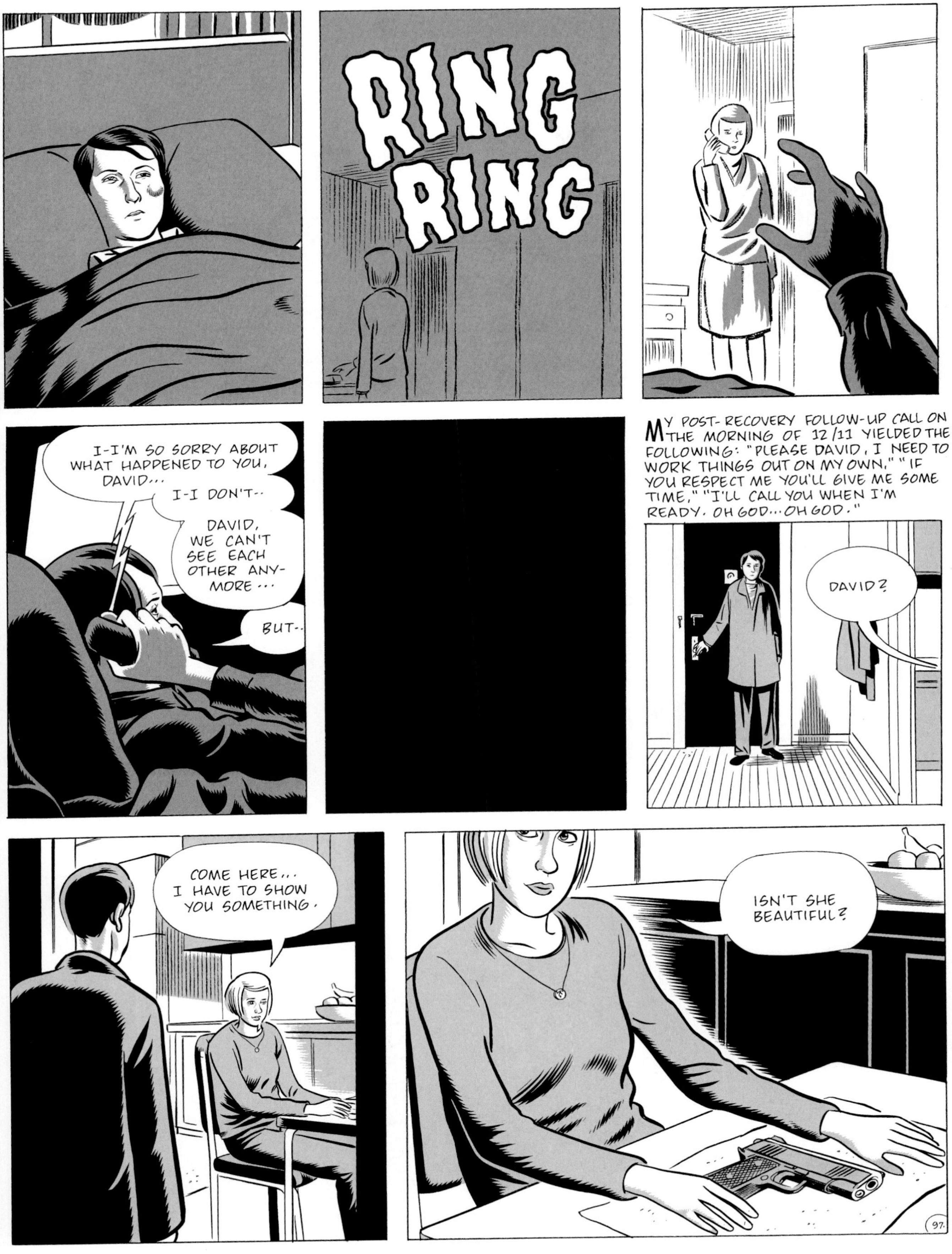
RING RING
I-I'M SO SORRY ABOUT WHAT HAPPENED TO YOU, DAVID...
I-I DON'T..
DAVID, WE CAN'T SEE EACH OTHER ANY-MORE...
BUT..
MY POST-RECOVERY FOLLOW-UP CALL ON THE MORNING OF 12/11 YIELDED THE FOLLOWING: "PLEASE DAVID, I NEED TO WORK THINGS OUT ON MY OWN," "IF YOU RESPECT ME YOU'LL GIVE ME SOME TIME," "I'LL CALL YOU WHEN I'M READY. OH GOD...OH GOD."
DAVID?
COME HERE... I HAVE TO SHOW YOU SOMETHING.
ISN'T SHE BEAUTIFUL?

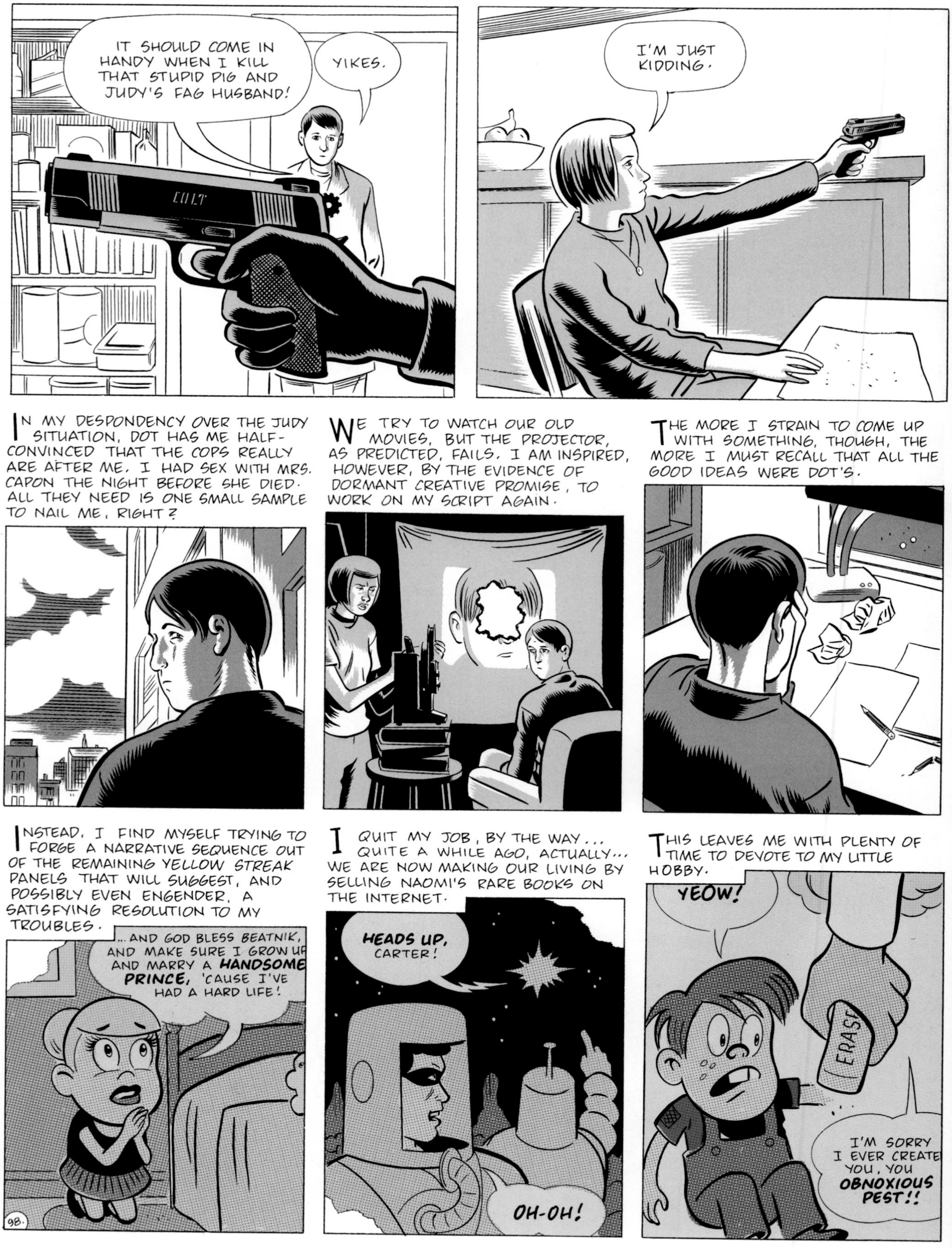
IT SHOULD COME IN HANDY WHEN I KILL THAT STUPID PIG AND JUDY'S FAG HUSBAND!
YIKES.
COLT
I'M JUST KIDDING.
IN MY DESPONDENCY OVER THE JUDY SITUATION, DOT HAS ME HALF-CONVINCED THAT THE COPS REALLY ARE AFTER ME. I HAD SEX WITH MRS. CAPON THE NIGHT BEFORE SHE DIED. ALL THEY NEED IS ONE SMALL SAMPLE TO NAIL ME, RIGHT?
WE TRY TO WATCH OUR OLD MOVIES, BUT THE PROJECTOR, AS PREDICTED, FAILS. I AM INSPIRED, HOWEVER, BY THE EVIDENCE OF DORMANT CREATIVE PROMISE, TO WORK ON MY SCRIPT AGAIN.
THE MORE I STRAIN TO COME UP WITH SOMETHING, THOUGH, THE MORE I MUST RECALL THAT ALL THE GOOD IDEAS WERE DOT'S.
INSTEAD, I FIND MYSELF TRYING TO FORGE A NARRATIVE SEQUENCE OUT OF THE REMAINING YELLOW STREAK PANELS THAT WILL SUGGEST, AND POSSIBLY EVEN ENGENDER, A SATISFYING RESOLUTION TO MY TROUBLES.
...AND GOD BLESS BEATNIK, AND MAKE SURE I GROW UP AND MARRY A HANDSOME PRINCE, 'CAUSE I'VE HAD A HARD LIFE!
98.
I QUIT MY JOB, BY THE WAY... QUITE A WHILE AGO, ACTUALLY... WE ARE NOW MAKING OUR LIVING BY SELLING NAOMI'S RARE BOOKS ON THE INTERNET.
HEADS UP, CARTER!
OH-OH!
THIS LEAVES ME WITH PLENTY OF TIME TO DEVOTE TO MY LITTLE HOBBY.
YEOW!
ERASE
I'M SORRY I EVER CREATED YOU, YOU OBNOXIOUS PEST!!

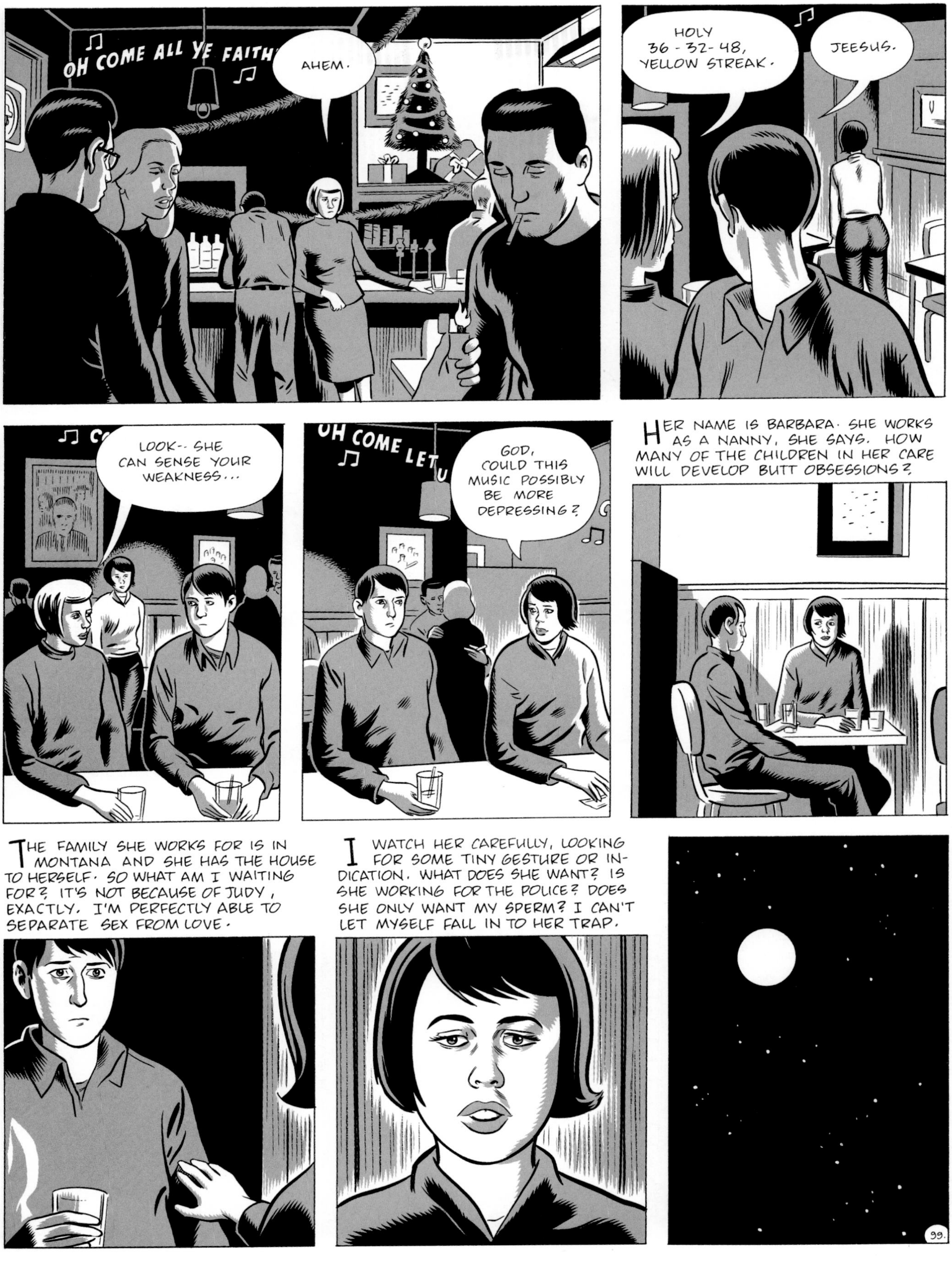
OH COME ALL YE FAITH
AHEM.
HOLY 36-32-48, YELLOW STREAK.
JEESUS.
LOOK-- SHE CAN SENSE YOUR WEAKNESS...
OH COME LET U
GOD, COULD THIS MUSIC POSSIBLY BE MORE DEPRESSING?
HER NAME IS BARBARA. SHE WORKS AS A NANNY, SHE SAYS. HOW MANY OF THE CHILDREN IN HER CARE WILL DEVELOP BUTT OBSESSIONS?
THE FAMILY SHE WORKS FOR IS IN MONTANA AND SHE HAS THE HOUSE TO HERSELF. SO WHAT AM I WAITING FOR? IT'S NOT BECAUSE OF JUDY, EXACTLY. I'M PERFECTLY ABLE TO SEPARATE SEX FROM LOVE.
I WATCH HER CAREFULLY, LOOKING FOR SOME TINY GESTURE OR INDICATION. WHAT DOES SHE WANT? IS SHE WORKING FOR THE POLICE? DOES SHE ONLY WANT MY SPERM? I CAN'T LET MYSELF FALL IN TO HER TRAP.

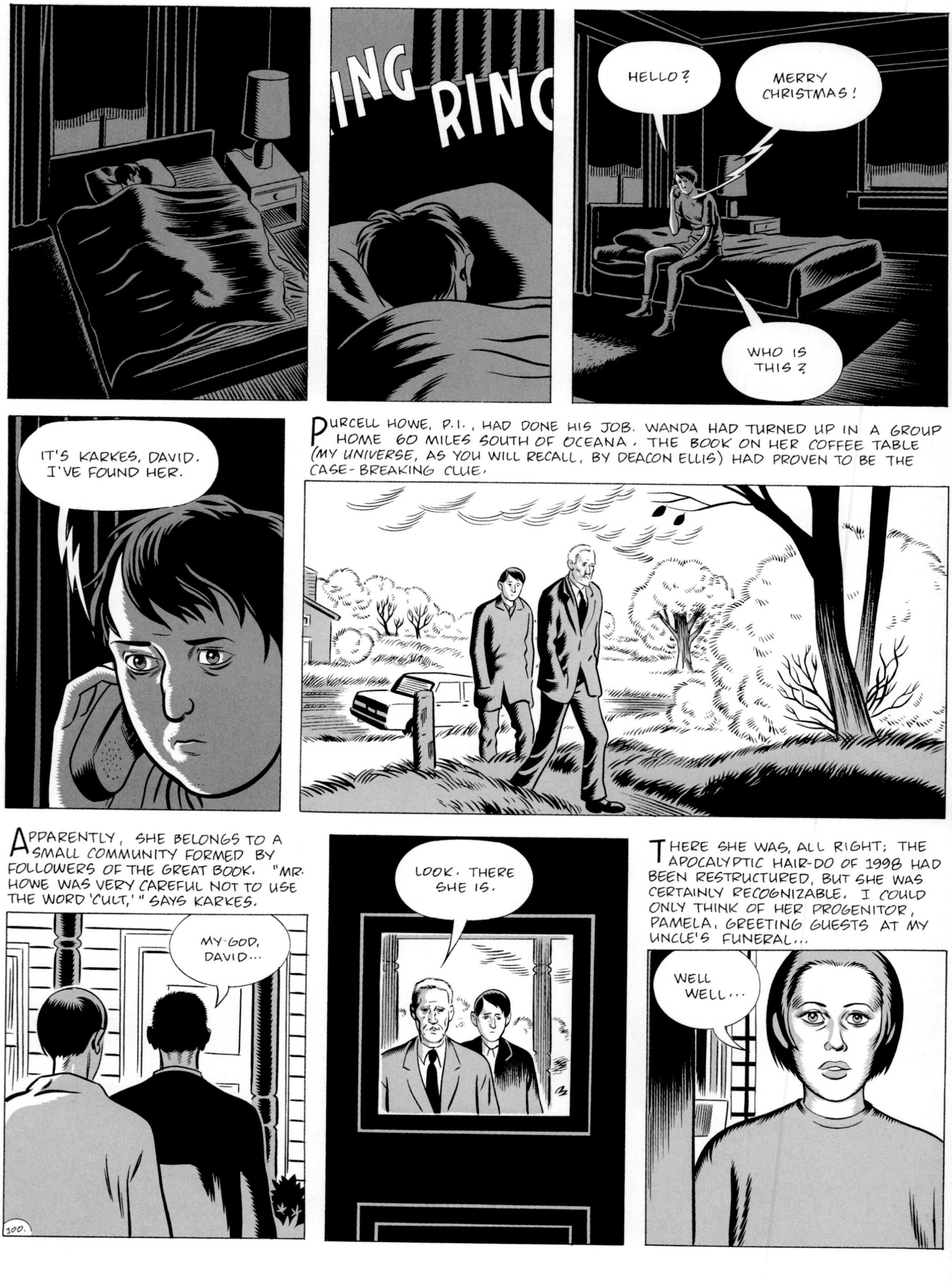

RING RING
HELLO?
MERRY CHRISTMAS!
WHO IS THIS?
IT'S KARKES, DAVID. I'VE FOUND HER.
PURCELL HOWE, P.I., HAD DONE HIS JOB. WANDA HAD TURNED UP IN A GROUP HOME 60 MILES SOUTH OF OCEANA. THE BOOK ON HER COFFEE TABLE (MY UNIVERSE, AS YOU WILL RECALL, BY DEACON ELLIS) HAD PROVEN TO BE THE CASE-BREAKING CLUE.
APPARENTLY, SHE BELONGS TO A SMALL COMMUNITY FORMED BY FOLLOWERS OF THE GREAT BOOK. "MR. HOWE WAS VERY CAREFUL NOT TO USE THE WORD 'CULT,'" SAYS KARKES.
MY GOD, DAVID...
LOOK. THERE SHE IS.
THERE SHE WAS, ALL RIGHT; THE APOCALYPTIC HAIR-DO OF 1998 HAD BEEN RESTRUCTURED, BUT SHE WAS CERTAINLY RECOGNIZABLE. I COULD ONLY THINK OF HER PROGENITOR, PAMELA, GREETING GUESTS AT MY UNCLE'S FUNERAL...
WELL WELL...

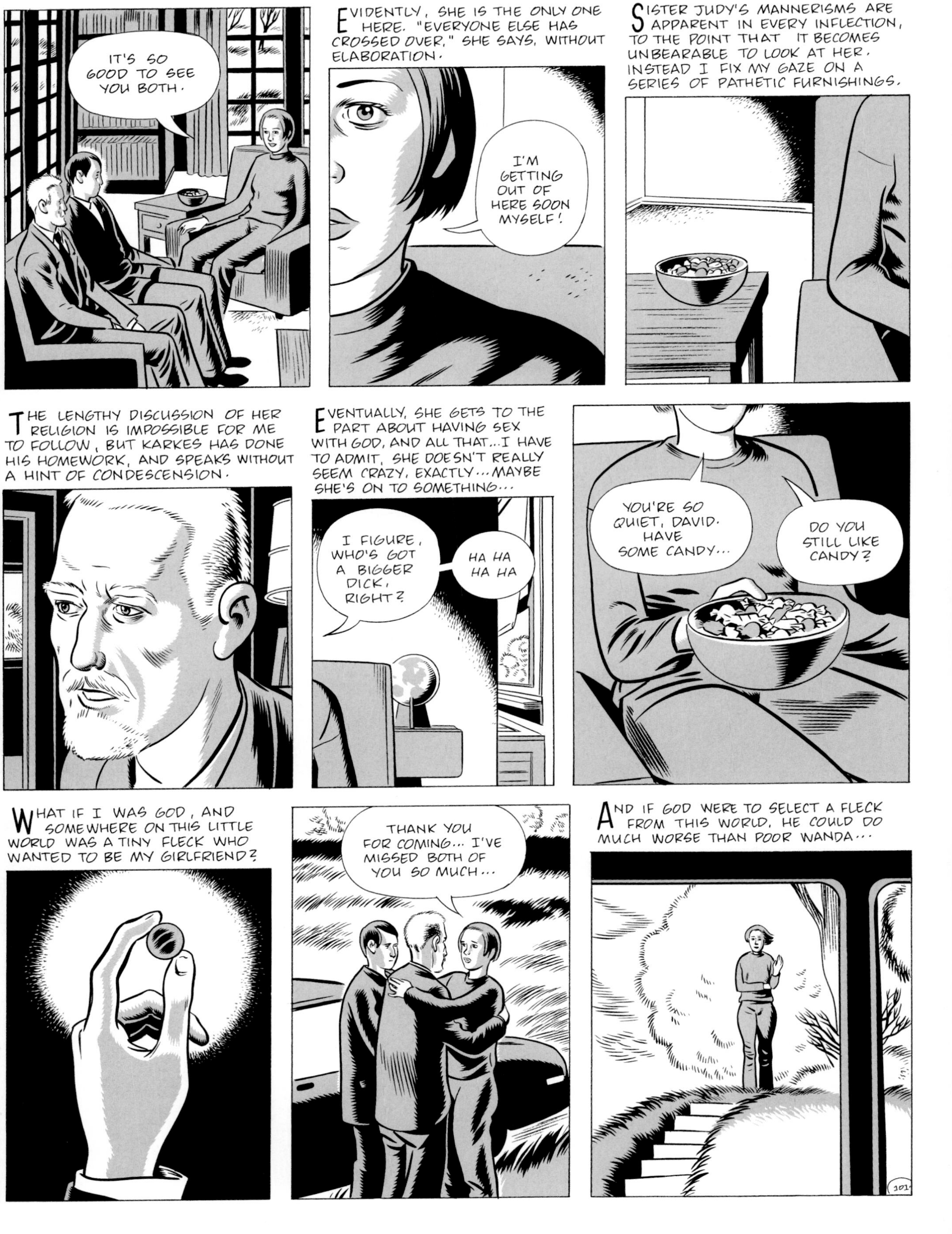
IT'S SO GOOD TO SEE YOU BOTH.
EVIDENTLY, SHE IS THE ONLY ONE HERE. "EVERYONE ELSE HAS CROSSED OVER," SHE SAYS, WITHOUT ELABORATION.
I'M GETTING OUT OF HERE SOON MYSELF!
SISTER JUDY'S MANNERISMS ARE APPARENT IN EVERY INFLECTION, TO THE POINT THAT IT BECOMES UNBEARABLE TO LOOK AT HER. INSTEAD I FIX MY GAZE ON A SERIES OF PATHETIC FURNISHINGS.
THE LENGTHY DISCUSSION OF HER RELIGION IS IMPOSSIBLE FOR ME TO FOLLOW, BUT KARKES HAS DONE HIS HOMEWORK, AND SPEAKS WITHOUT A HINT OF CONDESCENSION.
EVENTUALLY, SHE GETS TO THE PART ABOUT HAVING SEX WITH GOD, AND ALL THAT... I HAVE TO ADMIT, SHE DOESN'T REALLY SEEM CRAZY, EXACTLY... MAYBE SHE'S ON TO SOMETHING...
I FIGURE, WHO'S GOT A BIGGER DICK, RIGHT?
HA HA HA HA
YOU'RE SO QUIET, DAVID. HAVE SOME CANDY...
DO YOU STILL LIKE CANDY?
WHAT IF I WAS GOD, AND SOMEWHERE ON THIS LITTLE WORLD WAS A TINY FLECK WHO WANTED TO BE MY GIRLFRIEND?
THANK YOU FOR COMING... I'VE MISSED BOTH OF YOU SO MUCH...
AND IF GOD WERE TO SELECT A FLECK FROM THIS WORLD, HE COULD DO MUCH WORSE THAN POOR WANDA...
101

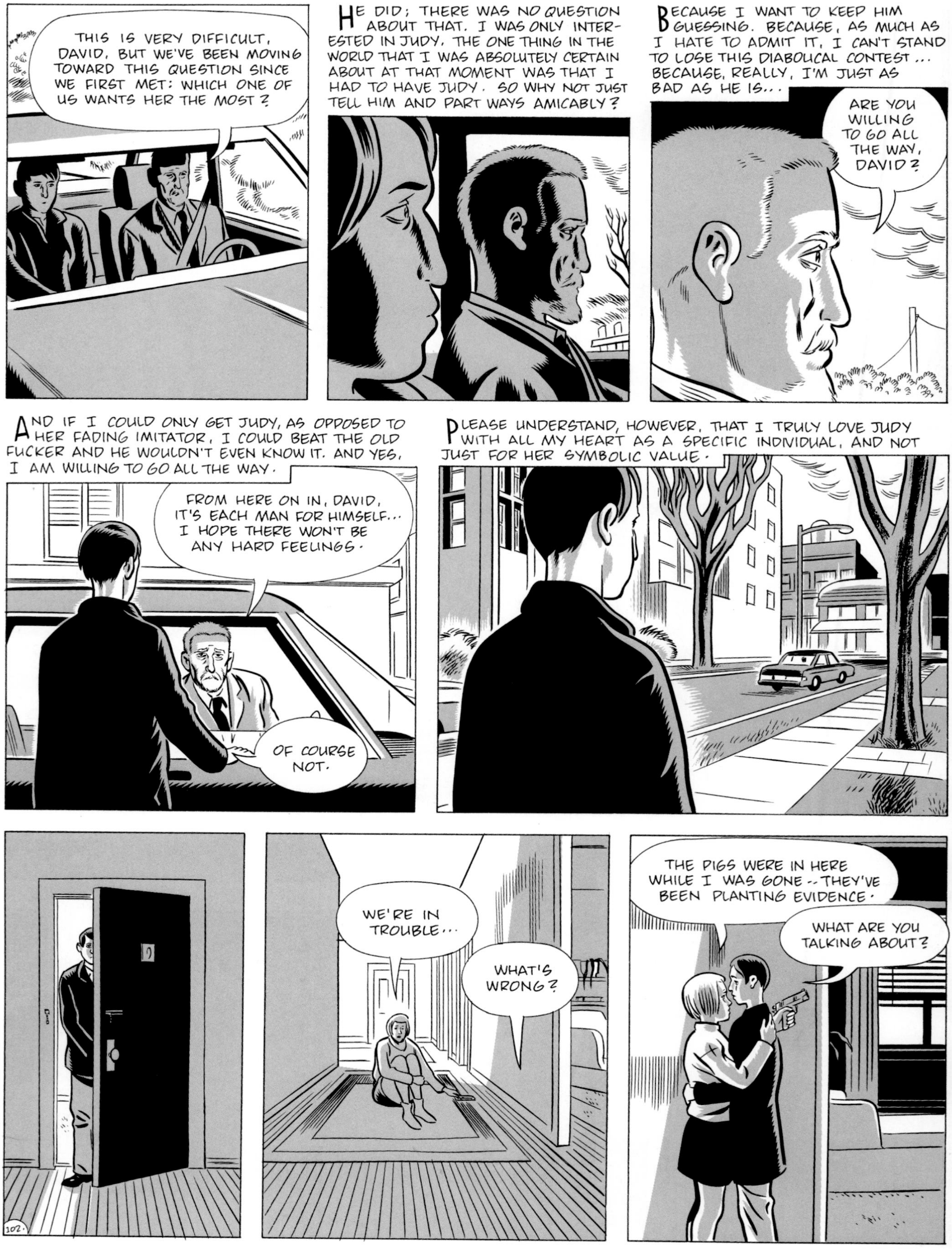
THIS IS VERY DIFFICULT, DAVID, BUT WE'VE BEEN MOVING TOWARD THIS QUESTION SINCE WE FIRST MET: WHICH ONE OF US WANTS HER THE MOST?
HE DID; THERE WAS NO QUESTION ABOUT THAT. I WAS ONLY INTERESTED IN JUDY, THE ONE THING IN THE WORLD THAT I WAS ABSOLUTELY CERTAIN ABOUT AT THAT MOMENT WAS THAT I HAD TO HAVE JUDY. SO WHY NOT JUST TELL HIM AND PART WAYS AMICABLY?
BECAUSE I WANT TO KEEP HIM GUESSING. BECAUSE, AS MUCH AS I HATE TO ADMIT IT, I CAN'T STAND TO LOSE THIS DIABOLICAL CONTEST... BECAUSE, REALLY, I'M JUST AS BAD AS HE IS...
ARE YOU WILLING TO GO ALL THE WAY, DAVID?
AND IF I COULD ONLY GET JUDY, AS OPPOSED TO HER FADING IMITATOR, I COULD BEAT THE OLD FUCKER AND HE WOULDN'T EVEN KNOW IT. AND YES, I AM WILLING TO GO ALL THE WAY.
FROM HERE ON IN, DAVID, IT'S EACH MAN FOR HIMSELF... I HOPE THERE WON'T BE ANY HARD FEELINGS.
OF COURSE NOT.
PLEASE UNDERSTAND, HOWEVER, THAT I TRULY LOVE JUDY WITH ALL MY HEART AS A SPECIFIC INDIVIDUAL, AND NOT JUST FOR HER SYMBOLIC VALUE.
WE'RE IN TROUBLE...
WHAT'S WRONG?
THE PIGS WERE IN HERE WHILE I WAS GONE -- THEY'VE BEEN PLANTING EVIDENCE.
WHAT ARE YOU TALKING ABOUT?
102.

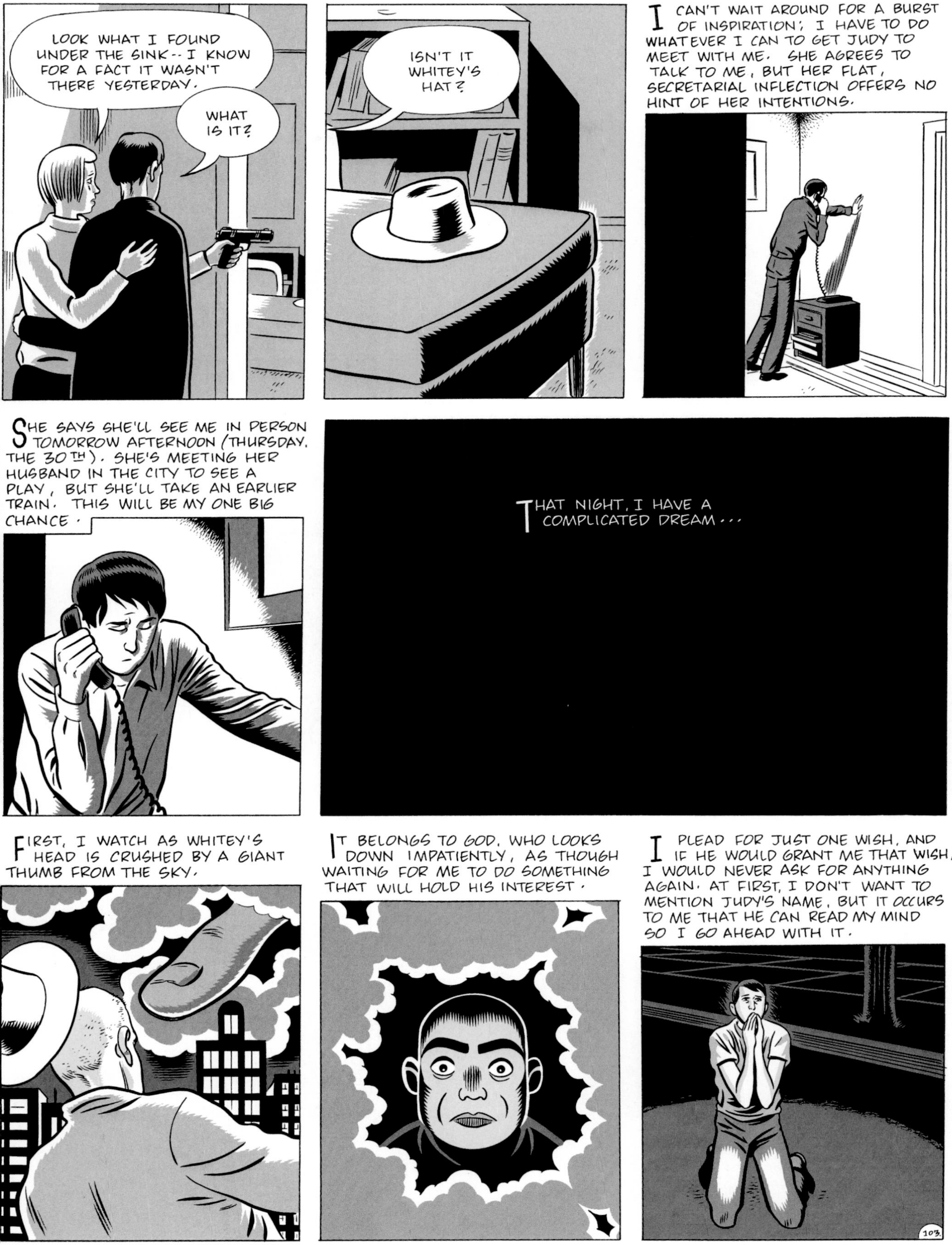
LOOK WHAT I FOUND UNDER THE SINK -- I KNOW FOR A FACT IT WASN'T THERE YESTERDAY.
WHAT IS IT?
ISN'T IT WHITEY'S HAT?
I CAN'T WAIT AROUND FOR A BURST OF INSPIRATION; I HAVE TO DO WHATEVER I CAN TO GET JUDY TO MEET WITH ME. SHE AGREES TO TALK TO ME, BUT HER FLAT, SECRETARIAL INFLECTION OFFERS NO HINT OF HER INTENTIONS.
SHE SAYS SHE'LL SEE ME IN PERSON TOMORROW AFTERNOON (THURSDAY, THE 30TH). SHE'S MEETING HER HUSBAND IN THE CITY TO SEE A PLAY, BUT SHE'LL TAKE AN EARLIER TRAIN. THIS WILL BE MY ONE BIG CHANCE.
THAT NIGHT, I HAVE A COMPLICATED DREAM...
FIRST, I WATCH AS WHITEY'S HEAD IS CRUSHED BY A GIANT THUMB FROM THE SKY.
IT BELONGS TO GOD, WHO LOOKS DOWN IMPATIENTLY, AS THOUGH WAITING FOR ME TO DO SOMETHING THAT WILL HOLD HIS INTEREST.
I PLEAD FOR JUST ONE WISH, AND IF HE WOULD GRANT ME THAT WISH, I WOULD NEVER ASK FOR ANYTHING AGAIN. AT FIRST, I DON'T WANT TO MENTION JUDY'S NAME, BUT IT *OCCURS* TO ME THAT HE CAN READ MY MIND SO I GO AHEAD WITH IT.

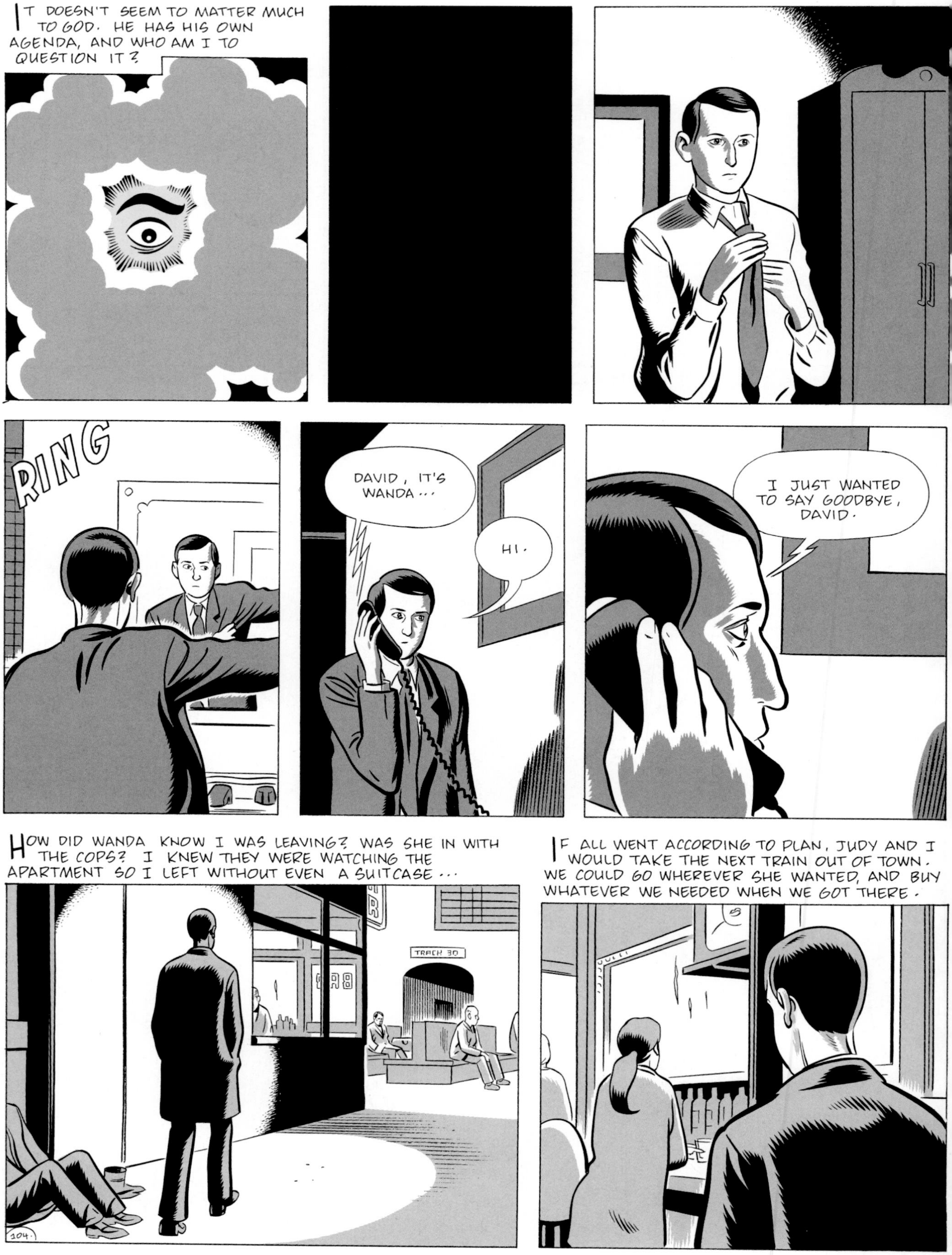
IT DOESN'T SEEM TO MATTER MUCH TO GOD. HE HAS HIS OWN AGENDA, AND WHO AM I TO QUESTION IT?
RING
DAVID, IT'S WANDA...
HI.
I JUST WANTED TO SAY GOODBYE, DAVID.
HOW DID WANDA KNOW I WAS LEAVING? WAS SHE IN WITH THE COPS? I KNEW THEY WERE WATCHING THE APARTMENT SO I LEFT WITHOUT EVEN A SUITCASE...
TRACK 30
IF ALL WENT ACCORDING TO PLAN, JUDY AND I WOULD TAKE THE NEXT TRAIN OUT OF TOWN. WE COULD GO WHEREVER SHE WANTED, AND BUY WHATEVER WE NEEDED WHEN WE GOT THERE.

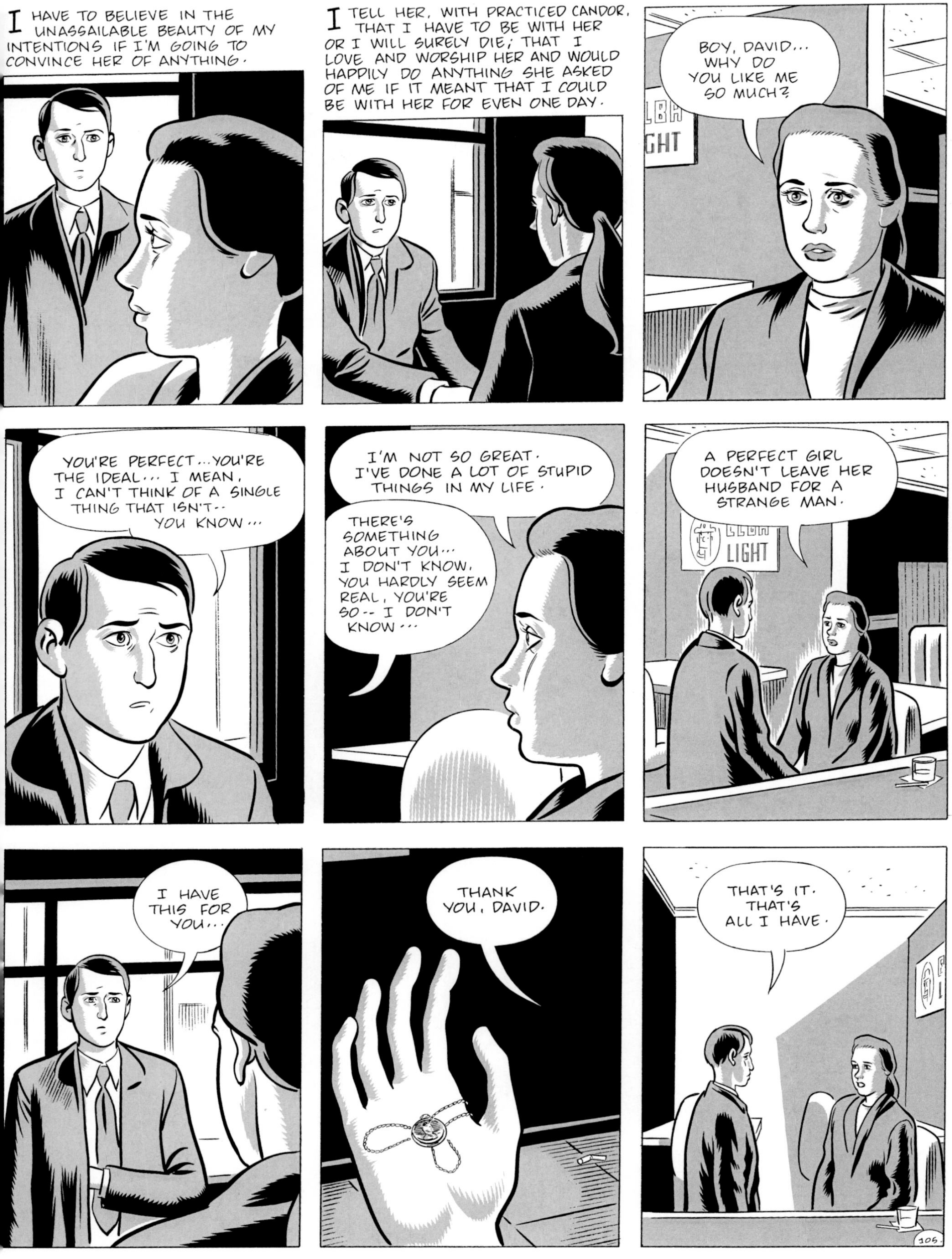
I HAVE TO BELIEVE IN THE UNASSAILABLE BEAUTY OF MY INTENTIONS IF I'M GOING TO CONVINCE HER OF ANYTHING.
I TELL HER, WITH PRACTICED CANDOR, THAT I HAVE TO BE WITH HER OR I WILL SURELY DIE; THAT I LOVE AND WORSHIP HER AND WOULD HAPPILY DO ANYTHING SHE ASKED OF ME IF IT MEANT THAT I COULD BE WITH HER FOR EVEN ONE DAY.
BOY, DAVID... WHY DO YOU LIKE ME SO MUCH?
LIGHT
YOU'RE PERFECT...YOU'RE THE IDEAL... I MEAN, I CAN'T THINK OF A SINGLE THING THAT ISN'T-- YOU KNOW...
I'M NOT SO GREAT. I'VE DONE A LOT OF STUPID THINGS IN MY LIFE.
THERE'S SOMETHING ABOUT YOU... I DON'T KNOW. YOU HARDLY SEEM REAL, YOU'RE SO-- I DON'T KNOW...
A PERFECT GIRL DOESN'T LEAVE HER HUSBAND FOR A STRANGE MAN.
LIGHT
I HAVE THIS FOR YOU...
THANK YOU, DAVID.
THAT'S IT. THAT'S ALL I HAVE.

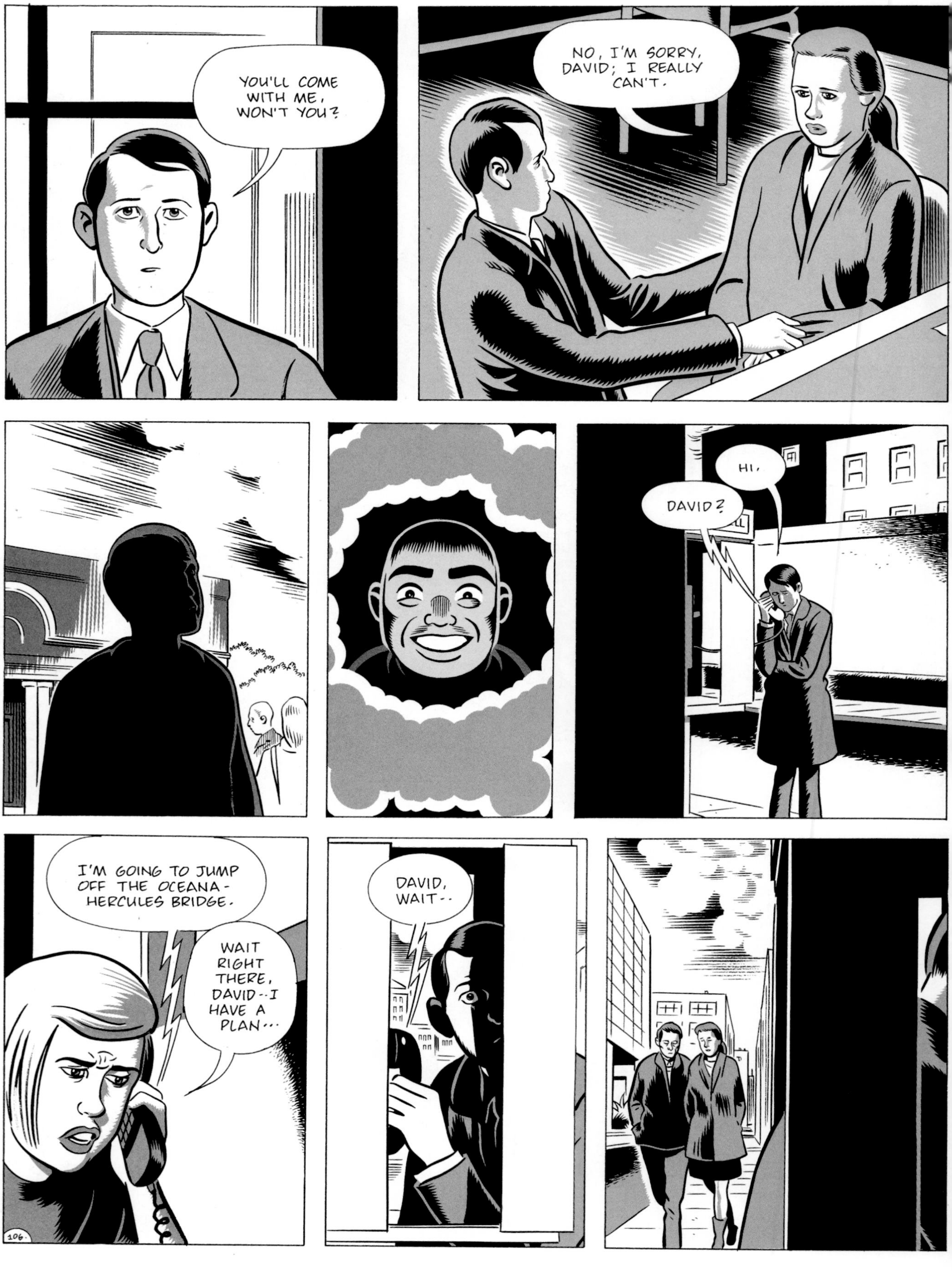
YOU'LL COME WITH ME, WON'T YOU?
NO, I'M SORRY, DAVID; I REALLY CAN'T.
HI.
DAVID?
I'M GOING TO JUMP OFF THE OCEANA-HERCULES BRIDGE.
WAIT RIGHT THERE, DAVID--I HAVE A PLAN...
DAVID, WAIT--.

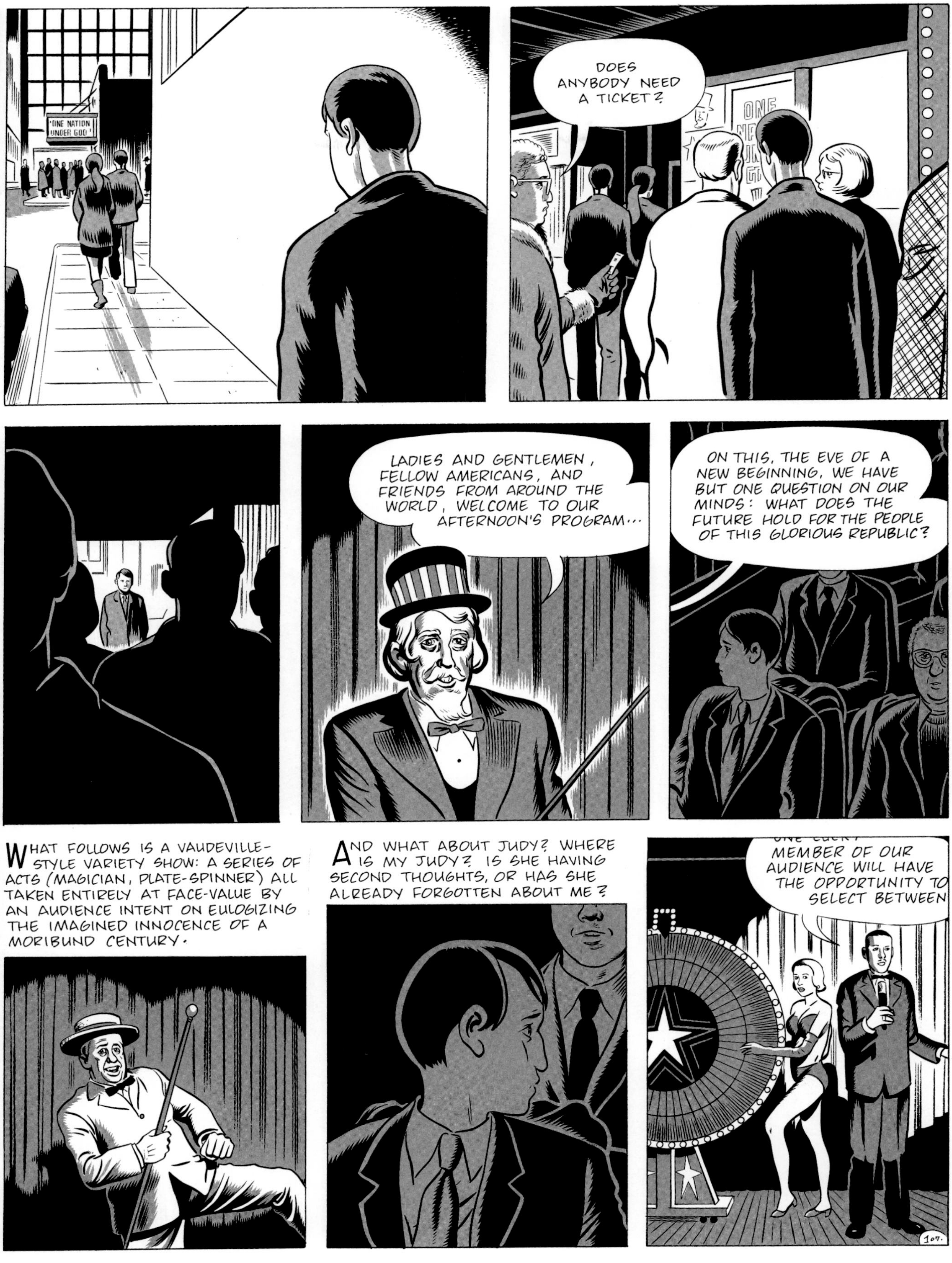
"ONE NATION UNDER GOD"
DOES ANYBODY NEED A TICKET?
LADIES AND GENTLEMEN, FELLOW AMERICANS, AND FRIENDS FROM AROUND THE WORLD, WELCOME TO OUR AFTERNOON'S PROGRAM...
ON THIS, THE EVE OF A NEW BEGINNING, WE HAVE BUT ONE QUESTION ON OUR MINDS: WHAT DOES THE FUTURE HOLD FOR THE PEOPLE OF THIS GLORIOUS REPUBLIC?
WHAT FOLLOWS IS A VAUDEVILLE-STYLE VARIETY SHOW: A SERIES OF ACTS (MAGICIAN, PLATE-SPINNER) ALL TAKEN ENTIRELY AT FACE-VALUE BY AN AUDIENCE INTENT ON EULOGIZING THE IMAGINED INNOCENCE OF A MORIBUND CENTURY.
AND WHAT ABOUT JUDY? WHERE IS MY JUDY? IS SHE HAVING SECOND THOUGHTS, OR HAS SHE ALREADY FORGOTTEN ABOUT ME?
MEMBER OF OUR AUDIENCE WILL HAVE THE OPPORTUNITY TO SELECT BETWEEN
107.

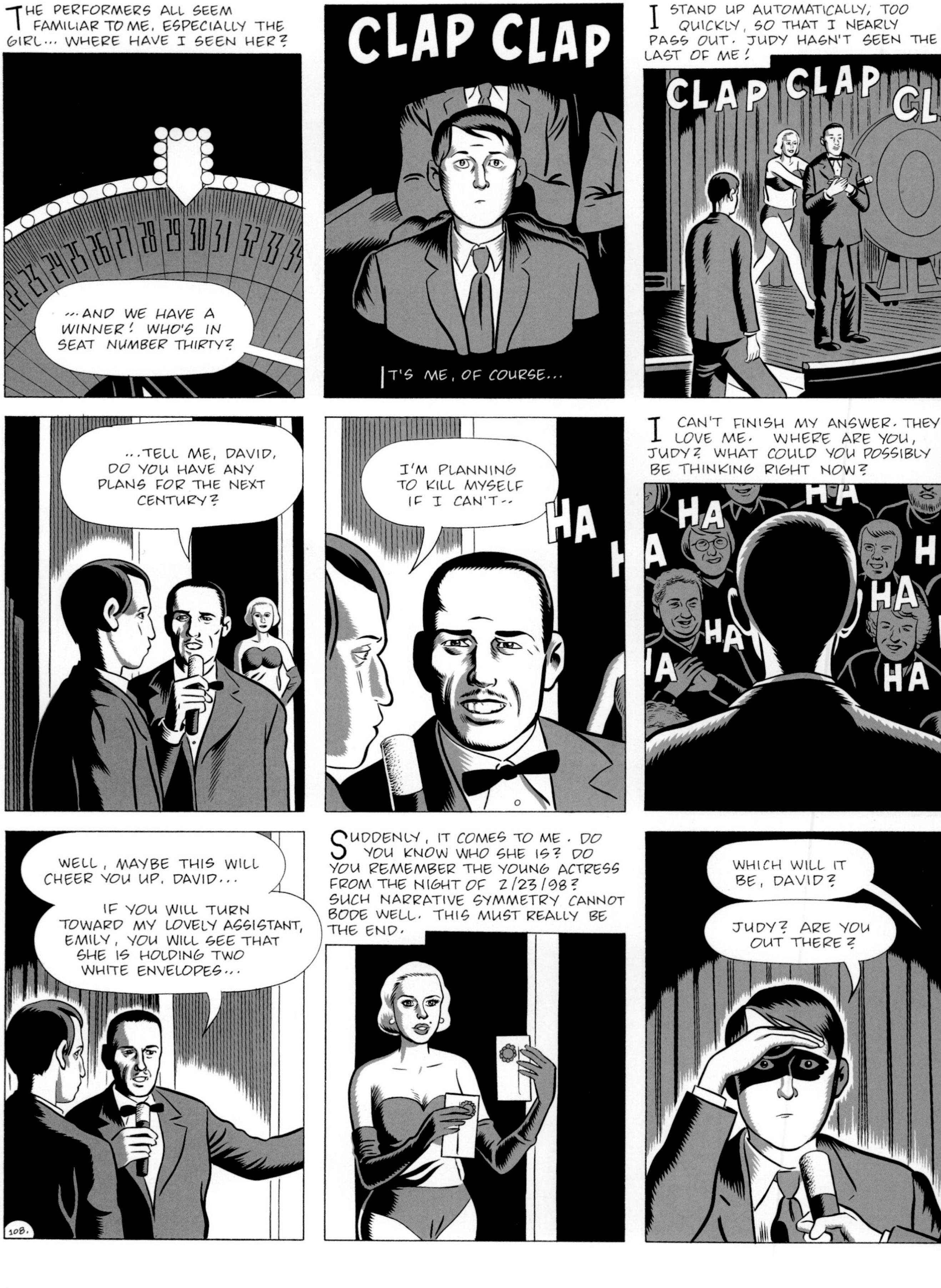
THE PERFORMERS ALL SEEM FAMILIAR TO ME, ESPECIALLY THE GIRL... WHERE HAVE I SEEN HER?
...AND WE HAVE A WINNER! WHO'S IN SEAT NUMBER THIRTY?
CLAP CLAP
IT'S ME, OF COURSE...
I STAND UP AUTOMATICALLY, TOO QUICKLY, SO THAT I NEARLY PASS OUT. JUDY HASN'T SEEN THE LAST OF ME!
CLAP CLAP
...TELL ME, DAVID, DO YOU HAVE ANY PLANS FOR THE NEXT CENTURY?
I'M PLANNING TO KILL MYSELF IF I CAN'T--
HA
I CAN'T FINISH MY ANSWER. THEY LOVE ME. WHERE ARE YOU, JUDY? WHAT COULD YOU POSSIBLY BE THINKING RIGHT NOW?
HA HA HA HA HA HA
WELL, MAYBE THIS WILL CHEER YOU UP, DAVID...
IF YOU WILL TURN TOWARD MY LOVELY ASSISTANT, EMILY, YOU WILL SEE THAT SHE IS HOLDING TWO WHITE ENVELOPES...
SUDDENLY, IT COMES TO ME. DO YOU KNOW WHO SHE IS? DO YOU REMEMBER THE YOUNG ACTRESS FROM THE NIGHT OF 2/23/98? SUCH NARRATIVE SYMMETRY CANNOT BODE WELL. THIS MUST REALLY BE THE END.
WHICH WILL IT BE, DAVID?
JUDY? ARE YOU OUT THERE?

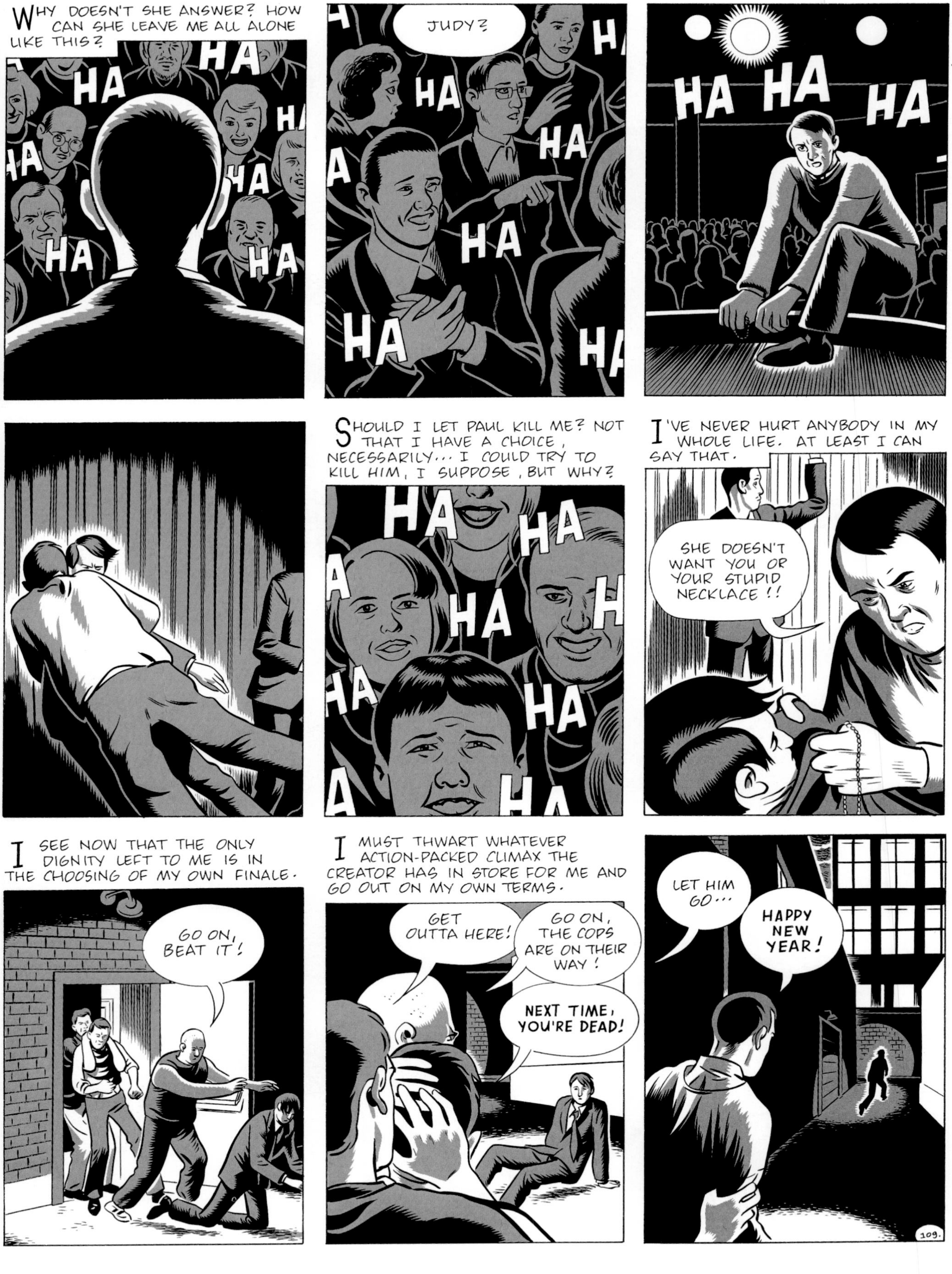
WHY DOESN'T SHE ANSWER? HOW CAN SHE LEAVE ME ALL ALONE LIKE THIS?
HA HA HA HA HA HA HA
JUDY?
HA HA HA HA HA HA HA
HA HA HA
SHOULD I LET PAUL KILL ME? NOT THAT I HAVE A CHOICE, NECESSARILY... I COULD TRY TO KILL HIM, I SUPPOSE, BUT WHY?
HA HA HA HA HA HA HA
I'VE NEVER HURT ANYBODY IN MY WHOLE LIFE. AT LEAST I CAN SAY THAT.
SHE DOESN'T WANT YOU OR YOUR STUPID NECKLACE!!
I SEE NOW THAT THE ONLY DIGNITY LEFT TO ME IS IN THE CHOOSING OF MY OWN FINALE.
GO ON, BEAT IT!
I MUST THWART WHATEVER ACTION-PACKED CLIMAX THE CREATOR HAS IN STORE FOR ME AND GO OUT ON MY OWN TERMS.
GET OUTTA HERE!
GO ON, THE COPS ARE ON THEIR WAY!
NEXT TIME, YOU'RE DEAD!
LET HIM GO...
HAPPY NEW YEAR!

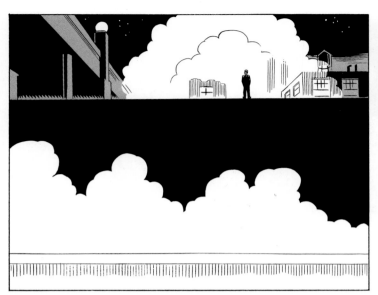

DAVID...

DAVID...

110.

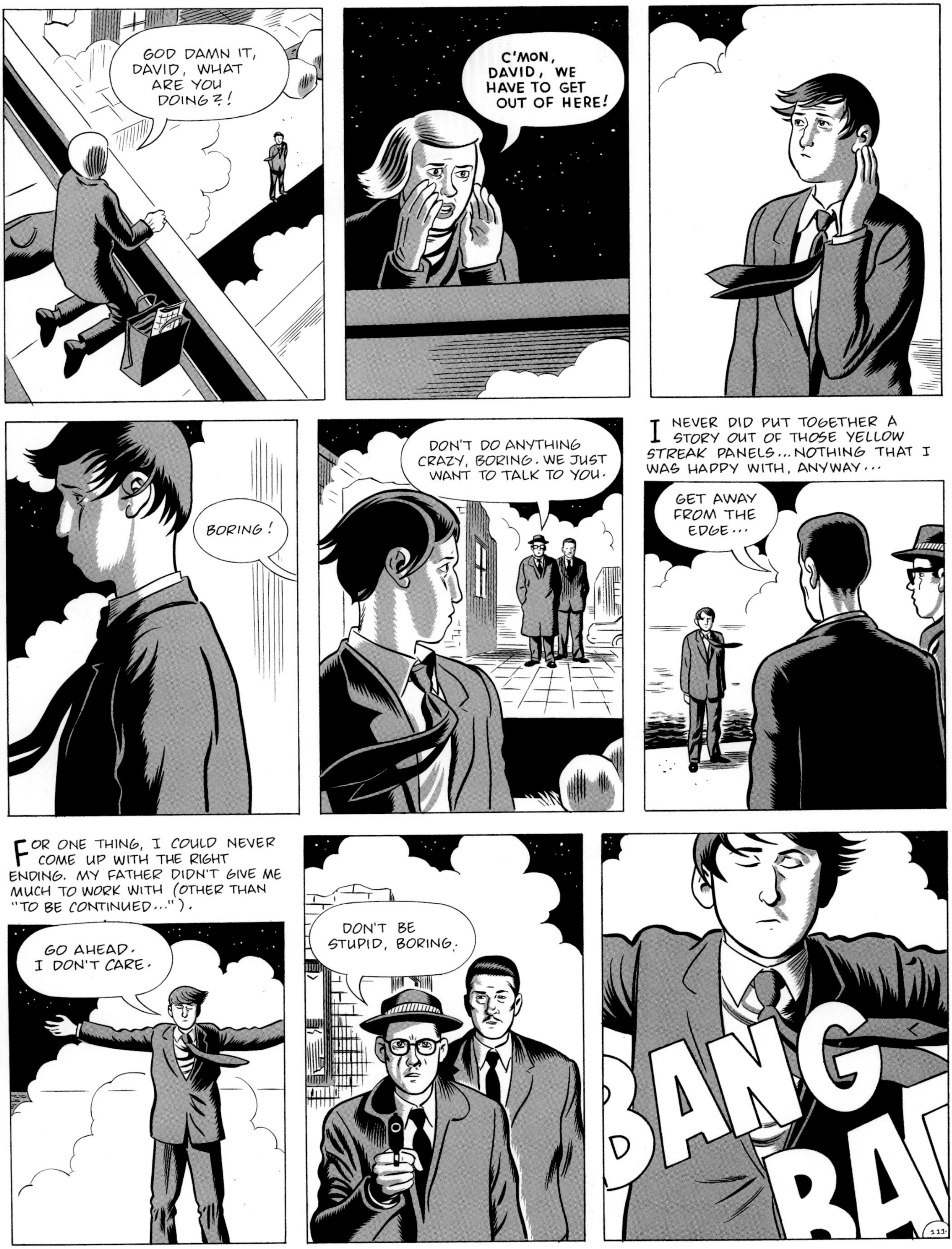
GOD DAMN IT, DAVID, WHAT ARE YOU DOING?!
C'MON, DAVID, WE HAVE TO GET OUT OF HERE!
BORING!
DON'T DO ANYTHING CRAZY, BORING. WE JUST WANT TO TALK TO YOU.
I NEVER DID PUT TOGETHER A STORY OUT OF THOSE YELLOW STREAK PANELS... NOTHING THAT I WAS HAPPY WITH, ANYWAY...
GET AWAY FROM THE EDGE...
FOR ONE THING, I COULD NEVER COME UP WITH THE RIGHT ENDING. MY FATHER DIDN'T GIVE ME MUCH TO WORK WITH (OTHER THAN "TO BE CONTINUED...").
GO AHEAD. I DON'T CARE.
DON'T BE STUPID, BORING.
BANG

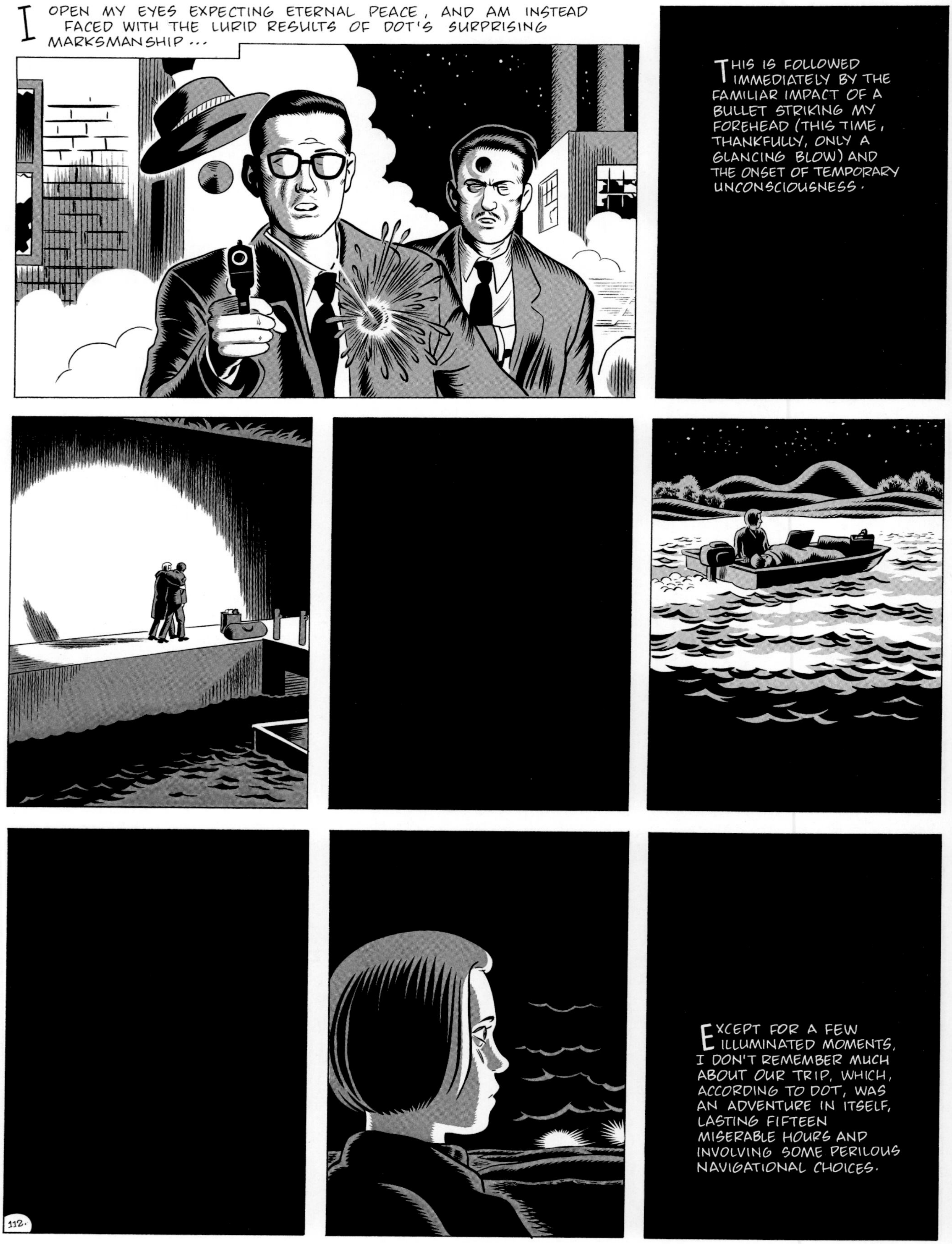
I OPEN MY EYES EXPECTING ETERNAL PEACE, AND AM INSTEAD FACED WITH THE LURID RESULTS OF DOT'S SURPRISING MARKSMANSHIP...
THIS IS FOLLOWED IMMEDIATELY BY THE FAMILIAR IMPACT OF A BULLET STRIKING MY FOREHEAD (THIS TIME, THANKFULLY, ONLY A GLANCING BLOW) AND THE ONSET OF TEMPORARY UNCONSCIOUSNESS.
EXCEPT FOR A FEW ILLUMINATED MOMENTS, I DON'T REMEMBER MUCH ABOUT OUR TRIP, WHICH, ACCORDING TO DOT, WAS AN ADVENTURE IN ITSELF, LASTING FIFTEEN MISERABLE HOURS AND INVOLVING SOME PERILOUS NAVIGATIONAL CHOICES.

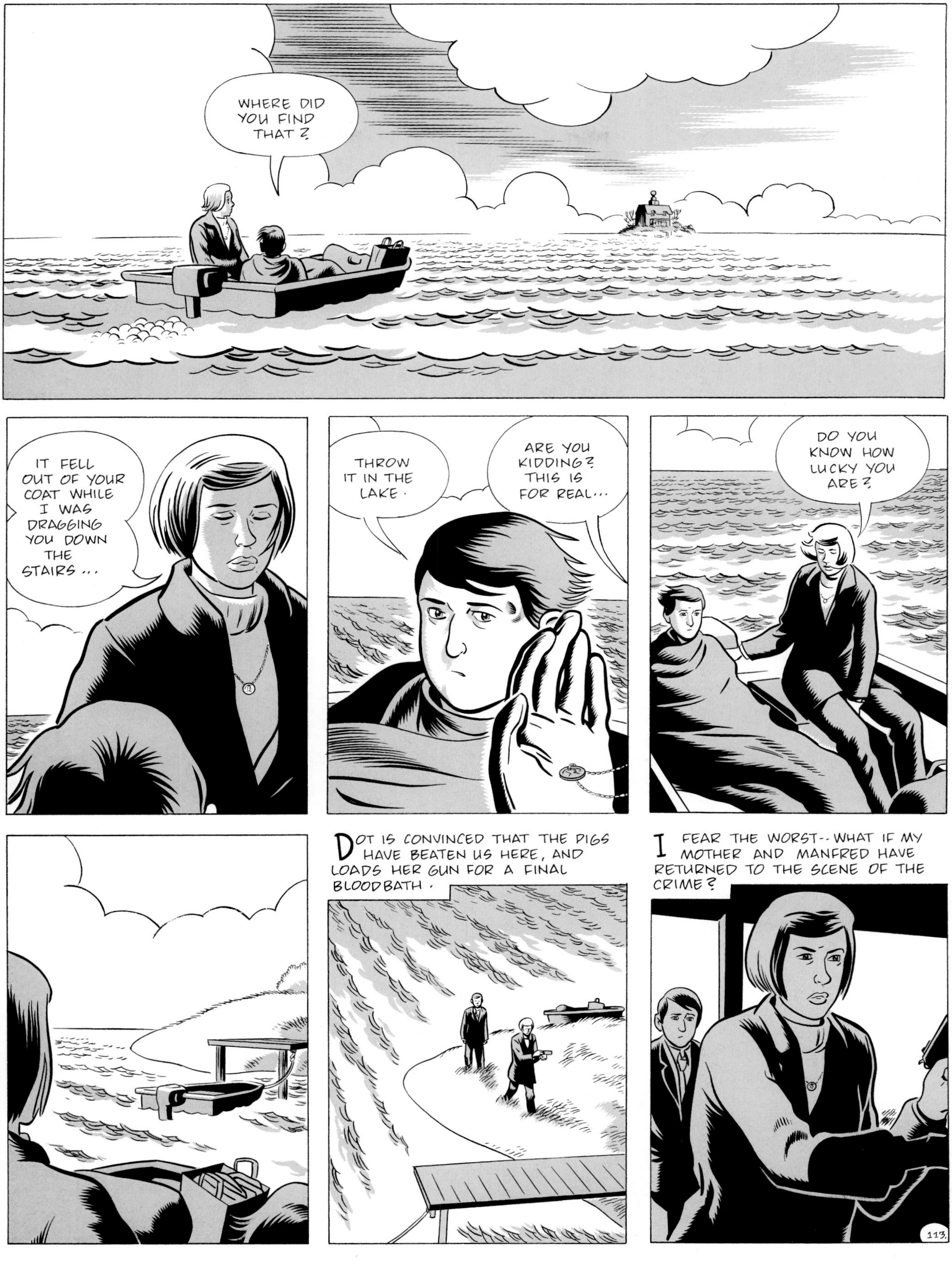

WHERE DID YOU FIND THAT?
IT FELL OUT OF YOUR COAT WHILE I WAS DRAGGING YOU DOWN THE STAIRS...
THROW IT IN THE LAKE.
ARE YOU KIDDING? THIS IS FOR REAL...
DO YOU KNOW HOW LUCKY YOU ARE?
DOT IS CONVINCED THAT THE PIGS HAVE BEATEN US HERE, AND LOADS HER GUN FOR A FINAL BLOODBATH.
I FEAR THE WORST--WHAT IF MY MOTHER AND MANFRED HAVE RETURNED TO THE SCENE OF THE CRIME?

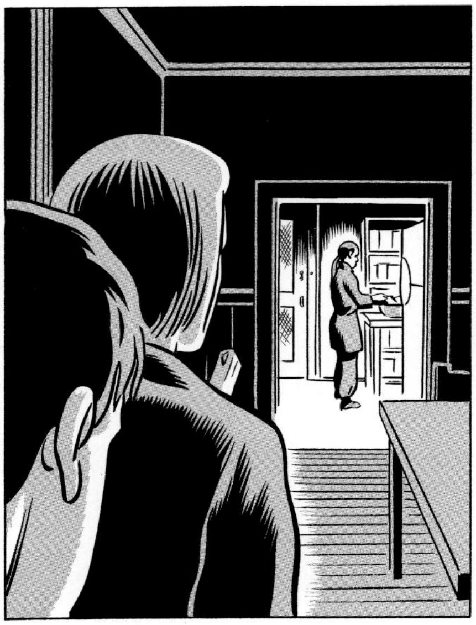

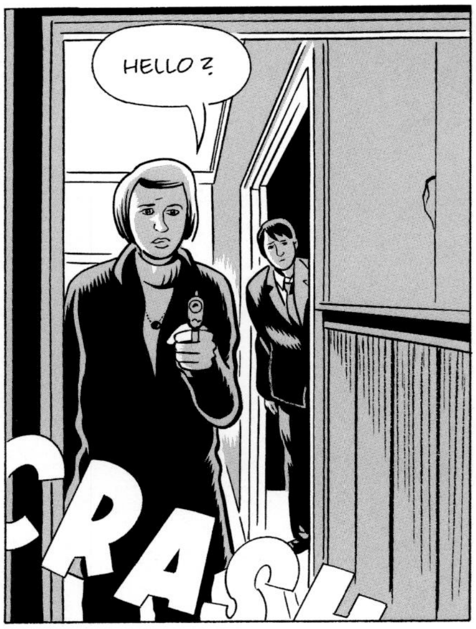
HELLO?
CRASH

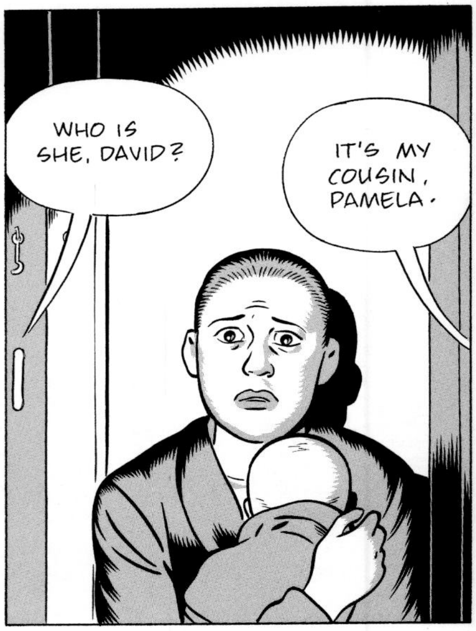
WHO IS SHE, DAVID?
IT'S MY COUSIN, PAMELA.

PAMELA HAS BEEN THERE SINCE THE 27TH, "JUST IN CASE THE TERRORISTS COME BACK," SHE SAYS. EVERYONE HAD PREDICTED AN ATTACK ON NEW YEAR'S EVE (WHICH IS TODAY, NOW THAT I THINK ABOUT IT) BUT DOT AND I HAVE BEEN TOO BUSY TO GIVE IT MUCH THOUGHT.

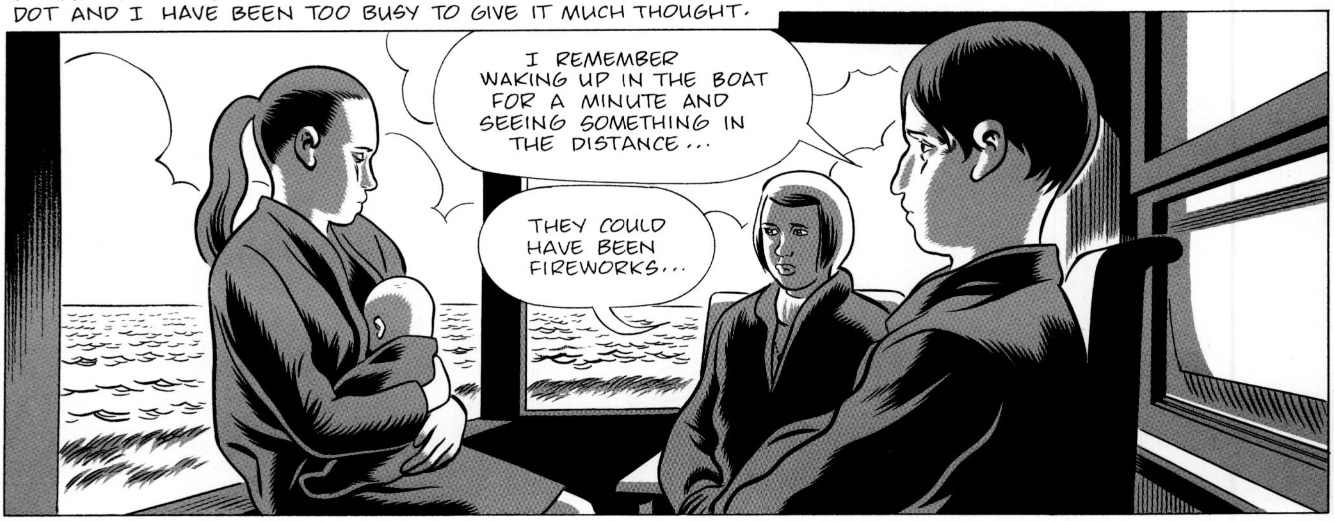
I REMEMBER WAKING UP IN THE BOAT FOR A MINUTE AND SEEING SOMETHING IN THE DISTANCE...
THEY COULD HAVE BEEN FIREWORKS...

"I'M NOT TAKING ANY CHANCES WITH HIM (GESTURES TOWARD BABY) IN THE PICTURE," SAYS PAMELA, THOUGH I SUSPECT SHE HAS A LOT TO GET AWAY FROM... SHE HAS ENOUGH DRY FOOD FOR SIX MONTHS AND PLANS TO START A VEGETABLE GARDEN IN THE SPRING, IF NECESSARY.

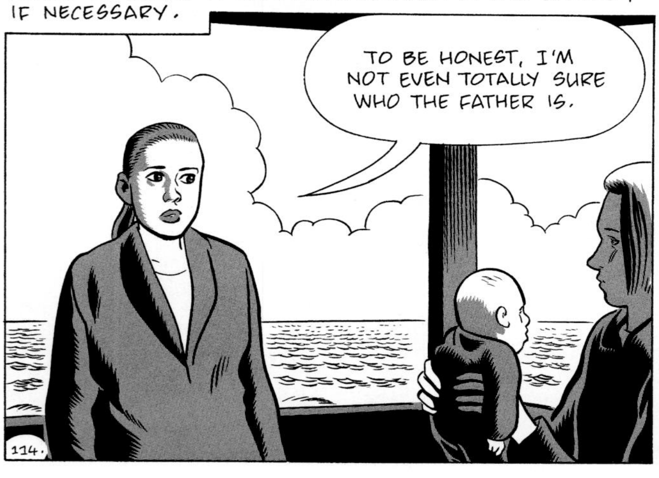
TO BE HONEST, I'M NOT EVEN TOTALLY SURE WHO THE FATHER IS.

A WEEK GOES BY AND THERE'S STILL NO SIGN OF THE POLICE. MAYBE SOMETHING REALLY HAPPENED THIS TIME. PAMELA HAS A LITTLE RADIO, BUT WE CAN'T GET A SIGNAL AND THE BATTERIES ARE DYING.

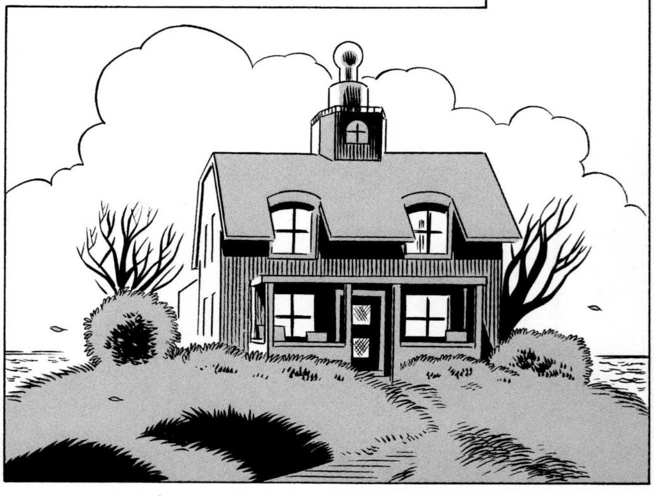

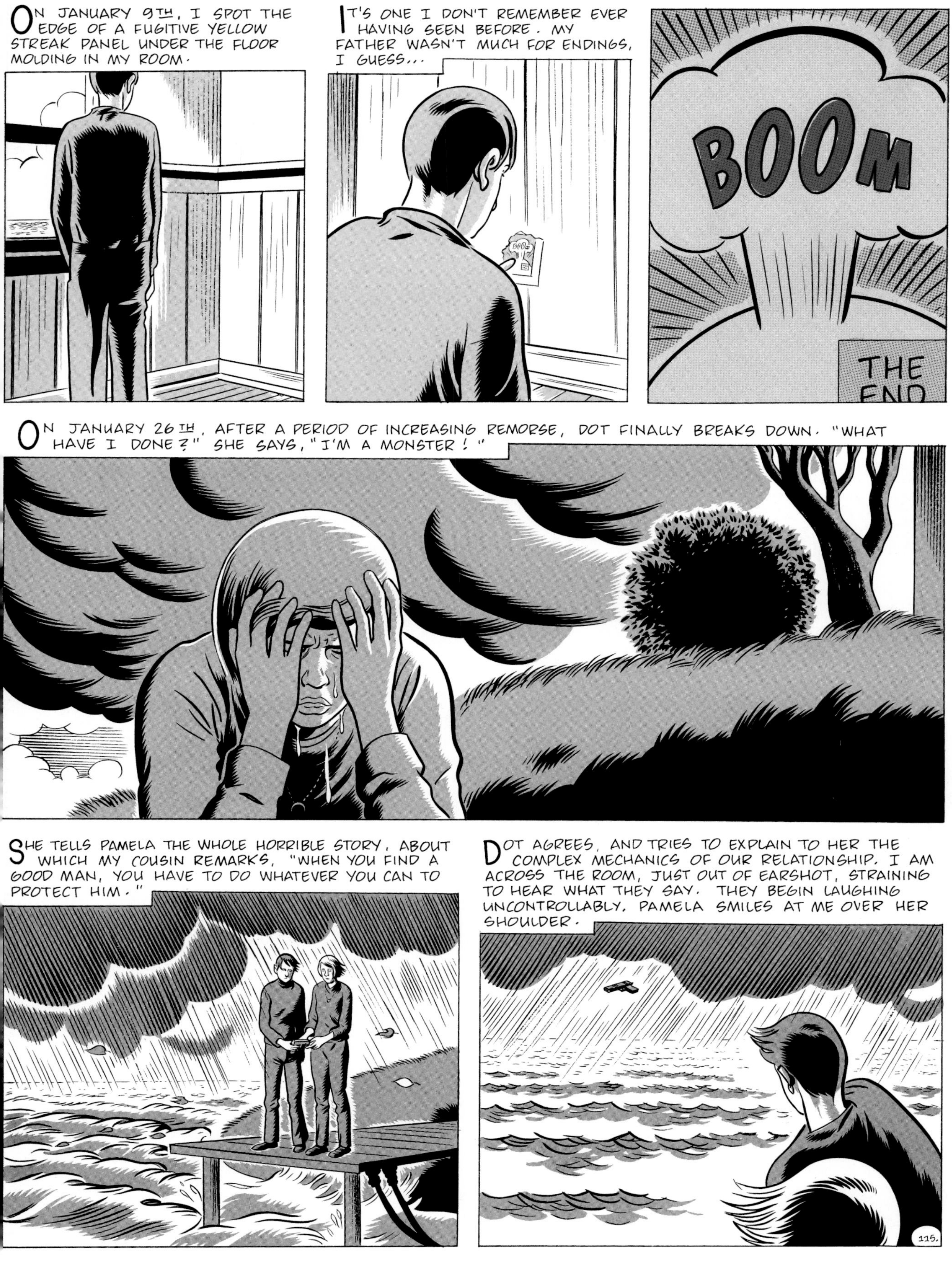
ON JANUARY 9TH, I SPOT THE EDGE OF A FUGITIVE YELLOW STREAK PANEL UNDER THE FLOOR MOLDING IN MY ROOM.
IT'S ONE I DON'T REMEMBER EVER HAVING SEEN BEFORE. MY FATHER WASN'T MUCH FOR ENDINGS, I GUESS...
BOOM
THE END
ON JANUARY 26TH, AFTER A PERIOD OF INCREASING REMORSE, DOT FINALLY BREAKS DOWN. "WHAT HAVE I DONE?" SHE SAYS, "I'M A MONSTER!"
SHE TELLS PAMELA THE WHOLE HORRIBLE STORY, ABOUT WHICH MY COUSIN REMARKS, "WHEN YOU FIND A GOOD MAN, YOU HAVE TO DO WHATEVER YOU CAN TO PROTECT HIM."
DOT AGREES, AND TRIES TO EXPLAIN TO HER THE COMPLEX MECHANICS OF OUR RELATIONSHIP. I AM ACROSS THE ROOM, JUST OUT OF EARSHOT, STRAINING TO HEAR WHAT THEY SAY. THEY BEGIN LAUGHING UNCONTROLLABLY. PAMELA SMILES AT ME OVER HER SHOULDER.

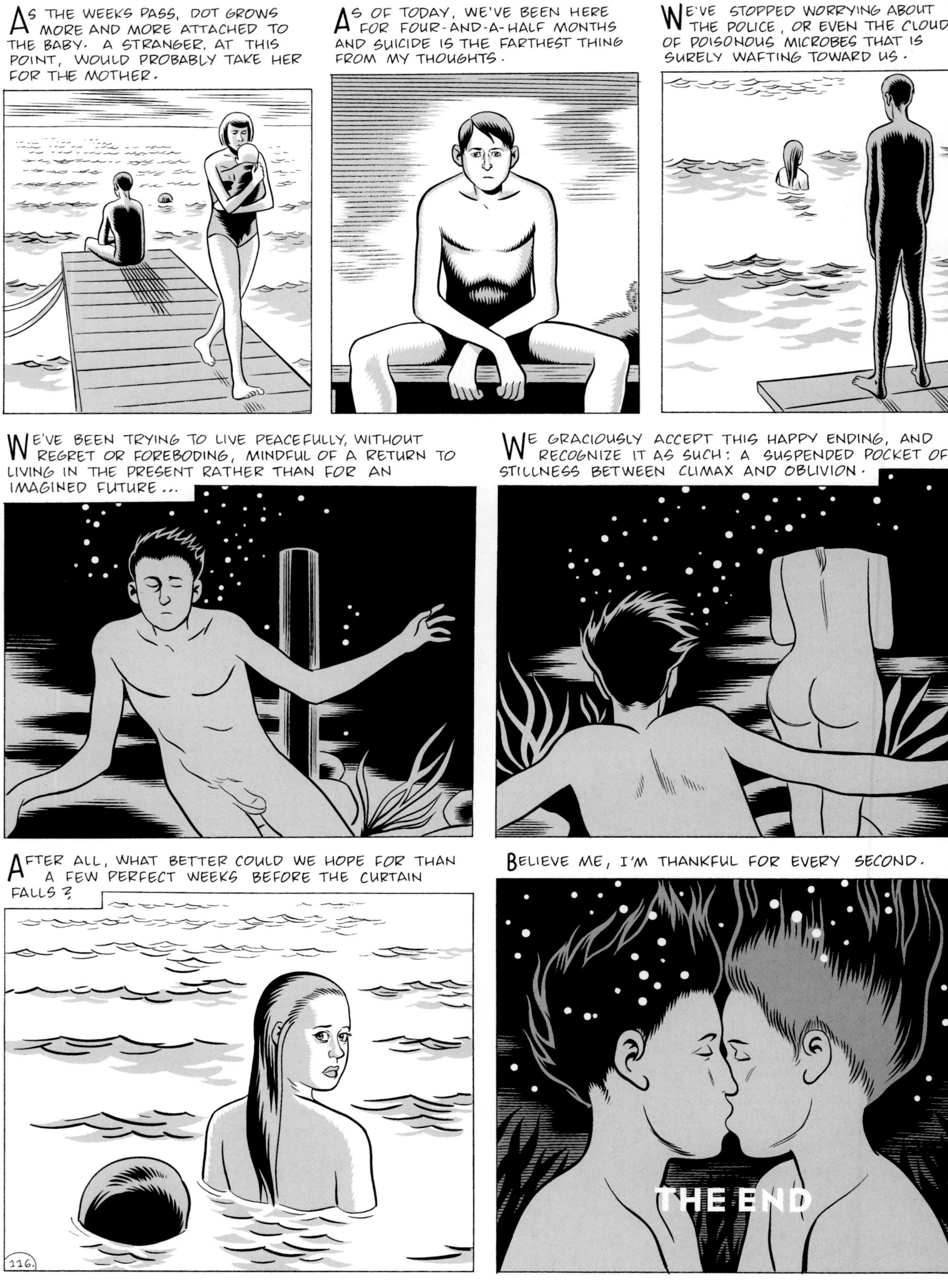
As the weeks pass, Dot grows more and more attached to the baby. A stranger, at this point, would probably take her for the mother.
As of today, we've been here for four-and-a-half months and suicide is the farthest thing from my thoughts.
We've stopped worrying about the police, or even the cloud of poisonous microbes that is surely wafting toward us.
We've been trying to live peacefully, without regret or foreboding, mindful of a return to living in the present rather than for an imagined future...
We graciously accept this happy ending, and recognize it as such: a suspended pocket of stillness between climax and oblivion.
After all, what better could we hope for than a few perfect weeks before the curtain falls?
Believe me, I'm thankful for every second.
THE END

FEATURING	(IN ORDER OF APPEARANCE)
NARRATOR	DAVID BORING
YOUNG ACTRESS	EMILY RANSOM
DAVID'S BEST FRIEND	DOT PAAR
BACKGROUND MAN	MR. BEARD
BACKGROUND WOMAN	MRS. BEARD
DAVID'S OTHER FRIEND	WHITEY WHITMAN
DOT'S DATE	GINGER FERGUSON
WHITEY'S DATE	CARLA S.
DAVID'S DATE	STEPHANIE B.
POLICE DETECTIVE	LT. ANEMONE
VAN DRIVER	BEN SOO
FIRST PASSENGER	PROF. JAFFE
SECOND PASSENGER	WANDA KRAML
PASTOR	PASTOR G. KNOOP
WHITEY'S COUSIN	DAGMAR HICKMAN
WHITEY'S STEPBROTHER	WARREN PAPPAS
MR. PIZZA EMPLOYEE	TREY BRAUN
DAVID'S MOTHER	MRS. BORING
STRANGE VISITOR	FERDINAND KARKES
MR. BEARD'S FRIEND	GLADYS X.
DAVE'S COUNTERMAN	DAVE JR.
COMPUTER JERK	ROB HILLOCKS
BARTENDER	BRAD CANDELARIA
GINGER'S BOYFRIEND	JEFF DRAKE
OTHER PROFESSORS	PROF. EDWARDS
	PROF. FAGG
	PROF. NUGENT
EERIE BOY	HIMSELF
GIRL IN WATER	PAMELA BROWN
CARETAKER	MR. HULLIGAN
DAVID'S SECOND COUSIN	HELEN CAPON
MRS. CAPON'S DAUGHTER	IRIS ROLAND
IRIS'S HUSBAND	MANFRED ROLAND
DAVID'S GREAT-UNCLE	AUGUST BROWN
RESCUER	KANDI LUTZ
RESCUER'S MOTHER	JANET LUTZ
DAVID'S GIRLFRIEND	NAOMI SORENSEN
COMIC DEALER	ROMAN JANACEK
COMICS EXPERT	GERRY BISHOFF

KARKES'S WIFE	MRS. KARKES
PRIVATE INVESTIGATOR	PURCELL HOWE
WANDA'S SISTER	JUDY LOWENSTEIN
FISHERMEN	CARL BECKMAN
	WILDER THORNE
FBI AGENT	ROY SMITH
JUDY'S HUSBAND	PAUL LOWENSTEIN
GIRL IN BAR	BARBARA HOPPER-STANGL
TICKET SCALPER	JACK DAHLMEYER
UNCLE SAM	FONTAINE FINNEGAN
STRAW HAT DANCER	CAL CALLISON
MC	DEAN LACEY
BOUNCERS	TUG TIMLIN
	TODD ZIMMER
PAMELA'S BABY	BABY BROWN
FEATURED EXTRAS	JANE ALLEN
	B.B. BOGLE
	SANDRA BUNCE
	D.G. CLOWES
	PARKER COLE
	JACK DAVIS
	LOUIS GOTTSCHALK
	POPEYE GROSSMAN
	PEPPER LACEY
	KIM LEE
	BRUCE MALM
	TROY MALM
	LUDWIG NELSON
	DENVER POLK JR.
	DOLORES POTTS
	KEN RUSK
	IRA SCHMERDEKNECHT
	DUANE SIKKENGA
	DOUG SIKKENGA
	EMILY SWAN
	SUMMER TUFTS
	BRUCE T. WAYNE
	C. C. WRIGHT
	GALE YEOMAN
	CON ZEIGLER

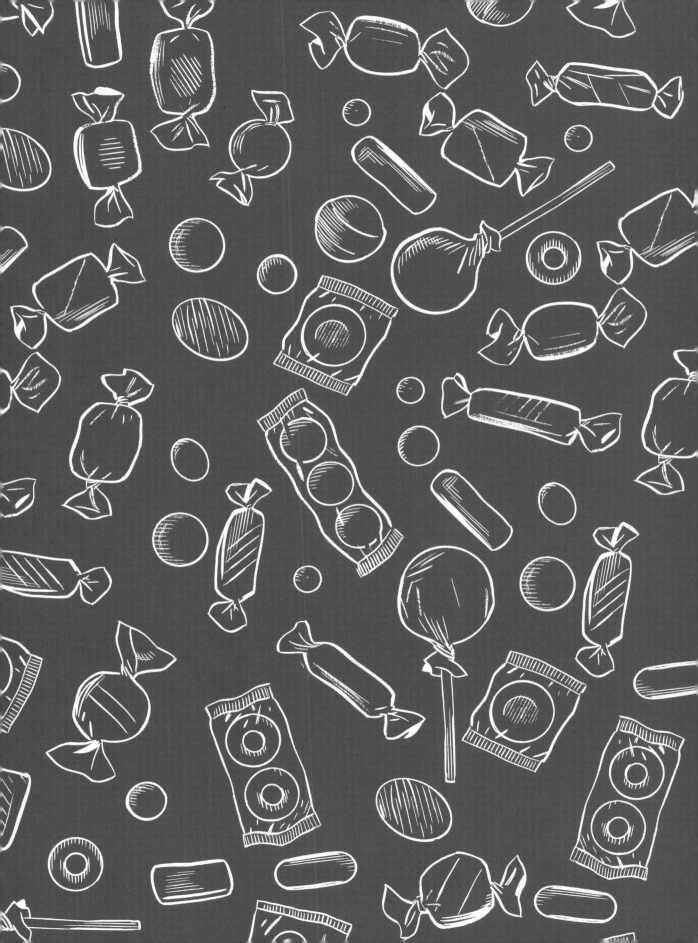

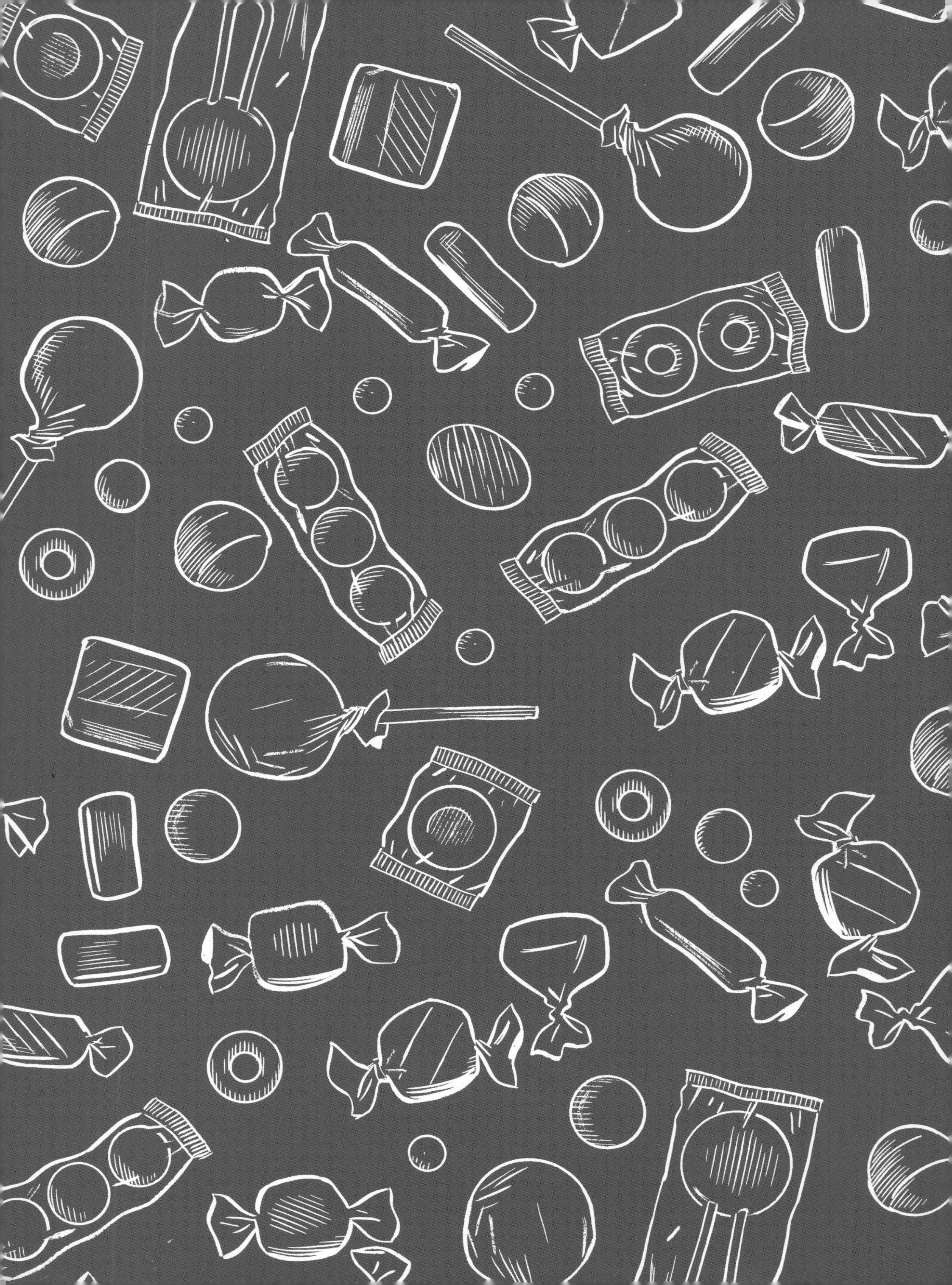